P9-AFR-544

# Chips Off the Old Benchley

# Books by ROBERT BENCHLEY

CHIPS OFF THE OLD BENCHLEY

BENCHLEY—OR ELSE!

BENCHLEY BESIDE HIMSELF

INSIDE BENCHLEY

AFTER 1903—WHAT?

MY TEN YEARS IN A QUANDARY,
AND HOW THEY GREW

FROM BED TO WORSE: OR COMFORTING
THOUGHTS ABOUT THE BISON

NO POEMS: OR AROUND THE WORLD
BACKWARDS AND SIDEWAYS

PLUCK AND LUCK

THE TREASURER'S REPORT, AND OTHER
ASPECTS OF COMMUNITY SINGING

20,000 LEAGUES UNDER THE SEA, OR
DAVID COPPERFIELD

THE EARLY WORM

LOVE CONQUERS ALL

OF ALL THINGS

# Chips Off the Old
# BENCHLEY

### By ROBERT BENCHLEY

*with an Introduction by* FRANK SULLIVAN
*and drawings by* GLUYAS WILLIAMS

HARPER & BROTHERS *Publishers* NEW YORK

CHIPS OFF THE OLD BENCHLEY. Copyright, 1949, by Gertrude D. Benchley.
Printed in the United States of America

*The following pieces were copyrighted in the years indicated, by:*

THE NEW YORKER MAGAZINE, INC. (formerly The F-R. Publishing Corp.) : *Boost New York!*, 1929; *So You're Going to New York*, 1929; *The Perfect Audience*, 1930; *"He Travels Fastest—,"* 1932; *A Belated Tribute*, 1932; *The Last of the Heath Hens*, 1933.

LIFE PUBLISHING COMPANY: *The Dying Thesaurus*, 1921; *The New Bone-Dust Theory of Behavior*, 1922; *Perrine's Return*, 1923; *Bayeux Christmas Presents Early*, 1927.

THE HEARST CORPORATION, NEW YORK MIRROR DIVISION: *Encore*, 1933; *"Good Luck,"* 1933; *Music Heavenly Maid*, 1933; *Memoirs*, 1933; *Looking at Picture Books*, 1933; *The Letter Box*, 1933; *Brain-Fag*, 1933; *Bird Lore*, 1933; *"Why I am Pale,"* 1933; *My Own Arrangement*, 1933; *Morale in Banking*, 1933; *Home Sweet Home*, 1933; *Learn to Write*, 1933; *Knowing the Flowers*, 1933; *Professional Pride*, 1933; *A Writers' Code*, 1933; *"Writers—Right or Wrong!"* 1933; *Your Change*, 1933; *Confession*, 1934; *My Subconscious*, 1934.

D. A. C. NEWS, INC.: *Down in Front*, 1921; *The Lure of the Rod*, 1923; *In the Beginning*, 1923; *How to Travel in Peace*, 1924; *Plans for Eclipse Day*, 1925; *The Menace of Buttered Toast*, 1930; *Browsing Through the Passport*, 1930.

LIBERTY MAGAZINE, INC.: *Ding-Dong, School Bells*, 1930; *Sporting Life in America—Watching*, 1930; *Sporting Life in America—Turkish Bathing*, 1930; *Take a Letter, Please*, 1930; *What Time Is It?*, 1930; *The Dear Dead Table d'Hôte Days*, 1930; *A Word About Hay Fever*, 1930; *Art Revolution No. 4861*, 1931; *My Five (or Maybe Six) Year Plan*, 1931; *"Greetings From—,"* 1931; *Future Man: Tree or Mammal?*, 1931; *Your Boy and His Dog*, 1932; *"Safety Second,"* 1932; *Imagination in the Bathroom*, 1932; *Good Luck, and Try and Get It*, 1933.

CHICAGO TRIBUNE-NEW YORK NEWS SYNDICATE, INC.: *The Mysteries of Radio*, 1929; *Hey, Waiter!*, 1929; *On or Before March 15*, 1930; *How to Get Things Done*, 1930; *The Questionnaire Craze*, 1930.

HEARST MAGAZINES, INC., Successors to International Magazine Co., Inc.: *Tiptoeing Down Memory Lane*, 1931.

BOOKMAN PUBLISHING CO., INC.: *Do I Hear Twenty Thousand?*, 1929.

THE CONDE NAST PUBLICATIONS, INC.: *A Warning Note in the Matter of Preparedness*, 1915; *On Saying Little at Great Length*, 1917; *Doing Your Bit in the Garden*, 1917; *The United States Senate Chamber*, 1918: *À Bas the Military Censor*, 1918; *"One Hundred Years Ago Today—,"* 1919; *Old Days in New Bottles*, 1926.

NEW YORK AMERICAN, INC.: *Are You an Old Master?*, 1934; *The First Pigeon of Spring*, 1934; *Literary Notes*, 1935; *Vox Populi*, 1936.

THE COLOPHON: *Why Does Nobody Collect Me?*, 1934.

THE TRIBUNE ASSOCIATION: *Picking French Pastry; a Harder Game Than Chess*, 1916.

*All rights in this book are reserved. No part of the book may be reproduced in any manner whatsoever without written permission except in the case of brief quotations embodied in critical articles and reviews. For information address Harper & Brothers.*

# CONTENTS

HARPER & BROTHERS
IS GRATEFUL TO MRS. ROBERT BENCHLEY
FOR HER WORK IN COLLECTING
THESE WRITINGS OF HER HUSBAND.

# INTRODUCTION

BY FRANK SULLIVAN

HERE, unexpectedly and delightfully, is a Benchley collection of articles, few of which have been seen before in book form. The publisher, optimistic soul, has an idea that I can deal with Mr. Benchley in a mere preface. I'll do my best.

Which Benchley do we take up first? The humorist and satirist? The drama critic? The book critic? The actor, stage, movie and radio? He was all of these at some time and some of them all of the time. Yet he liked to pretend that he was a lazy man. Or shall we talk about the New England Benchley from Worcester, Massachusetts? Or the Benchley who was Caliph of Manhattan? The Hollywood notable? The Scarsdale householder trying, usually unsuccessfully, to start the furnace, or the Benchley with a genius for friendship? A rather large biography might possibly encompass all these Benchleys.

I was first his fan and later, by my great good fortune, his friend but I was not as close a friend to him as I should have liked to have been. There was too much competition. Everybody, it sometimes seemed, wanted to be Mr. Benchley's close friend, and be with him all the time, and he, kindly and gregarious man that he was, would have liked to oblige, within reason. But there simply was not enough Benchley to go around. As it was he achieved remarkable results with the supply of Benchley that was available and when he died in 1945 he left friends in all the known walks of life and in a number of special walks invented to accommodate friends of his who did not fit into any of the conventional walks.

If "Mr. Benchley" seems a formal way of referring to the most informal and affable of men, let me explain. Some of us fell into the habit of calling him Mr. Benchley as often as we called him Bob because of a placard that held a prominent place over a doorway in that wonderful, cockeyed hotel apartment that was his Manhattan home for many years. It read: "**MR.** Benchley, *please*."

His tilts at windmills in this collection cover a number of the recent years but read as though they were written yesterday. He pays his respects and disrespects to the heath hen, to Gilbert and Sullivan audiences, bird fanciers, Sir Walter Scott, buttered toast; to people who applaud too long at theatres and men who run around the Central Park Reservoir every morning; to customers who are overbearing toward waiters, and to musicians who take a pleasant tune and "arrange" it until it is mangled out of all recognition. He suffered from hay fever and you may guess what he thought of people who were jocose about hay fever. In common with many of his fellow-Americans, he had great difficulty picking up change at movie-theatre windows, and it seemed to him that French pastry trays were rigged up just on purpose to make a selection excessively difficult. As for mankind's prospects he thought man would eventually become prettier but would have no legs.

There are not many subjects he did not probe at one time or another. Often he dealt with the same common or garden variety of subject other writers tackled, but a subject was rarely the same after Mr. Benchley got through with it. "Well," the reader would think, "here he goes on Turkish baths; now, even Benchley cannot think of anything new to say about Turkish baths." And then Benchley would say something new about Turkish baths.

Every sentence the reader traversed with him was apt to become an adventure. You never knew when you started where you would end but then neither did Mr. Benchley. Mr. Cassidy, in *Safety Second*, fell into a pulp machine and was "swashed around until all they had to do was dry him out and they could have printed the Sunday *Times* on him." A lesser man would have left Mr. Cassidy with this requiem. Not Mr. Benchley, who continues: "In fact that is just what they did do, and it was one of the best editions of the Sunday *Times* that ever was run off the presses. It had human interest."

The Benchley that Gluyas Williams understood and pictures so brilliantly did not take the Gadget Age, or Our Vaunted Civilization, lying down. He battled it to the end and sometimes gave as good as he got, though he usually came off second best in his encounters with machines, income taxes, banks, and daylight-saving time. He did not like daylight-saving time but, as he explains, he did not even like time, and his friends could add that he didn't think much of daylight, either. The Caliph of Manhattan was largely nocturnal in his habits, as a good Caliph should be.

He deals herein with his difficulties as a bank depositor and it is a pity that his bank was not given fifteen minutes for rebuttal. I should like to have seen this book enriched by a piece called "Banking With Benchley" by the Bankers' Trust Company. That institution remembers him with affection, though it was never quite the same after he bestowed his checking account on it. I understand the bank preserved some of his more uproarious checks, among them surely the one dated three A.M. at an uptown hot spot, made out to Cash, and endorsed something like this: "Dear Bank, having wonderful time. Wish you were here. Love to all. Bob."

In common with another great humorist named Dickens, Mr. Benchley had a talent for giving his characters lovely names, and in this book you will meet Mr. Manvogle, Mr. Cramsey, Mr. Anderson M. Ferderber, Mr. Wheer, Mr. Crolish, Mr. Reemis, Mr. McNordfy and, my favorite, Miss Janet MacMac, a faithful old Scotch retainer who, we are told, was for years family hemstitcher to the Benchleys.

If he sometimes won a battle over a gadget, Mr. Benchley never won one against Nature, which had him stopped cold. I find no more evidence in this book than in any of his works that he ever won in a tussle with a wild flower. He distrusted wild flowers. Tame flowers, too, especially azaleas. When he tried to take a sun bath, with the sun shining on his closed eyelids, "large, purple azaleas whirling against a yellow background" appeared, without invitation.

Birds were even worse. In Hollywood one night the *basso profundo* song of "a great big, burly bird with a long black beard" made him so nervous that he wished he were back in New York listening to the good old Sixth Avenue El rumbling past his diggings. Yet when he got back to Forty-fourth Street what turns up at his lattice to frighten the daylights—dawn would probably be the *mot juste* here—out of him but an ugly customer he describes as a bull pigeon.

He did not like exercise, sports, or the watching of sports. Since I knew this I was not surprised to meet him at the Saratoga races one August afternoon. Not caring particularly for horse racing, Mr. Benchley would of course be in some place where horses were racing. He was holding a talisman which he explained was to bring luck, through him, to a friend's horse in the big race of the day. But Mr. Benchley lost the talisman and the horse lost the race. It was probably a mistake to pick Mr. Benchley as a go-between to get in touch with the occult. That night he went to the yearling sales, where little horses are bought for great sums by the flicker of a millionaire's pinky. Bob brushed a mosquito from his cheek, the auctioneer misunderstood, and Bob found that the gesture had bought him a charming year-old filly. Mr. Benchley as an owner of race horses. What fascinating possibilities the thought suggests. But, as I never heard any more of the filly, I suppose some kind friend took her off his hands.

His lance pierced more shams than all the preachments of the indignation boys and do-gooders. He was the sanest of men and saw things clearly. He had humility, honesty and integrity. And he had a great, wholesome, hearty laugh which merely to hear made you smile and feel better. One of the chief troubles of the American theatre today is that Bob Benchley's laugh is no longer heard in it. To be in his company made you feel happy; he had a faculty for making you feel that you were far more brilliant and personable than you probably were. It is a talent given to few. Wholly without pretense, he would be ribald but patient at such fond words about him as these. I wish we could be assured that by some miracle a new Benchley collection like this would be unearthed and published annually for quite some time. It would make the future seem brighter. In the absence of the miracle, we can, of course, always reread this and the older Benchley books.

# Chips Off the Old Benchley

# THE NEW BONE-DUST
# THEORY OF BEHAVIOR

*Is Your Elbow All It Should Be?*

ALITTLE while ago it was your teeth that were to blame for everything. And now, after you have gone and had tin-types taken of your teeth, showing them riding in little automobiles or digging in the sand, some more specialists come along and discover that, after all, it is your glands that are the secret of your mental, moral and physical well-being.

A book called "The Glands Regulating Personality" claims that the secretions of the various glands throughout your body determine whether you are a good or a bad boy, cheerful or agile, Republican or Democrat. Anyone singing "For He's a Jolly Good Fellow" does not face the facts squarely. The words should go: "For he has jolly good glandular secretions, which nobody will deny."

In order to be at least two jumps ahead of the game, we are prepared to set forward another theory to take the place of the gland theory when that shall have become scratched. All enthusiasts who want to keep abreast of the times, will dip right into ours now; so that when the time comes they will be able to talk intelligently on the subject.

Briefly, the facts are these:

This wonderful body which Nature has given us is made up of just dozens and dozens of bones. Oh, so many bones! If you were to start counting now and should count bones until Daddy came home to supper, you would have counted only seven or eight of them, because it is almost time for Daddy now.

In the course of time, as we go about doing our daily work, these bones rub against one another, especially in the joints. It is true that Nature has provided little cups for the bones to fit into so that they will not rub, but what good are they? None. Of all the bungling, slip-shod jobs that Nature has done (and she has done a great many in her day) the friction of one bone upon another in the human form is among the worst. The truth about this has only just begun to come out.

Now, in this constant rubbing, due to people's constantly running up and down stairs, or prancing to keep warm, or jouncing babies on their knees, it is only to be expected that a quantity of bone-dust should be gradually worn off from the bones. You can't blame the bones. It's just one of those things that are bound to happen.

This bone-dust, once it is set loose, has no place to go except to swirl along in circulation with the blood. You are either a part of a bone or you are a part of the circulation of the blood. There is no middle course. And it is this visiting bone-dust, tearing about through one's system, that determines whether or not one is to be a criminal member of society or a pianist.

2

For example, the joints which shed criminal-breeding bone-dust are the elbow and knee. If dust from these predominates in your system (in other words, if you bend your elbows and knees more than you bend your fingers) you will have a tendency to steal little things or perhaps kill slightly. Dark circles will appear under your eyes and your friends will begin to shun you. You will be embarrassed when called upon to meet the president of the company and will, in all probability, have no speaking voice.

A very wealthy society woman, known to all of you by name, was brought to this office for treatment for stealing trinkets from Tiffany's. Ten years ago she would have been sent to a sanitarium as an incurable kleptomaniac. She was questioned about her reflexes and it was found that she was accustomed to bend her elbow constantly, just for the fun of the thing. A transfusion was made of the bone-dust of a young wolf who had no elbows, and in a few weeks the patient was as good as new. She has never had a recurrence of her throat trouble.

Thus it will be seen that the basis of our whole social structure today lies in the friction of the bones in our body and probably will lie there until Fall, when something else will be found to take the blame.

# BAYEUX CHRISTMAS
# PRESENTS EARLY

IT SEEMS rather strange that, in the very year which marks the nine hundredth anniversary of the birth of William the Conqueror, a strip of Bayeux tapestry should have been discovered in Bayeux, New Jersey, depicting the passage of that hero across the Channel. It seems so strange, in fact, that the police are investigating the matter.

The tapestry, it is alleged by the defense, shows four of the Conqueror's ships in mid-Channel. There seems to be some doubt among authorities as to the direction in which the ships are going—to or from Albion. We incline to the theory that they are on their way back to France. There must have been at least four boat-loads of Normans who were disappointed in England and who turned right around and went home.

Or, if we must be seasonal, we may hold to the theory that they are on their way back to Normandy for the Christmas holidays. Can you imagine the bustle and din there must have been in William's household along about December 20th of the first Christmas week following the landing? "Going home for Christmas?" must have been the question on all lips framed in probably the worst Norman-English ever heard. "Noël," they probably called it. The old oaken bucket that hung in Noël—to put it badly.

Any study of a Bayeux tapestry is made difficult by the fact that the old weavers were such bum draughtsmen. They may have known how to work looms but they couldn't draw for a darn. There is no way of telling from the tapestry whether or not William himself was aboard one of the ships, because all the men look alike, if you can even call it that. The man in the middle boat, the one bunking up with a horse, might be William, but the chances are against it. He is evidently so sick that he doesn't care *who* he is. He is making a mental resolution that, rather than cross this Channel again, he will spend the rest of his life in Normandy, or wherever it is he is headed for.

The little boat, which seems to be hanging in mid-air, is really, they tell us, in the distance. Its occupants are having a rather thin time of it and are evidently considering being ill, too. On the whole, the entire expedition would have done better never to have left land.

A word about the figureheads on the two ships which have them. The one on the boat at the extreme right would indicate that it is going in the opposite direction from the rest of the fleet, or else that somebody made an awful blunder in assembling the ship. It is on the stern, as near as we can figure it out, although the two boys amidships who are humming together confuse things by facing in opposite directions themselves. Judged merely as figureheads neither one is worth much, although we like the one on the right better than the big one at the left because the latter looks as if the designer had tried to be funny.

We gather that there was some vague idea of having the great black things held by the pilots look like rudders. Well, they don't—and that goes for the whole tapestry, too.

# THE LAST OF THE
# HEATH HENS

WELL, the Heath Hen has gone! We might as well face it. The sole surviving specimen of *Tympanuchus cupido*, which has been hopping and flitting about the island of Martha's Vineyard for the past few years under the fascinated gaze of the ornithologists, has disappeared, and, it is feared, has died without issue. It was not enough that the world should be tottering, its reason going, its standards gone. The Heath Hen must be taken from us.

We knew that it would have to happen some time, but it is hard to believe that there will never be another Heath Hen. We didn't mind so much when we were told that the Great Auk was extinct, or the Labrador Duck, or the Passenger Pigeon. Even the news about the Eskimo Curlews (although there is hope that there are still a few Eskimo Curlews left who are just playing possum or sulking) didn't give us that sinking feeling that we experienced when we heard about the Heath Hen. No more Heath Hens—*ever!* Thank God, John James Audubon did not live to hear that gloomy pronouncement. (He missed it by just three-quarters of a century.)

It seems only yesterday that I saw the Heath Hen at Martha's Vineyard. She looked as well then as she ever did, but she never was what you would call a robust bird. They did not keep her captive. She was too proud a spirit for that. But on one occasion, when she had lighted for a chat with Mr. McKinstry, her observer (Mr. McKinstry was paid by the state or somebody just to hang around Martha's Vineyard and keep tabs on the Heath Hen), they did attach two metal bands to her ankles, so that if she ever got lost or drunk, people would know that she was no ordinary grouse. She didn't like the bands, and felt that when one is the only surviving member of a proud race of birds, any sensitive person should recognize one without leg bands. "I don't like the idea of it, Joe," she said to Mr. McKinstry on one occasion. "Either I am a true princess or I am not."

One of the greatest sorrows in Mr. McKinstry's professional career as Heath Hen-watcher was that he could never find a mate for Miss Helen. (He called her Miss Helen because it seemed to suit her best.) The More Game Birds Foundation was very anxious that Miss Helen marry, not only because it would have made the bleak winters on Martha's Vineyard happier for her but because then, if things worked out right, she might not be the last of her breed in the world. And it was more or less up to Mr. McKinstry.

But either because there *were* no suitable mates for Miss Helen or because she rather fancied herself in her tragic rôle as the Last of the Heath Hens and deliberately snubbed any eligible suitors, the fact remains that she made no alliances and was always seen alone when she alighted on the farm of James Green every spring. It made it hard for Mr. McKinstry to make out his report, but there wasn't really very much that he could do about it.

"I see the position it puts you in, Joe," she said to him once, "but somehow I feel that I am in the right. I *can't* take anybody that comes along, and you wouldn't want me to. And if the Heath Hens are to go on, they must be the very best Heath Hens, worthy to carry on a fine tradition. And you don't know this Martha's Vineyard riffraff as I do."

And with that (according to Mr. McKinstry) she waddled into a thicket and wasn't seen again for weeks. Mr. McKinstry thinks that she spent a lot of her time in daydreaming and was really close at hand when she was supposed to be off on a tour of the island. It was also his idea that she had an independent income and kept to herself out of choice. When you are the Sole Surviving Specimen, you have a certain dignity to maintain.

And now she is gone. Spring has broken through again and no Heath Hen has come to James Green's farm. Somewhere on the hard-bitten ground of Martha's Vineyard Miss Helen lies in state, with two metal bands about her patrician ankles, and her proud spirit wings its way to the home of all those other Heath Hens who went before. We need sound no mournful tone for Miss Helen, for she kept her name unsullied to the end and her fame is secure on the records of ornithological royalty. But what, *what* is to become of Mr. McKinstry?

# ON OR BEFORE MARCH 15

I REALIZE that this is a fine time to be worrying about the Income Tax, a whole week after the returns were supposed to be in, but I am afraid that I shall have to be a little late this year in filing mine. Nobody regrets it more than I do and I want the officials to know that I am bending every effort to get the thing in just as soon as possible.

But I have struck several snags and my pencil keeps breaking and often I get so confused that I have to go and lie down, and all this takes time. I will get the return in. They needn't worry. But I won't be hurried. *March 15th! March 15th!* You would think to hear them screaming "March 15th" at you that there was no other date on the calendar. Well, I'll get mine in on or about March 28th or 29th, and they'll like it. I should think that they'd be busy enough in the tax offices messing around with the returns that *did* come in on time, so that they wouldn't have to have mine right away. Anyway, they're not going to get it.

It's their own fault that I am late. They print blanks for you to fill out, then pass a bill making the blanks no good, then send the blanks out anyway, with a little red slip telling you to disregard the blanks. If *I* had done a thing like that to *them*, what a howl they would have set up! I would have been just an old slipshod bungler, an impractical writer-man. But the Government can go out of its way to confuse and rattle *me*, and that's all right. Well, the Government makes me sick, that's what the Government does. And it always has, too.

In the first place, the little red slip got lost just as soon as I had taken it out of the envelope, so I never saw what it said. I can't sit right down the minute my blank comes and fill it out. I have certain other things which have to be attended to, although the Government may not think so. And a little red slip is very easily mislaid or lost these days. I don't suppose the Government ever loses anything, oh no! They're *perfect!*

Well, I lost the red slip and when I came to fill out my blank I filled it out according to printed instructions as every law-abiding citizen should. I took it for granted that the blank was right. I knew that it was gosh-darned unfair but I did think that it was technically correct. When a government is over a hundred and fifty years old one naturally assumes that it can, at least, put out correct printed matter. This is where I evidently made my first mistake.

My second mistake came in handling the "7's" and "8's." I always have had trouble in adding and subtracting "7's" and "8's." Even when I was in the thick of school arithmetic, adding and subtracting like mad every day of the year, the "7's" and "8's" seemed to me to be very complicated and tricky numbers and now that I have occasion to add and subtract only occasionally they throw me into something of a panic. If nobody is looking, I can get out of the jam by using my fingers to count on, but I rather hate, at my age, to be seen at it. In fact, I have been known to wait fifteen or twenty minutes until people left the room rather than count "7" and "8" on my fingers in front of them. All this time the mathematical problem at hand has been held up. If it is a rush job, and there are people in the room, I put my fingers in my pocket and rattle off the "7's" and "8's" there.

Also, this year, I got a book from my bank telling all about deductions, and this served only to confuse me. In the past, rather than go into the thing thoroughly, I have cheated myself unmercifully by claiming only the deductions that I could understand, such as two children and the Red Cross. (It is very evident that the Treasury officials have no children of their own if they think that $400 covers even the shoe-leather expense of one child.) But this year a businessman acquaintance told me that I was a fool not to deduct expenses to which I was legitimately entitled by the nature of my business, and gave me this book from the bank outlining the various forms of money-saving which come under the law.

I hadn't got very far in this book before I was tempted to go back to my old system of giving the Government everything except my two children and the Red Cross. Sec. 23 (b) mentions "a reasonable allowance for depletion in case of oil wells, mines, etc." Now, I don't own an oil well or a mine, but an oil well in which I had a small financial interest certainly was depleted during 1929, a depletion which amounted practically to complete elimination, and I ought to get a little something off on that, I should think. But I have also learned that most of the items which one would think could be legitimately deducted are just the ones which *can't* be.

My garden, for instance, which really ought to come in under the "etc." in the "oil wells, mines, *etc.*" clause, being a source of something or other (mostly radishes) which comes out of the ground, is probably not deductible. It was a big disappointment as a garden and I hardly got my bait back out of it, but I know that, if I went to the Government and said "Look at here! If a depleted oil well or mine can be written off, what about those string beans which I went to all the bother of planting (and my time is money, too) and which came up backwards and full of old threads?" I can just hear the Government laugh at the very suggestion. One of those nasty, unpleasant laughs.

A little farther on in the book I found, under Sec. 25 (a) "dividends received from domestic corporations, except corporations taxable under Section 251 of the law and corporations organized under the China Trade Act." Now I am frank to say that I do not know about the China Trade Act. I don't really suppose that it applies to me, but how am I to be sure? In Supplement K there is a paragraph (d) which is headed: "Definition of China" which says: "As used in this section the term 'China' shall have the same meaning as when used in the China Trade Act, 1922." This more or less brings us back to where we were in the beginning. If the Government thinks that it has cleared up anything at all in that "definition of China," it is crazy. I sometimes wonder if it isn't anyway.

This is where I stood on the evening of March 14th, the night before the Treasury Department's Christmas. I had about decided to let the whole thing go as it was and take my losses, when one of my neighbors, a brisk, rosy-cheeked man who always gets everything right, came in, glowing with health after a tramp through the country, and said: "Well, did you remember to make your one per cent reduction?"

At first I thought that he was kidding me about a tonic which I am supposed to be taking for my metabolism and said "Yes," very curtly.

"There'll be an awful lot of boobs who didn't," he said, smacking his lips.

"What do you mean—one per cent reduction?" I asked, trying not to appear too interested.

"In your income tax," he explained. "The thing Congress passed after the blanks were printed. The blanks are all wrong, you know." He began to suspect that I hadn't known about it and beamed accordingly.

"Oh, *that!*" I replied, not willing to give him the satisfaction of gloating over me. "Oh, sure!"

After he had gone, a little crestfallen, I made inquiries and learned about the little red slip which I had lost. I say "lost" because I suppose that I *did* have one in my envelope, although I wouldn't put it past the Government to have deliberately neglected to send me one. They will go to any lengths once they have got a grudge against you.

This meant that I had to do the whole thing over again. It didn't seem as if I could go through with it. Everything went black before my eyes and I sank down in my chair burying my head in my hands. When I was strong enough I got the blank out of the envelope which I had stamped all ready to send off. (I never trust those envelopes which say up in the corner that no stamp is necessary. It is worth two cents to be sure that your letter is really going to be delivered and not kicked about for months in a post office for insufficient postage.) I looked at the neat little figures in which I had done my reckoning—my figures may be wrong, but they *are* neat—and realized that I should have to get a new blank and begin fresh on the nightmare which had been tormenting me for two weeks. I must have fainted at this point, for I found myself in bed with an ugly gash on the back of my head. Perhaps I had even attempted suicide.

And now, after a week of trying to compute a tax of ½ per cent instead of 1½ per cent on the first $4,000 and a tax of 2 per cent instead of 3 per cent on the next $4,000 and a tax of 4 per cent instead of 5 per cent on the remainder (if there *is* a remainder), I have about decided to take a leaf from the Government's book and pull an "erratum" on them.

I will send in my tax-return just as I had it in the first place. In the envelope with it I will enclose a printed sheet headed "Instruction" on which I will say:

    1. Enter on Line 10, Art. 6, Sec. 11 all receipts, fiduciary

or otherwise, charged off to obsolescence of either subsection (b) or (c), if, for the taxable year 1926 or 1927 within the Provisions of the Revenue Act of 1926 or 1928 the amount of such net loss shall be allowed as a deduction in computing the net income for the two succeeding taxable years to the same extent and in the same manner as a net loss sustained for one taxable year under Art. 8, Sec. 3 of the China Trade Act, allowed as a deduction for the two succeeding taxable years.

2. Enter as Item 3 all items heretofore designated as Items 4, 6 and 9 in Schedule C, except such items as shall hereinafter be designated as Items 5, 2 and 7 if the net income for the period ending during the second calendar year which the portion of such period falling within such calendar year is of the entire period; and (2) any and all such items, 4 or otherwise, as you jolly well please.

To this sheet I will attach a little red slip reading: NOTICE TO INTERNAL REVENUE COLLECTORS. Read carefully before trying to make out Form 1040.

> Since the Individual Income Tax Return, Form 1040, for the Calendar Year 1929 was made out, the Joint Resolution of Congress reducing the rates of normal income tax for the calendar year 1929 has been called to my attention.
>
> Throughout this form, therefore, read ½% for 1½%, 3% for 4%, and 4% for 5%. Figure it out for yourself and fill in the enclosed blank check for whatever you make the amount due to be.

I know that the Government will gyp me if I leave it up to them like this, but I can't be bothered with the thing any more.

# THE MENACE OF
# BUTTERED TOAST

*Maybe I am a fool, but I want to go in for bulb cul-
ture. Oh, I know there is no money in it! I know that I shall
just get attached to the bulbs when I shall have to give them
away to somebody who wants to grow crocuses or tulips or
something, and there I shall be, alone in that great, big, lonely
old house that my grandfather, the Duke, left me.*

*This will mean, naturally, that I shall have to give up
writing for a living. This God-given talent which I have must
be tossed aside like an old mistress (or is it "mattress"?) and
my whole energy must be devoted to the creation and nurture
of little bulbs which someday will grow into great, big, ugly
crocuses, defacing beautiful green lawns all over the country.
But I feel the call, and what else is there to do?*

*Now, since I am resolved to abandon the belles-lettres, the
only decent thing is to pass on the secret of word magic to
someone else. Having held the reading public spellbound for
years with my witchery, I must disclose its secret in order that
some poor sucker may take it up and carry on the torch, bringing cheer to the sick and infirm and evasive notes to Brooks*

*Brothers and the Westchester Light and Power Company. I have therefore decided to set down here the magic formula, by means of which I have kept the wolf from getting upstairs into the bedrooms. Here is a sample of a typical Benchley piece:*

PERSONALLY, if you ask me (and, so far as I have heard, nobody has asked me yet, but I shall go right ahead just the same), I feel that we, as a nation (and when I say "as a nation" I mean "as a nation") eat too much buttered toast.

Buttered toast is all right, provided neither of my little boys butters it (my two little boys seem to have an idea that butter grows on trees, when everybody knows that it is cut in great sheets by a butter-cutter [butter-cutter, butter-cutter, where have you been?] whence it is shipped to the stamping-room where it is stamped by large blonde ladies with their favorite initials and done up in bundles of twenty-five to be sent to the Tissue Paper Department for wrapping), but I *do* think, and I am sure that you would think so, too, if you gave the thing a minute's thought, that there is such a thing as over-doing buttered toast.

In the first place, you order breakfast. (By ordering breakfast, I mean that you get up out of bed, go into the kitchen in your bathrobe, cut three slices of whatever happens to be in the bread box [usually cake], toast it, and butter it yourself.) The words "buttered toast" come naturally in any breakfast order. "Orange juice, two four-minute eggs, *buttered toast*, and coffee." Buttered toast and coffee must be spoken together, otherwise you will hear from the State Department.

Here is where we make our big mistake. If, for once (or even twice), we could say "coffee" without adding "buttered toast," it wouldn't be so bad, but, as my old friend President James Buchanan, used to say (he was President more as a favor to Mrs. Buchanan than anything else), "You can't eat your cake and eat it too."

It being Christmas Eve (or isn't it? I am all mixed up), we ought not to be very hard on buttered toast, because it was on a Christmas Eve that buttered toast was invented. There were six of us (five counting the Captain) all seated around an old stove (the stove was only eleven years old, but that seemed old in those days, and I guess that it *is* old for a stove), when up spoke Baby Puggy, the daughter of the termagant.

"What's all this?" said Baby Puggy. (All *what* never seemed to occur to her to explain, and if she was satisfied, what the hell are you kicking about?)

"I am in no state to bandy legs about," replied her uncle, who, up to this time, had entirely monopolized the conversation.

"I am getting awfully sick of this sort of thing," said Old Doctor Dalyrimple (they called Dr. Dalyrimple "old" because he was 107, and a very good reason, too, for calling him old), "and I have a good mind to go home and go to bed."

"You are in bed, but you're not at home," piped up little Primrose, a frightful child. "They gave your bed at home away to the Salvation Army."

"It serves them right—I mean the Salvation Army," said Old Doctor Meesky (who had changed his name from Dalyrimple to Meesky since we last saw him). And there, so far as anybody can tell, ends the story of Little Red Mother Hubbard, and, I can almost hear you say, "Who cares?"

But about buttered toast. (Not that I care about buttered toast, and not that I think you care.) If we are to have buttered toast brought to us on our breakfast trays (or is it "drays"?) I would suggest the following ways to get around the unbearable boredom of the thing:

1. Have the Football Rules Committee decree that no buttered toast shall be dunked in coffee which does not fill at least one-half (¾) the cup. This will do away with fumbling.

2. Nobody connected with the theatre, either in a managerial capacity (this includes calling "half-hour" and holding up the left leg of the tenor's trousers while he is stepping into the right leg) or as an actor (God knows what this includes) shall sell tickets to any performance for more than $11.50 over and above the box office price—or, at any rate, shall not boast about it.

3. My two small boys shall not throw paper aeroplanes so that they hit Daddy any nearer his eye than his temple.

4. I forget what this rule is.

5. I remember this, but wish I hadn't.

6. Nobody named "Cheeky" shall be allowed to compete.

This, I think, will fix matters up. And if you find that your buttered toast has become soggy after having lain under a small china Taj Mahal with a hole in the top (maybe the *real* Taj Mahal has a hole in the top, for all I know. It ought to have, to let all those people in and out) then just send for the Captain (you remember the Captain!) and tell your troubles to him (song cue: "Tell Your Troubles to the Captain. He Will Weather or Not").

But I *do* think that something has got to be done about buttered toast. I am not one to cavil (cavil me back to Old Virginny) but I do think, if you ask me (and I don't remember anyone's asking me [oh, I guess I said that in the beginning of this article. Sorry!]), I do think, personally, that— where was I?

# A BELATED TRIBUTE

I AM terribly sorry about being so late in paying some attention to the Sir Walter Scott centenary. I don't know what you will think of me, and as for the Scots—Good Lord, I won't dare show my face around there for a year!

Well, all that I can say is that I was out of town during September, when the centenary was going on, and even after I got back, it was a good month before I got any news of the literary world (a *very* good month, in fact). Of course, nobody ever took the trouble to let me know there was a centenary on. Oh, no! I must keep track of such things myself. Oh, yes! If it weren't for the fact that I have been waiting a hundred years to take a crack at the Waverley Novels (or "Leatherstocking Tales," as I used to call them on my examination papers), I would be tempted to let the whole thing slide, now that it has gone this long.

But I happen to have a peculiar lack of interest in Scott, and so may be able to contribute something unique to Waverliana, in view of the fact that, in my youth, every time I changed schools (which was quite often, my grandfather having been King of the Gypsies), the new English class was just beginning to study "Ivanhoe." I am the boy who has taken every word out of "Ivanhoe" and put it back eight times. There was a time when I had "Ivanhoe poisoning" so badly that, at the sight of the Ginn & Co. edition, I would scream and yank the tablecloth off with all the dishes on it. I still twitch my withers slightly at the mention of the name Rowena. I don't suppose that one should speak disparagingly of the dead, but there was a long time when I could have easily done without Sir Walter Scott.

It was in this mood, then, that I began my studies into the life and times of the creator of the Waverley Novels, and, after many trips to Abbotsford, Liddesdale, and all over the place, I now find myself with a collection of some of the worst-fitting data to be found in the Highlands, which, I am sure, will match in interest most of the anecdotes which have been distributed recently in honor of the centenary. In addition, I also saw many interesting sights in London.

We hear a great deal about the financial remuneration which Sir Walter's writings brought him in. It is said that his income was £10,000 a year (I have just discovered that I have a £ sign on my typewriter! I am afraid that you will have to pardon me while I use it just a little more. It comes out so neat and black. £50,000 minus £30,000 equals £20,000 plus £15,000, £5,000, £8,000—oh well, while I'm at it I might as well make it good—£500,000, £750,000, £3,000,000! There, I feel better!) Let's see, where were we?

Oh, yes! Even with £10,000 a year, he was able to get an advance of £19,000, which, as any publisher will tell you today, is a tidy advance, even in these boom times in the book trade. I have been able to dig up a letter from Scott to his publishers which not only gives an idea of the delightful style of the great novelist but shows him to have been a man not without humor, or, to put it more succinctly, a man *with* humor. After reading some of his recently published correspondence, I also think it leads the lot in sparkle:

"Dear Joe: How's chances for a little advance of, say, £15,000? Abbotsford and all that, you know. There's a good old publisher!

"Yours, Walter."

Not bad, considering that Scott didn't learn English until he was forty.

A favorite place in London to which Scott often repaired (in the original this reads "*was* repaired," but I have taken the compiler's liberty of changing it) was No. 22 Sussex-place, Regent's Park. This house is the same now as it was in Scott's time, except that the front wall has been torn down and a marble façade erected in its place with a Turkish-bath establishment crowded in behind it. The street number has also been changed to No. 50, Albemarle Street, Edinburgh. It was here that Scott dined with Coleridge and made his famous remark: "Sam, the more I see of gooseberries, the sicker I get of them. Honest, I do." He got £15,000 for this.

Although Abbotsford took most of his money (£10,000 a year with advances of £19,000, £15,000, £12,000, and such at various times, which were never paid back), it was in London that Scott had most of his literary contacts. Byron (George Byron, that is), Coleridge, Lady Caroline Lamb, Joanna Baillie, £30,000, and a whole slew of others, all used to get together and write letters to each other from the next room, all of which have, oddly enough, been found in a good state of preservation and published in a book called "Swift's

Letters to Stella." It is from this book that most of our knowledge of London of that day (Tuesday) has been culled. It doesn't make very good reading.

It is only because of the imminence of the Scott centenary that I have presumed to bring these little incidents to light, and I suppose it will be another hundred years before I can print any of the others which I have saved up. By then, I suppose, I shall have read "Ivanhoe" eight more times, and will be in the mood again.

# ART REVOLUTION NO. 4861

ACCORDING to advices from Paris (if you want to take advices from such a notorious town), a new painter has emerged from the ateliers of Montparnasse who bids fair to revolutionize Art. Art has been revolutionized so many times in the past twenty years that nothing short of complete annihilation can be considered even a fist fight, to say nothing about a revolution; but it looks now, however, as if the trick finally had been turned. A French boy of forty-five has done it.

The artist in question is Jean Baptiste Morceau Lavalle Raoul Depluy Rourke (during the Peninsular campaigns a great many Irish troops settled in Paris and the authorities were unable to get them out—hence the Rourke). He is a little man, who has difficulty in breathing (not enough, however), and not at all the type that you would think of as a great painter—in fact, he *isn't*. But hidden away in the recesses of that small head is an idea which, some say, is destined to make a monkey out of Art.

Here is the Idea: All Art is Relative although all Relatives are not Art. (The gag is not mine. I am merely reporting.) If we look at a chair or a table or an old shoe box of picnic lunch, what we see is not really a chair, or table, or shoe box full of picnic lunch, but a glove, a sponge, and a child's sand set. This much is obvious.

*Now*—if Art is to be anything at all in the expression of visual images, if, as someone has said, it is to hold Nature up to the mirror, then we must (I am still quoting Rourke, although I am thinking of stopping shortly) put down on our canvas *not* the things that we see but the things that see *us*. Or do I make myself clear?

Perhaps the best way for us to study this new theory of painting is to put on our thinking caps and consider Rourke's famous painting, Mist on the Marshes. The committee of the French Academy refused to hang this picture because, they said, it wasn't accompanied by a stamped, self-addressed envelope and, besides, it didn't have enough paint on it. This, however, was an obvious subterfuge on the part of the committee. The fact was that they didn't understand it, and, in this world, what we don't understand we don't believe in. And a very good rule it is, too.

If you examine the picture closely you will see that it is really made up of three parts—Maine, New Hampshire, and Vermont. The leg, which doesn't seem to belong to anybody, is mine—and I want it back, too, when you have finished looking at the picture. The pensive-looking old party who appears to be hanging on the cornice of a building which isn't shown in the picture is a self-portrait of the artist. He painted it by holding a mirror in one hand and a harmonica in the other and then looking in the other direction. In this way he caught the *feeling* rather than actual physical details.

Now, as you will see, what we have here is not so much a

picture as a feeling for Beauty. Although the artist is still feeling for it, it is quite possible that it may not be as far beyond his grasp as it seems. You can't go on feeling around like that without striking something, possibly oil.

For example, a great many people resent the fried egg in the upper left-hand corner. They claim that it looks too much like the sun. On the other hand, sun worshipers claim that it looks too much like a fried egg. As a matter of fact, friends of the artist, who caught him in a communicative mood one night when he was drunk, report that it is really a badge of a parade marshal, symbolizing the steady march of Art toward the picnic grounds. Whatever it is, you cannot deny that it is in the upper left-hand corner of the picture. And that is something.

In the Sur-Réaliste school of painting (of which Monsieur Rourke was a member until he was suspended for swimming in the pool when there was no water in it) there is an attempt to depict Spirit in terms of Matter and both Spirit and Matter in terms of a good absinthe bun.

Thus, the laughing snake in the lower left-hand corner of Mist on the Marshes is merely a representation of the *spirit* of laughing snakes, and has nothing to do with Reality. This snake is laughing because he is really not in the picture at all. It also pleases him to see that snakes are coming back as figments of delirium tremens, for there was a time when they were considered very bad form.

A good imaginative drunk of five years ago would have been ashamed to see such old-fashioned apparitions as snakes, the fad of the time being little old men with long beards who stood in corners and jeered.

"Seeing snakes" was held to be outmoded and fit only for comic characters in old copies of Puck. If you couldn't see little old men, or at least waltzing beavers, you had better not see anything at all.

But the Sur-Réalistes have brought back the snake, and this one is pretty tickled about it. After all, old friends are best.

The crux of the whole picture, however, lies in the fireman who holds the center of the stage. Here the artist has become almost photographic, even to the fire bell which is ringing in the background.

The old-fashioned modernist painters, like Matisse and Picasso, were afraid of being photographic, but the new boys think it is heaps of fun. This could not possibly be anything but a fireman and a fire bell, unless possibly it is a fisherman and a ship's bell. At any rate, it is a man and a bell, and that is going a long way toward photographic Art.

As for the silk hat, the ladder, the rather unpleasant un-attached face, and the arrow and target, they belong to another picture which got placed by mistake on top of this one when the paint was still wet. Monsieur Rourke feels rather upset about this, but hopes that you won't notice it.

# DING-DONG, SCHOOL
# BELLS

## Or *What the Boy Will Need*

ALTHOUGH it hardly seems credible, it is almost time to begin packing the kiddies off to school again. Here they have been all summer, the rascals, tracking sand into the dining room, rolling Grandma about, and bringing in little playmates who have been exposed to mumps (when Daddy himself hasn't had mumps yet, and mumps for Daddy would be no fun), and in all kinds of ways cheering up the Old Manse to the point of bursting it asunder.

And now the school bells will be ringing again! A sure sign of the coming outbreak of education is the circulars which come in the mail from the clothing and general outfitting stores with lists of "required articles for the schoolboy and for the schoolgirl," just as if the schoolboy and the schoolgirl couldn't tell you themselves exactly what they are going to need—and more, too. Some day I want to get one of those list-compilers to come around and listen to my son and my daughter make out *their* lists. They will have him crying his heart out with chagrin inside of three minutes. "One rubber slicker," indeed! "One green slicker, one tan slicker, one old-rose slicker," is more like it. That is in case the rain comes in three different colors.

I can remember the time (by pressing my temples very hard and holding my breath) when the opening of school meant simply buying a slate with a sponge tied to it and a box of colored crayons. No one, to my knowledge, ever used a slate and a sponge. They were simply a sentimental survival of an even earlier day which the man in the stationery store forced on children who were going to school. The colored crayons were, of course, for eating.

But we bought our slates and our sponges and our crayons (sometimes with a ruler for slapping purposes), and then never used them, for the school furnished all the pencils and pads of yellow paper which were necessary. One of the great releases of my grown-up life has been that I don't have to write on a yellow sheet of paper with blue lines ruled on it half an inch apart. I don't *like* to have to write my lines half an inch apart, and now that I am a great big man, I don't do it. That is one of the advantages of graduating from school.

Today, however, although the slate and the sponge have been removed from the list, there are plenty of "incidentals" even for those children who go to what are known as public schools. What with the increase in high-school fraternities and fixings, high school today resembles the boarding school of yesterday, the boarding school of today resembles the college of yesterday, and the college of today (let's see if I can keep this up) has turned the corner and resembles the public school of yesterday. Is that clear? Or shall we go over it just once again?

Of course, according to the clothing-store lists, once your child gets into a so-called private school (which means that no child who has killed an uncle, an aunt, or any nearer relative, can enter) he is in for an outfitting such as hasn't been seen since Byrd started for the South Pole. You wouldn't think that merely sleeping away from home, in a nation as strict as ours, would entail so many extra clothes for a child.

And not night clothes, either. A boy, when he is living at home, may just sit around the house reading and grousing all day, but the minute he gets away to school (according to the lists) he goes in for fox-hunting, elk-hunting, and whatever it is they hunt with falcons (Falcon hood, $45.50). Then for caber-tossing, you can get a good caber for $24, but the suit that you have to wear must be made by a Scottish tailor out of regulation St. Andrews heather, made up into a smart model for $115.

As I remember my school requirements (I am both a public and a private school boy myself, having always changed schools just as the class in English in the new school was taking up Silas Marner, with the result that it was the only book in the English language that I knew until I was eighteen— but, boy, did I know Silas Marner!), I would substitute a list something like the following in place of that sent out by the clothing store:

One sheet of note paper (with envelope to match) for letter home. This should do for the school year. Requests for money can be made by telegraph, collect.

Five hundred pairs of socks, one to be thrown away each day.

One hat, in a hatbox, the key of which will be left with the school principal for safekeeping until the end of the term.

One overcoat, to be left with the hatbox key, *unless* the overcoat is of raccoonskin, in which case it should be made adaptable for wear up to and including June 10.

One copy, in clear English translation, of each of the following books: The Æneid, Odyssey, Immensée, La Fontaine's Fables (be sure that this follows the original French; there are a lot of fancy English adaptations which will get you into trouble with words which aren't in the text), Nathan the Wise, and Don Quixote. There should be plenty of room between the lines in these books, to allow for the penciling in of a word now and then.

One rubber mouth appliance, for making the sound commonly known as "the bird."

One old model Ford, with space for comments in white paint.

One pipe, with perhaps an ounce of tobacco, for use about four times, then to be discarded or lost.

One pocket lighter, made to harmonize with the other bureau ornaments.

Three dozen shirts, with collars already frayed to save the laundry's time.

One very old T-shirt.

Three dozen neckties, for use of roommates.

One set of name tags, to be sewn on clothing to insure roommates getting them in return for clothing marked with roommate's name.

There is no sense in trying to provide handkerchiefs.

Here, then, Mr. Boy's Outfitter, is my list. I think that it takes care of everything. I am not prepared to go into as much detail as to the requirements for a girl's school, because my daughter (if I had one) is not old enough. But I don't want to get any more intimations that I am not doing right by my boy if I don't buy him a red hunting coat. If he wants a red hunting coat, he can let the sleeves of mine down an inch or so and wear that.

# MY FIVE- (OR MAYBE SIX-) YEAR PLAN

I HAVE decided to start my own five-year plan: All that is necessary is for me to find out just what a five-year plan is.

As I understand it, you take five years to start all over again. You throw out all your old systems, clean out the rubbers in the hall closet, give to the Salvation Army all those old bundles of the National Geographic you have been saving, and tell your creditors to wait for five years and that they will be surprised to see how well you pay. It sounds like a good plan to me. I haven't asked my butcher about it yet.

When a nation goes in for a five-year plan it reorganizes everything, eliminates competition, buys everything on a large scale, sells everything in amalgamations, and, in general, acts up big. I can't do that, because I shall be working alone and on my own, but I *can* reorganize, and I figure that it will take me about five years to do the thing right. Let's say six and be on the safe side.

In the first place, my whole financial system has got to be gone over. It is in such bad shape now that it can hardly

35

be called a system. In fact, I don't think that it can even be called financial. It is more of a carnival. I shall have to go through all those old checkbook stubs and throw them out, for, under my present method of keeping books, there was no need of saving them, anyway. You see, it has been quite some time since I subtracted the amounts of checks drawn from what I smilingly call the "balance." In fact, there are often great stretches of time when I don't even enter the amounts at all. This latter irregularity is due to a habit of making out checks on blank forms supplied by hotels and restaurants, on which even the name of the bank has to be filled in, to say nothing of the number of the check and its amount. I like to make these out, because I print rather well and it is a great satisfaction to letter in the name of my bank in neat capitals exactly in the middle of the space provided for that purpose. I have sometimes made out a blank check just for the satisfaction of seeing "BANKERS' TRUST CO., 57th St. Branch" come out in such typographical perfection from the point of my pen. I am sure that it is a satisfaction to the bank, too. They often speak of it. What they object to is the amount which I fill in below. It seems too bad, they say, to have such a neat-looking check so unnegotiable. All of this will be changed under my five-year plan, for I intend not only to give up making out blank checks, but to enter and subtract those which I do make out. I cannot guarantee to subtract them correctly, for I am not a superman and can do only one thing at a time, but I will at least get the figures down on paper. The bank can handle the rest, and I am sure that they will. That is what they pay men to do, and they have never failed me yet.

Which brings us to the second part of my new economic reorganization—production. Some way has got to be found to turn out more work. One solution would be, I suppose, to do more work, but that seems a little drastic. I ought to be able to combine with somebody to speed up mine without making a slave of myself as well. If I could get a dozen or so fellows who are in the same line of business, we could work up some division of labor whereby one of them could think up the ideas, another could arrange them in notes, another could lose the notes, and yet another could hunt for them. This would take a lot of work off my hands and yet save time for the combination.

By then we would be ready for a fifth member of the pool to walk up and down the room dictating the story from such of the notes as could be found, while a sixth took it down in shorthand. We could all then get together and try to figure out the shorthand, with a special typing member ready to put the story down on paper in its final form. All that would now remain would be to put the stories in envelopes and address them, and it is here that I would fit in. That neat printing that I have been doing on blank checks all my life could be turned to good account here. It makes a great difference with an editor whether or not the contribution is neat, and it might turn out that I was the most important member of the pool. I don't think there is any doubt that the stories would be better.

So much for production. With my financial system reorganized and my production speeded up, the problem would be my world market. Here is where the fun would come in. You can't get a world market without personal contact. You couldn't very well write letters to people in Germany and Spain and say: "I am a little boy forty years old and how would you like to buy a piece that I have written?"

You would have to *go* to Germany and to Spain and see the people personally. This is why I feel that my five-year plan may take possibly six years to carry out. I shall have to do so much traveling to establish a world market. And I *won't* want any of my associates in the pool along with me, either. They will have plenty to do with thinking up ideas at home—and writing them.

This is what appeals to me about the idea. I want to be given a little rest from all this nagging and eyebrow-lifting and "What about that article you promised?" and "Your account shows a slight overdraft." I want to have something definite to hold out to these people, like: "In five years' time I will have my whole system reorganized, with a yearly production of 3,000,000 articles and monthly deposits of $500,-000. Can't you have a little faith? Can't you see that a great economic experiment is being carried on here?" (This, I think, ought to do the trick, unless they have no interest in progressive movements at all. And, from what I hear about them, they haven't.)

# BOOST NEW YORK!

IT IS high time that results were beginning to come in from that pamphlet prepared a while ago by the Merchants' Association and sent broadcast to the newspapers of the country with some idea of boosting New York. Presumably the purpose was, as stated, "to get bigger business coming from an increased number of visitors," although it hardly seems credible that any organization in its right senses would deliberately go out of its way to get *more* visitors to New York. We residents can get hardly any sleep as it is.

I thought at the time of distribution of the pamphlet that the subject-matter was not exactly that which would stir people throughout the country to come rushing to New York on a visit, but I didn't say anything. For instance, it didn't seem that the news that in New York a baby is born every four minutes and six seconds would make lethargic provincials throw some things into a bag and take the first train to the metropolis, unless perhaps they happened to want a baby very badly. And even then they might have to wait quite a time until a free four-minute-and-six-second interval came along, for there would be a lot of people ahead of them. The Merchants' Association went on to state that, using a twelve-hour day for computation, fourteen couples get married every hour, and certainly those who get married in New York ought to get the call over mere visitors in the matter of baby distribution. By the time the visitors got around to their turn, they would have automatically become residents.

It also seemed that the Merchants' Association hadn't dressed its statistics up in very attractive form to lure outsiders into town. To say that the 6,056,000 people in New York eat 3,500,000 tons of food a year, 2,659,632 quarts of milk and 7,000,000 eggs daily, wouldn't strike one as being the best possible argument for coming to New York on a visit. It is hard to imagine a man who has never been out of Des Moines picking up his newspaper and saying to his wife: "Marion, get out your good clothes—we're going to New York. It says here that people there eat three and a half million tons of food a year." Or his wife saying: "But how many eggs a day do they eat?" and, on hearing that it is seven million, replying: "Good! That's all I want to know. We're off!" If I had never been to New York (and sometimes I wonder if it wouldn't have been better) I certainly would not have been moved to come by such tactics.

At times in the pamphlet it almost seemed as if the Merchants' Association was trying actually to discourage people from visiting. "More than one hundred and ninety persons pick up the telephone-receiver every second," they said. Is that any way to boost your town? Immediately the question presents itself in the mind of the reader: "And how many put it down without getting their number?" Picking up a telephone-receiver is nothing to boast of. How many calls are actually put through? The picture of one hundred and ninety people trying to get numbers every second presents a picture bordering on that of Bedlam as seen from the air. Any Westerner would be a fool to leave his home-town on such a prospect, even if his own telephone has to be cranked before and after using.

What I am trying to find out now is whether or not the Merchants' Association has noticed any increase in visitors since the good news was broadcast over two months ago. Perhaps it is too soon to tell, but the summer is when most people visit New York just for the sake of visiting. There ought to have been a few from the larger automotive cities, like Detroit, who would have been excited by the item of there still being fifty thousand horses in daily use in New York, although they are in for a big disappointment if they come and bring their riding togs expecting to ride them. They may not even see them.

Practically the only item of surefire interest to non-residents was that telling of the two hundred and fifty-two theatres in which the spoken drama is played (cut, during the summer, to fifteen which were available). It is probably ten years since a lot of people outside of New York have seen spoken drama and it will take a trip to New York to convince them that they haven't missed much.

But the things that potential visitors really want to know, such as how many night-clubs there are, what speakeasies to go to, and what to do after 3 A.M., the Merchants' Association omitted entirely from its prospectus. You will get no visitors by telling them how many horses there are in New York, or how many babies are born every four minutes, or even that the 1,584 churches are worth more than $286,000,000. At least, I don't think so. But, as I said before, who *wants* more visitors? That's why I didn't point all this out before.

# ADVICE TO GANGSTERS

I WANT it strictly understood right at the beginning of this article that I am *not* trying to interfere in any gang war. Let me make that clearer. Out of any ten thousand men you might question, you would not find one who wanted to interfere in a gang war less than I do. Not only am I averse to interfering in a gang war, but I would rather not meet any gangsters socially. "Live and let live" is my motto—especially "live."

But I would like to help the gangsters if I can. When I say "help," I don't mean that I want to go out with them some night and help them ring doorbells and take off fence-gates. I don't want to go out with them at all. (Although, mind you, I am sure that they are all charming young men, and that we could have quite a jolly time if we got together.) What I mean by "helping" them is what is commonly meant when anyone says he wants to help—that is, I want to give some advice. Well, perhaps "advice" is too strong a word. I want to make a few little suggestions as to how they can carry on their business more efficiently—and then I want to run like hell.

I do hope that any gang-members who happen to pick this

magazine up in their club library and see this article will take it in the proper spirit and will not go off in a huff. They must know as well as I do that the system can be improved upon and there is no need of being so touchy with anyone who tries to point out a few things which would aid in a reorganization of the business. If we are going to have gang wars, let us, by all means, have good ones and not go around the country wasting bullets and derby hats.

In the first place, there isn't a good morale among racketeers. The boys don't trust each other. If they were able to devote as much time to getting good beer into the country as they do to spying on each other, the beer situation wouldn't be in the frightful state that it is today. A man can't buy a good glass of beer for his little boy today without having the fear that the child will be going around the house all the next day moaning and holding onto its head and snapping at its parents. And why? Because the bootleggers, who are supposed to be supplying the country with good stuff, are spending all their time tiptoeing around after each other with machine guns.

And this machine-gun racket is another point on which the gangsters could take a tip or two. Of course, I realize that, for a man who isn't a very good shot with a revolver or rifle, a machine gun reduces the risk of missing to almost a minimum. With three hundred bullets sweeping through the area occupied by the intended victim, it is a pretty jumpy gangster who can't get his man—or, at least, a part of him. But it is an awful waste of bullets. Five good marksmen with a revolver could be hired for a little more than it takes to pay a machine-gun squad, and the saving in bullets and ordnance would be tremendous. As it is, when the gunmen have to rely on their

*The "Deadly Gang" would run on occasion*

revolvers, even though five or six of them take shots at a man, the worst that he can die of is lead-poisoning.

Of course, I am only kidding, boys. You know that, don't you? Aha-ha-ha-ha! There are a million laughs in me if you'll only stick around and not get sore. Or even just not get sore. What the hell? Life is too short. Life is too short as it *is*, I mean.

When I was a little boy I used to belong to a gang, and it seems to me that we handled our gang-matters a little better than the older boys today are doing. In the first place, we limited the gang war to just two gangs, the so-called "Deadly Gang" (my idea, if I do say so) who lived on one side of King Street hill and Eddie Foley's gang, who lived on the other slope. The "Deadly Gang" wasn't so deadly that it wouldn't run on occasion, especially when Eddie Foley got his two big brothers and a friend of theirs who had a paper route, to join them. But, if left to themselves, the two gangs were nearly a match for each other. And some very pretty mêlées took place, too. I think that, man to man, more of our boys actually faced each other in open battle than the boys today do. Automobiles weren't so common then, so we couldn't sneak up, throw an icy snowball at a single opponent, and then drive away. And somehow I rather doubt if we would have done it if we could. Or perhaps I am just getting sentimental about it.

Each gang had one leader and only one leader (if possible in long pants or, at any rate, overalls) and that leader, so long as he led the charges himself and was not knocked down *too* many times, was safe from insubordination. There was none of this "you rat!" or "you double-crossing so-and-so!" stuff. We devoted our whole attention to Eddie Foley's gang, and Eddie Foley's gang devoted its whole attention to us. (I have a scar on my knee to prove it, a scar, I am sorry to say, received in a nasty fall during a retreat. We were outnumbered.)

Now I am afraid that I have said too much. I am afraid that something I have said will be taken amiss. Isn't that always the way? You try to do a good turn for somebody and what do you get? A long ride in the country, ending in the entrance to a culvert.

# "HE TRAVELS FASTEST—"

IF THIS year, because of some silly old reason, you feel that it won't be possible to take the whole family abroad unless the children tend cattle, by no means let this deter you from making the trip yourself. It will eventually mean money in the family coffers, for it will restore that old personal morale you lost somewhere on Broad Street between the corners of Wall and Exchange Place. Next to a shot of some good, habit-forming narcotic, there is nothing like traveling alone as a "builder-upper."

In the first place, you become very good-looking. In your contacts with frank friends and solicitous relations during the past year there may have been some remarks passed which have tended to shake your confidence in your personal appearance, remarks like "When are you going to get fitted to a new dinner-coat?" or perhaps just a simple "Gee, you look awful!" But once you step on board an ocean liner alone, you flip a magic cloak over your left shoulder and become your own Dream Prince. The mirrors in staterooms being none too explicit, there is no reason why you should look just about as you have always wanted to look, for certainly no strangers are going to come up to you and tell you that you are mistaken.

If you dress for dinner every night in solitary distinction, take a quiet apéritif (preferably some un-American-looking liquid like *anis deloso* or *amer picon*) and stand up a great deal straighter than you do at home, you may even become a mystery man before the trip is over, at least in your own mind. Once, on a ten day trip alone, I even got myself to thinking that my hair was quite gray at the temples and that I had an interesting scar across my cheek. On short runs, like that of the *Bremen*, about the best you can do is swing yourself into the belief that you look like a man with a secret sorrow.

Dressing for dinner when traveling alone is essential to this revival of narcissism, but, during the daytime, even your old sport coat with the tear down one side of the pocket becomes rather distingué, and trousers that you had some doubts about even packing take on an air of unostentation which no one ever commented on when you wore them around town. ("The sort of man who can wear any old thing and look well dressed" would be your way of phrasing it.) Leaning over the rail in an ensemble of odds and ends and watching the foam rush back from the prow in determinedly lonely contemplation, the solitary traveler can almost hear people say as they pass by: "There's that man we saw last night in the smoking-room. I wonder who he is!" The fact that nobody really knew that he was on the ship need not come out until, after landing, he meets the beautiful lady he thought was being tortured most by the mystery of it all and hears her say: "Why, were *you* on the *Ile* that trip? Where did you keep yourself?" By then he will have lost his new-found morale anyway.

But in the smoking-room at night, in your immaculate evening dress (if you had had a companion you would have

48

been told that your tie was up under one ear and that one stud had slipped out) you can become enough of a superman to carry you through at least a month of routine when you get back on the job. It is a good idea to take along a book into your hermit corner over by the bar, preferably some work by Bertrand Russell or perhaps a limp leather edition of Hazlitt's *Winterslow*, for, under these conditions your perceptions are razor-sharp and everything you read, if it contains an ounce of inspiration, will feed your personal integrity to the bursting point. Little sentences which you might have skipped had you been dozing by your bed-light at home, suddenly stand out like inscriptions carved on a monument, and you stop and re-read them again and again, saying "How true, how true!" and resolve to begin to live according to them the minute the ship docks—or maybe as soon as you are unpacked. You almost forget that you are the cynosure of all eyes which should be on their bridge hands, and, if you forget sufficiently, along about eleven-thirty, you can allow a few tears to well up into your eyes, rather fine, true eyes, if you do say so yourself.

It usually ends by your making yourself the hero of an imaginary wreck at sea, on this very ship, perhaps. You are sitting right where you are now, when the terrifying news comes that the ship is sinking. Calmly you slip your book into your pocket, button your coat about you and light a cigarette (or better yet, a pipe). You even allow yourself to become slightly British on this occasion, for British men are more the type. This mysterious stranger, who has been sitting alone the entire voyage ("I looked over his shoulder once and he was reading Hazlitt," one of the survivors will report)

*You may even become a mystery man*

becomes a tower of strength on the sinking ship, encouraging women here, assisting the crew there, and, with a wry little smile, jesting with the children as he lifts them into the life-boats. If you had not already been in evening dress, it would be a rather fine gesture to go below and put it on for the last Great Adventure, as you once read of someone's doing under similar circumstances. (It might almost be worth-while *not* to dress first, so that this bit of pardonable theatricalism might be saved for the big moment.) If possible, without sacrificing too much poise, it would be a little better if you too could be saved at the last moment (much against your will) but if not —then heigh-ho—*c'est la guerre!*

If at this point the ship begins to pitch a little and you decide that, since there is no immediate danger or need for your services, you might just as well go below and get a little sleep before it gets too rough, you are still aglow with your recent heroism and the prospect of the fine, new life which stretches out before you when you land, and not even a slight lurch into a table on your way out can make you anything less than a giant among men and possibly the next great leader of the world—or, at any rate, the Atlantic seaboard.

All of this exaltation and spiritual revival is dependent on traveling alone, and is open to anyone who can scrape together the price of a round-trip ticket. Or perhaps just one way would be enough, for, by the time you reach Cherbourg you will be an important enough personage to have the line offer you a free trip back, just for the publicity. Don't say that you can't afford it. You can not afford not to.

# "GREETINGS FROM—"

URING the Christmas and New Year's season there was an ugly rumor going the rounds of the counting-houses and salons (*Note to Printer: only one "o," please!*) of the town that I was in jail. I would like to have it understood at this time that I started that rumor myself. I started it, and spent quite a lot of money to keep it alive through the use of paid whisperers, in order that my friends would understand why they got no gifts or greeting cards from me. They couldn't expect a man who was in jail to send them anything. Or could they?

I have now reached an age and arterial condition where this business of selection of gifts for particular people throws me into a high fever (102) and causes my eyes to roll back into my head. It isn't the money that I begrudge. I spend that much in a single night on jaguar cubs and rare old Egyptian wines for one of my famous revels. It is simply that I am no longer able to decide what to get for whom. In other words, that splendid cellular structure once known as my "mind" has completely collapsed in this particular respect. (I am finding other respects every day, but we won't go into that now.)

It is not only at Christmas and New Year's that I am confronted with this terrifying crisis. When I am away on my summer vacation, when I go away on a business trip, or even when I wake up and find myself in another city by mistake, there is always that incubus sitting on my chest: "Which post card shall I send to Joe?" or "What shall I take back to Mae?" The result is that I have acquired a full-blown phobia for post-card stands and the sight of a gift shop standing in my path will send me scurrying around a three-mile detour or rolling on the ground in an unpleasant frenzy. If I knew of a good doctor, I would go to him for it.

On my last vacation I suddenly realized that I had been away for two weeks without sending any word home other than to cable the bank to mind its own business and let me alone about that overdraft. So I walked up and down in front of a post-card shop until I got my courage up, gritted my teeth, and made a dash for it. I found myself confronted by just short of 450,000 post cards.

Taking up a position slightly to the left and half facing one of those revolving racks, I gave it a little spin once around, just to see if it was working nicely. This brought the lady clerk to my side.

"Some post cards?" she asked, perhaps to make sure that I wasn't gambling with the contraption.

"I'm just looking," I reassured her. Then, of course, I *had* to look. I spun the thing around eighty or ninety times, until it began to look as if there were only one set of post cards in the rack, all showing some unattractive people in a rowboat on a moonlit lake. Then I started spinning in the opposite direction. This made me dizzy and I had to stop altogether. "Let

*"I'm just looking," I reassured the lady clerk*

me see," I said aloud to myself in order to reassure the lady that I really was buying cards and not just out on a lark, "who—whom—do I have to send to?"

Well, there were four in my own family, and Joe and Hamilton and Tweek and Charlie (something comical for Charlie)—oh, and Miss McLassney in the office and Miss Whirtle in the outer office and Eddie on the elevator, and then a bunch of kidding ones for the boys at the Iron Gate and— here I felt well enough to start spinning again. Obviously the thing to do was to take three or four dozen at random and then decide later who to send each one to. So I grabbed out great chunks of post cards from the rack, three out of this pack showing mountain goats, six out of this showing a water-colored boy carrying a bunch of pansies (these ought to get a laugh), and seven or eight showing peasants in native costume flying kites or something.

"I'll take these," I said, in a fever of excitement, and dashed out without paying.

For four days I avoided sitting down at a desk to write those cards, but at last a terrific mountain storm drove me indoors and the lack of anything to read drove me to the desk. I took the three dozen cards and piled them in a neat pile before me. Then I took out my fountain pen. By great good luck, there was no ink in it. You can't write post cards without ink, now, can you? So I leapt up from the desk and took a nap until the storm was over.

It was not until a week later that I finally sat down again and began to decide which cards to send and to whom. Here was one showing an old goat standing on a cliff. That would be good for Joe, with some comical crack written on it. No,

I guess this one of two peasant girls pushing a cart would be better for Joe. I wrote, "Some fun, eh, kid?" on the goat picture and decided to send it to Hamilton, but right under it was a colored one showing a boy and a girl eating a bunch of lilies of the valley. That would be better for Hamilton—or maybe it would be better for Charlie. No, the goat one would be better for Charlie, because he says "Some fun, eh, kid?" all the time. . . . Now let's do this thing systematically. The goat one to Charlie. Cross off Charlie's name from the list. That's one. Now the boy and girl eating lilies of the valley— or perhaps this one of a herd of swans—no, the boy and girl to Hamilton because—hello, what's this? How about *that* for Hamilton? And how about the boy and girl eating a herd of swans in a cartful of lilies of the valley on a cliff for Eddie or Joe or Miss McLassney or Mother or Tweek or—

At this point everything went black before me and when I came to I was seated at a little iron table on a terrace with my face buried in an oddly flavored glass of ice. Not having had a stamp, I didn't send even the card I had written to Charlie, but brought them all home with me in my trunk and they are in my top desk drawer to this very day.

The question of bringing home little gifts is an even more serious one. On the last day before I start back I go to some shop which specializes in odds and ends for returning travelers. I have my list of beneficiaries all neatly made out. Here are some traveling clocks. Everyone *has* a traveling clock. Here are some embroidered hand bags. (As a matter of fact, I have come to believe that the entire choice of gifts for ladies, no matter where you are, is limited to embroidered hand bags. You ask a clerk for suggestions as to what to take to your mother, and she says: "How about a nice embroidered hand bag?" You look in the advertisements in the newspapers and all you can find are sales of embroidered hand bags. The stores at home are full of embroidered hand bags and your own house is full of embroidered hand bags. My God, don't they ever think of anything else to make?)

I roam about in shop after shop, thinking that in the next one I shall run across something that will be just right. Traveling clocks and embroidered hand bags. Perfumes and embroidered hand bags. Perfumes and traveling clocks. And all of them can be bought at home right down on Main Street and probably a great deal better. At this point, the shops all close suddenly, and I am left with my list and lame ankles to show for a final day's shopping. It usually results in my sneaking out, the first day that I am home, and buying a traveling clock, some perfume, and an embroidered hand bag at the local department store and presenting them without the telltale wrappings to only moderately excited friends.

This is why I pretend to be in jail around Christmas and New Year's. It may end up in my pretending to be (or actually being) in jail the year round.

# SO YOU'RE GOING TO
# NEW YORK

TO THE traveler who is returning to New York after a summer in Europe, full of continental ways and accustomed to taking in with an appraising eye such points of interest as have been called to his attention by the little books he bought at Brentano's, perhaps a few words will not be amiss to refresh his memory about his homeland. One forgets so easily.

We approach New York by the beautiful North River, so-called because it is on the west of the island, the scene of many naval battles during the Civil War and referred to by Napoleon as *"le robinet qui ne marche pas"* ("the faucet which does not work"). All true Americans, on sailing up the harbor, will naturally feel a thrill of pride as the tall towers (incorrectly called "the tall towers of Ilium") raise their shaggy heads through the mists, and will naturally remark to one another: "Well, after all, there isn't anything like Little Old New York." These will be the last kind words they speak of New York until they are abroad again next year.

The word for douanier is *customs-house officier*, and you

will find that the American customs are much less exacting than those of foreign countries, owing to the supremacy of American industries and their manufacturing efficiency which makes it possible for them to make better goods at lower prices than those of Europe. The only articles which one is not allowed to bring into America in any quantity are:

Wearing apparel, jewelry, silks, laces, cottons (woven or in the bale), living equipment, books, gifts, raw hides, marble slabs, toothpaste, sugarcane, music (sheet or hummed), garters (except black with a narrow white band), sun-burn acquired abroad, moustaches grown abroad (unless for personal use), cellulose, iron pyrites, medicine (unless poison), threshing-machines, saliva, over four lungfulls of salt air, and any other items that you might possibly want to bring in.

The customs thus disposed of, we take a cab and tell the driver to drive slowly to our hotel. This will be difficult at first, owing to the hold which the French or German language has got on us. We may not have noticed while we were abroad (and certainly the foreigners never noticed it) how like second-nature it comes to speak French or German, but, on landing in America, we shall constantly be finding ourselves (especially in the presence of friends who have been at home all summer) calling waiters *"Garçon"* or saying to drivers: *"Nicht so schnell, bitte!"* This will naturally cause us a little embarrassment which we will explain away by saying that we really have got so used to it that it is going to take us a couple of days to get the hang of English. Some way should be found to make Americans as glib in foreign languages while they are abroad as they are when they get back to New York. Then there will be no more wars.

American money will cause us quite a lot of trouble, too. Compiling statistics ahead of time, we may say that roughly one million returning Americans will remark to friends, during the month of September: "Say, I thought I had a ten-shilling note here," or "I'll be giving one of these dollars for ten francs the first thing I know." The fact that they are not the same size at all will not enter into it. Sharp-tempered people who have been in New York throughout the torrid season may have to take the matter into their own hands and shoot a great many returned travelers.

American money will, however, present quite a problem, owing to the tendency of those who have been accustomed to wadding five- and ten-franc notes (to keep them from falling apart) to leave dollar bills similarly wadded around in peignoir pockets or toss them off as tips. New York waiters, during the month of September, will probably reap a harvest of wadded dollar-bills. Or maybe, when it is a matter of a loss of seventy-five cents, the travelers will catch themselves just in time and remember that they are back in America.

Now that we are safe and sound at our hotel, or home, or favorite bar, we have the whole of marvelous New York before us. New York was founded by the Dutch in the Seventeenth Century (the editors will not give you the exact date because by looking it up for yourself you will remember it better) and is a veritable gold-mine of historic associations. We must divide our days up wisely, in order to get the most out of our stay here, and to renew old friendships and revisit familiar scenes. We shall also spend a few days looking over old bills which we neglected to pay before sailing.

The old friendships will not be so difficult to renew. The

first old friend we meet will say: "Hi!" cheerily and pass on. The second will say: "Not so hot as it was last week, is it?" and the third will say: "When are you going to take your vacation?" This will get us back into the swing again, and we can devote the rest of our time to studying points of interest. Most of these will either have been torn down or closed.

There is an alternate, or Trip B, from Europe to New York. If we follow this, we stay right on the boat and go back to Cherbourg.

# FUTURE MAN: TREE OR MAMMAL?

THE study of Mankind in its present state having proven such a bust, owing to Mankind's present state being something of a bust itself, scientists are now fascinating themselves with speculation on what Mankind will be like in future generations. And when I say "future," I don't mean 1940. Add a couple of ciphers and you'll be nearer right. It's safe enough to predict what Man will be like in that kind of future, because who'll be able to check? We know what Man was like in the Pleistocene Age. He was awful. If he stood upright at all he was lucky, and, as for his facial characteristics, I would be doing you a favor if I said nothing about them. Somehow or other he knew enough to draw pictures of elephants and mammoths on the walls of his caves, but I have always had a suspicion that those elephant pictures were drawn by some wag who lived in the neighborhood along about 1830 and who wanted to have some fun. You can't tell me that anyone who carried himself as badly as the Neanderthal Man could have held a piece of crayon long enough to draw an elephant. However, this is none of my business. I can't draw an elephant either, which is probably why I am so bitter.

But when it comes to predicting what Man will be like in 100,000 years (I put it at 100,000 years because, when it gets up into figures like that, it doesn't make any difference; 100,-000 years—50,000 years—who cares?), when it comes to predicting that far ahead, it is anybody's racket. I can do it myself.

When we look back and see how Man has developed through all those corking stages from the Palaeozoic Age, from sponge to tadpole to jellyfish (maybe we're on the wrong sequence—we don't seem to be getting any nearer Man), anyway, through all those stages before he came on up through the ape to the beautiful thing we know today as J. Hamilton Lewis or Grover Whalen, and when we consider how many aeons and aeons it took for him to develop even arms and legs, to say nothing of pearl shirt-studs and spats, we realize that we must go very carefully before we predict what he will be like in an equal number of aeons. By then he may be a catalpa tree. Stranger things *have* happened.

I am basing my prediction on the part which protective coloration has played in the development of Man from the lower animals. It was only those jellyfish which had the same color as the surrounding country which survived the rigors of evolution. (Name six rigors of evolution, beginning with Head Colds.) Birds which are the same color as the foliage in which they nest are less likely to be disturbed by other birds who want to drop in and chat, and therefore last longer. The chameleon is a good example of protective coloration carried to ridiculous extremes. If all the animals had been possessed of this ability to change colors at the drop of a hat, we should be living in a madhouse today.

According to my theory, however, the principle of protective coloration will be working, from now on, in exactly the opposite manner from that in which it functioned in past ages. It will be only those men and women whose color differs most sharply from the surrounding country who will survive. If you will stop that incessant whispering and fidgeting and will come up in single file and drop your chewing gum into the wastebasket, Teacher will continue to explain what he means.

Let us say that A and B are two citizens living in a modern city. A dresses in clothes which are of a dull slate color or perhaps low-class marble. When he goes out on the street he blends in with the color of the buildings, especially if he happens to be hung-over and not looking in the best of health. (Most people today do not look in the best of health owing to not being in the best of health.) What happens? He is run down by an automobile, the driver of which cannot distinguish him from the background of buildings and passing vehicles (unless a circus band wagon happens to be passing at the time, a contingency which it would be well not to count on too much), or he is shot by accident by a gunman who is aiming at a comrade and doesn't see the drab-colored citizen at all.

The other citizen, whom we have called B but whose name is probably W, dresses in bright reds and yellows and has a complexion which makes him stand out from his fellow men. (Drinking will do this for one.) He can cross the street with impunity, because he is conspicuous, and automobile drivers will sometimes run right up on the sidewalk and knock down a dozen drab-colored citizens rather than crash into him. Gunmen can also see him clearly and will recognize him as *not* one of their number, for gunmen are notoriously quiet dressers. It is B then (or W, as you will) who survives.

But the man who doesn't go out into the street at all will survive even longer than B. We call him $B^1$, or better yet $^2B$. This wise man stays right in his room and reads magazines all day, with an occasional look at the clock to see how late he would have been if he had kept that luncheon appointment. He has his meals brought in to him, and, when it is bedtime, he sends for a lot of friends and they play backgammon. In time, owing to never having to walk, he loses the use of his legs, and, after several centuries, his breed have no legs at all. I therefore predict that Man will, in 3,000 years, have no legs, for all of those men who once had legs and have gone out into the streets will have been killed off.

This may seem fantastic and I shall probably be refused membership to the American Academy of Sciences because of promulgating this doctrine. See if I care. I still maintain that the Man of 1,900,031 will be very highly colored and will have no legs. His arms, however, owing to the constant raising and lowering of highball glasses (to preserve the high coloring) and centuries of turning on and off television dials (by means of which he will be kept in touch with the outside world), will have attained a remarkable flexibility and may reach five times the length of the distance now attained by what we fatuously call "modern man." He will not be very pretty-looking, according to modern standards, but he will be alive, which is something.

However, since we are in a period of transition right now, the best that we can do is to hasten this pleasant state of inactivity in behalf of our descendants. We ourselves cannot hope to reap its benefits. But we can attain to something of the charm and peace of that future state by resolving to stay indoors as much as possible, to increase our coloring to what others may consider an alarming degree, and to do nothing which will impede Nature's progress toward her inevitable goal, the elevation of Mankind to the condition of the beautiful catalpa tree.

# ENCORE

NEW YORK has been in for its annual revival of Gilbert and Sullivan operas. Sometimes I'm glad when they are announced, and sometimes I'm sorry.

I am glad because I happen to like Gilbert and Sullivan. Not *all* of Gilbert and Sullivan, but enough to rate as a fan. And I am sorry because most Gilbert and Sullivan audiences drive me crazy.

A real Gilbert and Sullivan audience has much to recommend it. It is made up of obviously nice people, most of them past middle-age, and many of them unaccustomed to going to the theatre in these days when going to the theatre is such a gamble. They would rather stay at home, and you have a feeling that staying at home with them would be no hardship. They look like people who would talk well at their own dinner-table, and are the only group of theatre-goers who look as if they hadn't put on evening clothes just to go to the theatre. They may not be the latest thing in dinner-clothes, but you have a feeling that these people would have had them on anyway, theatre or no theatre.

But there their attractiveness ceases. Possibly because they do *not* go to the theatre regularly, or possibly because they are just thoughtless (people who dress for dinner at home *can* be thoughtless, too), they do not realize that the fact that they have loved "Dear Little Buttercup" all their lives does not warrant them keeping it being repeated ten times by their applause. A lot of other people are sick of "Dear Little Buttercup," if only because they have heard it in the Civic Center so many times sung by the real-estate agent's wife. Neither does it warrant them humming it to each other, half a beat ahead of the singer.

Furthermore, a great many of the lines in Gilbert's dialogue are *not* funny now, especially after one has heard them for forty years straight. They couldn't be funny to anyone who did not know, and feel strongly about, the topics of the day in which they were written. And yet, to hear your G. & S. fans laugh, you would think that they came like a bolt from the blue and hit the nail right on the head. I am afraid that a lot of these nice people are pretending just a teenty-weenty bit.

But take "Iolanthe"! There's a Gilbert and Sullivan opera that I could hear over and over again three times in the same evening! And don't think I let them get away with a couple of encores to each song, either.

# SPORTING LIFE IN
# AMERICA

## *Watching*

IF THERE is one sport which we Americans go in for
wholeheartedly it is the grand old outdoor exercise of
"watching." By "watching" is not meant "kibitzing," for
a kibitzer takes things more personally than does a
watcher. A kibitzer gets very close to whatever he is watching,
usually a game of cards. Sometimes he is almost in the cards.
Sometimes he even gets hit.

The watcher, on the other hand, is more or less detached
and does his observing from a distance, as, for instance, a
railing surrounding a building excavation. He offers no advice, as the kibitzer does. He doesn't understand much about
what is going on down in the excavation. His game is more
gazing than really watching. After a certain period of time he
seems to have crossed the border between human beings and
plant life and become a form of fungus. This is our watcher.

The most common watching-fields are found around the
above-mentioned cellar excavations. Just dig a hole in the

ground big enough for a donkey engine to chug around in, surround it with a fence to keep people from dropping in, and you will in three minutes have a crowd of busy Americans (oh, the rush and bustle of this money-mad land!) settled along the railing, who will follow the project through to the bitter end. If the hole is big enough, and you set some compressed-air drills to work, you will have half the population of the town fascinated to the point of stupor.

The rules for the game of watching, or unprofessional observation, are fairly simple. The watcher takes his position leaning against a wooden fence, resting the elbows on the top rail with the body inclined out into the sidewalk at an angle of perhaps twenty degrees. (There is an Australian game in which the players' bodies rest at a forty-degree angle, but in this game the player is supposed to sleep part of the time. There is no sleeping among American watchers, no siree!)

Once in position, the player fixes his eyes on some one object in the excavation below and follows it carefully. This object is known as the "quarry." It may be either a workman, a chunk of rock, or the revolving wheel of an engine. As it moves about, either under its own steam or by some outside force, the player keeps careful watch of it until it has stopped. This counts him ten. If he loses sight of it somewhere in its course, either because of defective vision or because it gets behind some intervening object, he loses ten. If he can find two or more quarries which he can watch all at once, he becomes a master-watcher and may wear a gold eyeball on his watchchain. The game is over when one watcher has got a thousand points, but as it begins again immediately, the result is not noticeable to passers-by.

Excavation-watchers, as a class, are very conscientious sportsmen. You very seldom catch them watching anything else when they are on an excavation job. Fire engines may go by in the street behind their backs, old ladies may faint over their very heels, and even a man with a sidewalk stand of bouncing dolls may take up his position on the curb across the street, but the cellar-hole boys stick to their post without ever so much as batting an eyelash. In fact, the eyelash-batting average of some of the old-timers has gone as low as .005 in a busy season.

They are also not averse to night work. If the boss decides that the job requires coming back after supper and digging by the light of flares and torches, the watchers are on hand without a word of complaint and may even bring along a couple of friends as helpers. I myself have been caught up by the spirit of the game at night and, in amateur circles, am known as something of a speed demon at night-excavation-watching. My eyes are a little weak for daytime work, but when the flares are throwing their hellish light over the jagged walls of rock and the little men are darting about like demons in purgatory (it must be the mystic in me that is fascinated) I find it hard to pass by without giving at least fifteen or twenty minutes of my time to a general survey of the scene. One night I became so enthralled by the inferno-like spectacle that I allowed my top hat to fall off into the abyss, where naturally it was lost and will probably turn up in a hundred years or so embedded in the wall of the foundations. This will cause no end of speculation among archaeologists, for it had my initials in it and they will know that I never went in much for building, even in my heyday. "Jack-of-all-trades-and-master-of-none" will probably be the sobriquet under

*My silk hat fell in*

which I shall go down in history as a result of this little incident. And even then they won't quite understand what I was doing laying foundations in a silk hat.

Once the framework of the building is up and the wooden observation bridge removed, the game of watching becomes a little more difficult. The players may then move on to the next excavation or get jobs in offices across the street where they can carry on their watching from the windows. In several offices where I have worked I should say that at least two-thirds of the office force had been recruited from the ranks of old excavation-watchers who had come up from the wooden bridge to keep an eye on the job as it progressed. It had become almost a religious frenzy with them. Give them a desk by a window overlooking a new building across the way and put a sheet of figures in their hands to be checked up and copied by four o'clock, and long before that time they will have had six large steel girders in place and twenty red-hot bolts tossed through the air, to say nothing of having assisted at the raising and lowering of a temporary elevator at least forty times. If it is possible to place a water cooler by the window which commands the best view of the construction work, you will soon have everybody playing the game.

Of course, excavation- and construction-watching is not the only form this recreation takes. There are always drug-store windows. There is more variety in drug-store-window-watching, but it attracts a slightly more superficial crowd than an excavation. Their hearts aren't in it, and they stop and pass by with perhaps only a ten- or fifteen-minute wait. This is probably because of the frivolous nature of the exhibits.

A train of cars made out of coughdrop boxes running round

73

and round in a circle may be all right for a quarter of an hour's fun, but it isn't getting buildings built. A man may profitably spend a few hours a week watching a red ball disappear in a mound of peanuts, but the human brain demands a little more to work on.

Of course, if there happens to be a man in the window demonstrating a strap which holds the trousers up and keeps the shoes on at the same time, *then* it would be worth while to stick around a bit. This comes under the head of scientific investigation. An hour would not be too much to devote to this, especially if you have a bundle to deliver or an appointment to keep in half an hour.

Unfortunately, however, window-demonstrating seems to be dying out as a trade. I don't think that I have seen a man standing in a window in his underclothes for over a year. There are still a few ladies who do legerdemain with day-beds, but that doesn't strictly come under the head of scientific research. Everyone knows how to work a day-bed by now. What we want is to see a new way to open bottles without a corkscrew, or a combination cuff and spat. Where have all those men gone who used to hold up three fingers at you through the glass, meaning that three times they had tried to break a watch crystal and now admitted themselves hopelessly defeated? Where are those martyrs to health who used to allow themselves to be shaken to a froth by electric vibrators? Wherever they are, they are holding up the wheels of window-watching, one of the noblest of America's outdoor games.

# SPORTING LIFE IN
# AMERICA

*Turkish Bathing*

ONE of the more violent forms of exercise indulged in by Americans today is Turkish-bath sitting. This invigorating activity has almost entirely replaced the old-fashioned tree chopping and hay pitching which used to work our fathers up into such a rosy glow and sometimes land them in an early grave. Turkish-bath sitting has the advantage of not only making you perspire freely, but of giving you a chance to get your newspaper read while perspiring. And you can catch cold just as easily after a Turkish bath as you ever could after pitching hay. Easier.

A man seldom thinks of taking Turkish baths until it is too late. It is usually at that time of life when little diamonds of white shirt have begun peeping out between the buttons of his vest, or when those advertisements showing men with a large sector of abdomen disappearing under the influence of a rubber belt have begun to exert a strange fascination for him. Then he remembers about Turkish baths. Or when he wakes up some morning with his head at the foot of the bed and the lights all going and the windows shut. Then, somewhere in the recesses of what used to be his mind, there struggles a puny thought vaguely connected with steam rooms and massage.

"That might do me some good," he thinks, and promptly faints. In both of these cases he is anywhere from one day to one year too late.

However, he takes a chance. He totters to the nearest emporium which features pore-opening devices, checks his watch and what is left of his money, and allows a man to pull off his shoes. Just in time he remembers that he has on the lavender running drawers which someone once sent him as a joke, and quickly dismisses the attendant, finishing disrobing by himself and hiding the lavender running drawers under his coat as he hangs them up. Not that he cares what the attendant thinks, but you know how those guys talk.

Then, coyly wrapping a towel about himself, he patters out into the hot room. A hot room in a Turkish bath is one of the places where American civilization appears at its worst. One wonders, on glancing about at the specimens of manhood reclining on divans or breathing moistly under sheets, if perhaps it wouldn't be better for Nature to send down a cataclysmic earthquake and begin all over again with a new race. It is slightly comforting in a way, however, because no matter how far along you have allowed your figure to get, there are always at least half a dozen figures on view which make yours look like that of a discobolus.

I can imagine no lower point of self-esteem than to find yourself one day the worst-looking exhibit in a Turkish bath.

They should keep a pistol handy for just such cases. And you might shoot a couple of others while you are at it. It would save them all that bother of lacing up their shoes again.

In the hot room there isn't much to do. You can read a newspaper, but in a couple of minutes it gets a little soggy and flops over on your face, besides becoming so hot that turning over a page is something of an adventure. If, by any chance, you allow an edge of it to rest on an exposed bit of your anatomy, it isn't a quarter of a second before you have tossed it to the floor and given up reading. Then comes the period of cogitation.

As you sit waiting for your heart to stop beating entirely, you wonder if, after all, this was the thing to do. It occurs to you that a good brisk walk in the open air would have done almost the same thing for you, with the added advantage of respiration. People must die in hot rooms, and you wonder how they would identify you if you were quietly to smother.

The towel around your waist would do no good, as they are all alike. You regret that you were never tattooed with a ship flying your name and address from the masthead. The only way for them to tell who you were would be for them to wait until everybody else had gone home and find the locker with your clothes in it. Then they would find those lavender drawers. So you decide to brave it out and not to die.

Conversation with your oven mates is no fun either. If you open your mouth you get it full of hot air and you are having trouble enough as it is keeping body and soul together. In the second place, you know that you look too silly to have your ideas carry any weight.

I remember once sitting on a sheet-covered steamer chair

with my head swathed in a cold towel to keep my hair from catching on fire and thinking that there was something vaguely familiar about the small patch of face which was peering at me from under a similar turban across the room. As the owner of the face got up to go into the next torture chamber I recognized him as an English captain whom I had last seen in the impressive uniform of those Guards who sport a red coat, black trousers, and an enormous fur busby with a gold strap under the chin. I at once hopped to my feet, and, clutching my towel about me with one hand, extended my other to him.

"Well, fancy seeing you here!" was about all that seemed suitable to say. So we both said it. Then we stood, perspiring freely from under our head cloths, while he told me that he was in New York on some military mission, that the King and Queen were both well, and that England was counting a great deal on the coming Naval Conference to establish an entente with America.

In my turn, I told him that I was sure that America hoped for the same thing and that, to my way of thinking, the only impediments to the success of the conference would be the attitude of France and Italy. He agreed in impeccable English, and said that he had some inside information which he wished that he might divulge, but that, all things considered—

And then, as my mind began to stray ever so slightly, the idea of this gentleman in a sheet and a head towel having any secrets from *any*one struck me as a little humorous. To make things worse, a picture came to my mind's eye of how he would look if he had that busby on right now, with the gold strap under his chin, and I gave up my end of the conversation.

He must have, at the same time, caught a picture of me standing behind a none-too-generous towel, giving it as my opinion that France and Italy were the chief obstacles to international accord in naval matters, for he stood slightly at attention and, bowing formally, said: "Well, I'll be toddling along. See you again, I hope." There was an embarrassed shaking of hands and more formal bowing and he went his way, while I went out and flung myself into the pool.

There is one feature of Turkish bathing which I have not had much experience in, and that is the massage. Being by nature very ticklish, I usually succeed in evading the masseur who follows me about suggesting salt rubs, alcohol slaps, and the other forms of violence. I tell him that I am in a hurry and that I really shouldn't have come at all. He chases me from one room to another, assuring me that it won't take long. Then I plead with him that I have got a bad knee and am afraid of its flying out again. This just spurs him on, because bad knees are his dish.

Once in a while I slip on the wet tiles and he gets me, but I prove to be such a bad patient, once he has me down on the slab, that he passes the whole thing up and gives that irritating slap which means, in the language of the masseur: "All right! Get up—if you can."

Once, while I had my back turned, he played a powerful stream from two high-powered hydraulic hoses on me from clear across the room, which threw me against the wall and dazed me so that I went back into the hot room again instead of getting dressed. I would rather that the masseurs let me alone when I am in a Turkish bath. *I* know what I want better than they do.

As a matter of fact, I don't know why I go to a Turkish bath at all. I emerge into the fresh air outside looking as if I had been boiled with cabbage for five hours, with puffy, blood-shot eyes, waving hair, and the beginnings of a head cold. It is all I can do to get back to my room and go to bed, where I sleep heavily for eleven hours.

And invariably, on weighing myself, I find that I have gained slightly under a pound.

However, it is a part of the American sporting code and we red-blooded one hundred percenters must carry on the tradition.

# TAKE A LETTER, PLEASE

P ROBABLY one of the most potent causes of war in the world's history (this shapes up like a pretty broad statement, but my attorney tells me that I have adequate proofs) has been the giving out of statements, sometimes by mistake, which the giver-out is too proud to take back. A king or a dictator, a little behind in his phrase-making, has pulled a quick one like "Beyond the Alps lies Italy," "*L'Etat, c'est moi,*" or "Never give a sucker an even break," and then has had to go through with it to save his face. A great many times all the trouble could have been avoided if the original speechmaker had been willing to say: "I guess I must have been cockeyed. I don't remember having said any such thing."

That is one reason why I am afraid to dictate a letter. I probably couldn't start a war between any nations worth noticing, but I could get myself into an awful jam. There is something about a stenographer sitting with pencil poised waiting for my next word which throws me into a mild panic. Anybody, in order to be a secretary or even a stenographer, has got to have a certain amount of concentrative power and a good common-school education. This means that while they are sitting there waiting for a word or two, they are passing judgment on me; for my own education, although lengthy, is what you might call "sketchy." Almost any stenographer could write a better letter than I can.

With this uppermost in my mind I sit down with a young

lady facing me and try to sound businesslike. "Take a letter, please, Miss Keegle," I say. Miss Keegle always seems to be an exceptionally intelligent young lady, and always has the appearance of disapproving of me right at the start.

The first part of the letter goes like wildfire. I have the name and address of the man right in front of me. "To

Mr. Alfred W. Manvogle, Room 113, Butchers' and Bakers' Bank Building, St. Louis." So far, so very good. Miss Keegle is obviously impressed.

" 'My-er-dear Mr. Manvogle,' or rather, I guess—'Dear Sir. (*Confidential aside to Miss Keegle:* I don't know him at all. *Miss Keegle nods, as if to say,* What of it?) In reply to your letter of September 11th (*long pause to figure out just what the reply is going to be. I should have thought this out before*). In reply to your letter of September 11th would say that, although I agree with you on the main principles of your argument (*I don't agree with him at all, but am saying this in order to give the girl something to write down*), I feel that—er—I feel that—ah—(This is awful!)—I feel that it would be better if your Mr. Cramsey and I could get together again some afternoon this week. (I *don't* want to see Mr. Cramsey again, and I haven't got any afternoon this week that I can see him, but I have got to say something. This girl has been waiting there fifteen minutes already.) I —er—or rather you—ah—seem to be laboring under the de- lusion—' No, I guess cross that out. Ah— 'Your ideas about how we should go ahead in this matter—' No, I guess never mind that. (I should really get some sort of instrument to dictate into—but then think of the records I would waste!) Where was I, Miss Keegle?"

Miss Keegle says that I really wasn't anywhere.

In desperation I continue, in a much more belligerent mood than I otherwise would have been, simply to get the thing over with: "I don't see how we can get together on this thing unless you are willing to listen to reason."

Miss Keegle reminds me that I have already said that I

would like to talk to Mr. Cramsey again. Which do I mean?

"Cross that out about Mr. Cramsey. I don't want to see him. I don't want to see anybody. I want to get this whole thing out of the way. Just send the letter as it is, Miss Keegle—and thank you."

Miss Keegle then goes away, and a letter goes out to Mr. Manvogle which gives quite the wrong impression of my attitude in the matter. If Mr. Manvogle were France and I were the United States, there would be a war, simply because I blurted out something under the harassing fear of Miss Keegle, which I really didn't mean. Of course, I should have to stand by my guns when the matter came up before the World Court, and I should expect all the young men of the country to stand by my guns with me. Or, perhaps, I should expect them to stand by *their* guns while I dictated some more letters.

Of course, one can correct a letter when it comes back from the typist, but, after correcting a few letters until they looked like a manuscript of Victor Hugo's, with long sentences written out in the margin running upward and long sentences on the end of a string running downward from the middle of the sheet, I have given up postdictation correction, and just sign my name. In fact, I have given up dictation entirely, and write out my letters longhand, to be copied by anybody who can read them. I am thinking now of giving up writing letters.

But this giving out snap judgments and snap answers, simply because somebody is waiting and making you nervous, is a very dangerous business. This is especially true if the language in use happens to be one with which you are unfamiliar. If given plenty of time to mutter the thing over to myself, and perhaps write it out on a little card, I can understand what a Frenchman is saying to me. But when he rattles it off like mad (and show me a Frenchman who doesn't) and is obviously impatient for an answer, I am quite likely to commit myself to something I don't want to do, just out of sheer nervousness.

I once got into a French barber's chair (no small feat in itself) and asked, in French which I had rehearsed out in the corridor for five minutes before entering, for a shave. During the process the barber said something to me which, because of its rising inflection at the end, I took to be a question. In fact, it was one of those questions which seem to demand an answer in the affirmative, like "It's a nice day, isn't it?" or "Is the razor all right?" (And, by the way, did anyone ever answer this last question by saying that the razor *wasn't* all right?) So I said *"Oui, oui!"* out from my lather and shut my eyes again. In about half a second my hair was on fire. At the same moment, a boy rushed up from the back of the shop and started taking my shirt off.

I realized that I had said *"oui"* to the wrong thing, but was ashamed to admit it. So I clung to my chair and took my beating. It seems that, in addition to having agreed to have my hair singed, I had got myself in for a treatment for congestion of the lungs (French barbers still maintain the old medieval office of surgeon and will treat you for anything up to, and including, the birth of a small child), and before I got out of the chair, I had had four little cups burnt on the small of my back so that they hung there by force of suction (all the air having been drawn out by flaming cotton, a charming process known as *"ventouse,"* which I had mistaken for *"vendeuse,"* which means "saleslady"). And all this because I had said *"oui"* to something I didn't understand. At least, I know enough now to say *"non"* to everything. I may miss a little fun, but I am playing safe.

It doesn't have to be a foreign language to cause misunderstanding. I can answer questions that I don't understand in English just as easily and get into just as much trouble. It all comes from not wanting to ask for a repeat, especially after the second time. I have signed up for hotel rooms with Italian gardens attached and Roman swimming pools adjoining, simply because the man at the desk muttered something as I signed my name which I took to be a little pleasantry calling for a genial "Yes, indeedy" in reply. I have bought suits with belts in the back, hats with green feathers in them, and shoes which would throw a Chinese lady on her face, all because I misunderstood the clerk and didn't have the nerve to crawl. If I were just learning about life, I would try to correct this fault. But it is a little late now.

The best that I can do is bluff the thing out, and make believe each time that I am getting exactly what I wanted. But, as we noted in the beginning, that is one of the reasons nations get themselves mixed up in wars. And I certainly don't want to have another war until we get this last one paid for. It is quite a problem.

# THE MYSTERIES OF RADIO

I WOULDN'T be surprised if I knew less about radio than any one in the world, and that is no faint praise. There may be some things, like horseshoeing and putting little ships in bottles, which are closed books to me, but I have a feeling that if someone were to be very patient and explain the principles to me I might be able to get the hang of it. But I don't have any such feeling about radio. A radio expert could come and live with me for two years, and be just as kind and gentle and explicit as a radio expert could be, and yet it would do no good. I simply never could understand it; so there is no good in teasing me to try.

As a matter of fact, I was still wrestling with the principle of the telephone when radio came along, and was still a long way from having mastered it. I knew that I could go to a mouthpiece and say a number into it and get another number, but I was not privy to the means by which this miracle was accomplished. Finally I gave up trying to figure it out, as the telephone company seemed to be getting along all right with it, and it was evident from the condition my own affairs were getting in that there were other things about which I had much better be worrying. And then came radio to confuse me further.

Of course, I know all about the fact that if you toss a stone into a pond it will send out concentric circles which reach to the shores. Everybody pulls that one when you ask them how sound is transmitted through the air. If I have been told

about tossing a stone in a pond once I have been told it five hundred times. I have even gone out and done it myself, but I guess that I didn't have the knack, for the concentric circles ran for only about two feet and then disappeared.

But the stone in pond explanation is really no explanation

at all, for there you have at least the stone and the pond to work with, whereas in radio you have nothing, absolutely nothing. If people tell me about the stone in the pond once again I shall begin to think that it is a gag worked up by those who don't understand the thing either. They have got to be more explicit if they want me to understand. Perhaps they don't care. I almost think that nobody cares whether I am enlightened or not. Certainly nobody seems to be putting himself out to help me. (I am sorry if I sound bitter about the thing, but I have stood it just about as long as I can.)

Somebody once did say something which made a great impression on me, but which I can hardly believe. He said that the air had always been full of these sounds, and that all the radio did was to give us some means of catching them. This is a horrible thought. To think that the room in which the Declaration of Independence was signed would have, by the mere installation of radio, been echoing with the strains of something corresponding to "I Kiss Your Hand, Madame," or that Robert and Elizabeth Browning held hands in a chamber which was at that very moment teeming with unheard syllables explaining how to make bran muffins! Reason totters at the thought, and I mention the supposition here only to show how absurd the whole thing is.

But the suggestion is a haunting one, even though you, as I have done, discard it as impractical. If the air has always been full of music and voices which we have only just recently learned to make audible, what else might it not be full of right now which, perhaps in a hundred years, will also be dragged out into the light? If by the installation of a microphone at the other end and a receiving set at my end I learn that my room has all the time been full of noises made by the Little Gypsy Robber Sponge quartet over in Newark or a man employed by some slipper concern in Michigan, why isn't it possible that it is also full of things I don't know about, such as the spirits of the men who murdered the little princes in the tower, or perhaps a couple of Borgias? It simply makes a mockery of privacy, that's all it does. A man ought to have some place where he can go and be alone without feeling that he may be breathing in a lot of strangers and what nots.

I will even concede that the air of out of doors may be full of sound waves, but you can't make me believe that they can get through the walls of great big houses. They might get through the walls of a summer hotel, or even come through an open front door and work their way upstairs. I will even go so far as to recognize the possibility of something erected on a roof catching them and bringing them down into the living room to disturb daddy when he is trying to take a nap. But to ask me to believe that a box which has no connection at all with the outside can be carried about a house which is securely locked, and still keep on playing sounds which have pushed their way through stone walls, is just a little too much. For this reason I have refused to turn on my portable radio set which was given to me on my birthday. I will not allow myself to be made a party to any such chicanery.

My biggest argument that the whole thing is a fake is the quality of the stuff that comes out of the air. It is the same thing which makes me distrust spiritualism—the quality of the material offered us from the spirit world. I am really a very simple minded man at heart and will believe most anything as long as the person who tells me has a pleasant face. I might very easily be won over to spiritualism, just as I have in the past been won over to Buddhism, osteopathy, and Swedish bread. But when I go into a darkened room with the expectation of hearing something out of the great unknown which will help clear up this mystery of life and death and find out merely that the uncle of some person in the room is still having that trouble with his hip which he had before he died, or that those old gray gloves which I thought I had lost are in my winter overcoat hanging in the hall closet, it all seems hardly worth the trouble.

It is much the same with radio. Scientists have gone to all the trouble of rigging up apparatus which will pull out of the air sounds which we were never able to hear before, the whole ether is thrown into a turmoil, the south pole is placed in connection with Greenland and modern life is revolutionized by the utilization of these mysterious sound waves. And with what result? We in New York hear Miss Ellen Drangle in Chicago singing "Mighty Lak a Rose." The mountain which brought forth a mouse did a good day's work in comparison.

All of this, however, is probably none of my business. I had better not sit here criticizing others for something which I couldn't possibly do myself. Probably that is what upsets me so—that I don't understand how it works. I have seen other people make it work and that has more or less discouraged me. They get so unpleasant about it. It would seem as if contact with such cosmic natural elements as electricity and sound waves and WJZ would have a tendency to make a man broadminded and gentle, but it doesn't work out that way. It just makes them nasty.

I had a cousin once who built a radio. It seemed to me to be a foolhardy thing to do in the first place, monkeying around with electricity and tubes and things, but I said nothing. He read books on the subject and bought a lot of truck and sat around trying to fit things together for weeks and weeks, not speaking to his family except to tell them to get away from there and, in general, behaving in a very boorish manner.

Finally he got the thing so that it would work and picked up some kind of concert which was being broadcast from a station about half a mile away. The selection was a marimba band playing "Moonlight Waves," and he was tickled to death. Everyone had to come in and listen and congratulate him. "You certainly are a wonder, Ed," they exclaimed, and he said nothing to dispute it. Then he tried another station and broke in on the middle of another marimba band playing "Moonlight Waves." He was so pleased at being able to get another station, however, that he let it finish. That happened to be the end of that program; so he tried what he called "Cleveland, Ohio." Well, it seemed that "Cleveland, Ohio," was specializing that day on marimba band selections of "Moonlight Waves" and Ed got another load of that for half an hour. By this time the rest of the family had tiptoed out of the room.

The upshot of it was that Ed never moved away from that radio set for ten days and nights, always turning little knobs and looking up charts, always hoping against hope, but always getting a marimba band playing "Moonlight Waves." He refused food that was brought to him, but somehow had some whisky smuggled in, which he consumed in great gulps to keep his courage up. Pretty soon this began to tell on him, and he grew emaciated and trembly and nobody dared go near him. His wife got the doctor to come, but he wouldn't let anyone come into the room, simply showing his teeth and growling like an old fox terrier every time the threshold was crossed. And all the time the moaning strains of "Moonlight Waves" dragged through the room, from Detroit, Chicago, Los Angeles, and Boston, until finally his family had to move over to the grandmother's and leave him to his ultimate breakdown, which took the form of crawling into the cabinet himself and singing "Moonlight Waves" until he collapsed and could be carried out.

They never found out quite what had been the matter. Some people said that he had built a gramophone by mistake, and that the marimba band number was a record which kept on playing and playing. Others said that he had stumbled on some new form of sound reproduction and had isolated a certain number of sound waves so that they never could get free. Articles were written about it in scientific journals and he was hailed as an inventor, but it didn't do him any good, as no one would want to buy a lot of sound waves which did nothing but play "Moonlight Waves" over and over again. The whole thing was very tragic.

It only goes to show, however, that even the people who know a lot about radio and electricity really don't know an awful lot, and makes me all the more contented to stick to my old banjo. I don't know many chords on it, but I do know where they come from.

# YOUR BOY AND HIS DOG

PEOPLE are constantly writing in to this department and asking: "What kind of dog shall I give my boy?" or sometimes: "What kind of boy shall I give my dog?" And although we are always somewhat surprised to get a query like this, ours really being the Jam and Fern Question Box, we usually give the same answer to both forms of inquiry: "Are you quite sure that you want to do either?" This confuses them, and we are able to snatch a few more minutes for our regular work.

But the question of Boy and Dog is one which will not be downed. There is no doubt that every healthy, normal boy (if there is such a thing in these days of Child Study) should own a dog at some time in his life, preferably between the ages of forty-five and fifty. Give a dog to a boy who is much younger and his parents will find themselves obliged to pack up and go to the Sailors' Snug Harbor to live until the dog runs away— which he will do as soon as the first pretty face comes along.

But a dog teaches a boy fidelity, perseverance, and to turn around three times before lying down—very important traits in times like these. In fact, just as soon as a dog comes along who, in addition to these qualities, also knows when to buy and sell stocks, he can be moved right up to the boy's bedroom and the boy can sleep in the dog house.

In buying a dog for a very small child, attention must be paid to one or two essential points. In the first place, the dog must be one which will come apart easily or of such a breed that the sizing will get pasty and all gummed up when wet. Dachshunds are ideal dogs for small children, as they are already stretched and pulled to such a length that the child cannot do much harm one way or the other. The dachshund being so long also makes it difficult for a very small child to go through with the favorite juvenile maneuver of lifting the dog's hind legs up in the air and wheeling it along like a barrow, cooing, "Diddy-ap!" Any small child trying to lift a dachshund's hind legs up very high is going to find itself flat on its back.

For the very small child who likes to pick animals up around the middle and carry them over to the fireplace, mastiffs, St. Bernards, or Russian wolfhounds are not indicated—that is, not if the child is of any value at all. It is not that the larger dogs resent being carried around the middle and dropped in the fireplace (in fact, the smaller the dog, the more touchy it is in matters of dignity, as is so often the case with people and nations); but, even though a mastiff does everything that it can to help the child in carrying it by the diaphragm, there are matters of gravity to be reckoned with which make it impossible to carry the thing through without something being broken. If a dog could be trained to wrestle and throw the child immediately, a great deal of time could be saved.

But, as we have suggested, the ideal age for a boy to own a dog is between forty-five and fifty. By this time the boy ought to have attained his full growth and, provided he is ever going to, ought to know more or less what he wants to make of himself in life. At this age the dog will be more of a companion than a chattel, and, if necessary, can be counted upon to carry the boy by the middle and drop him into bed in case sleep overcomes him at a dinner or camp meeting or anything. It can also be counted upon to tell him he has made a fool of himself and embarrassed all his friends. A wife could do no more.

The training of the dog is something which should be left to the boy, as this teaches him responsibility and accustoms him to the use of authority, probably the only time he will ever have a chance to use it. If, for example, the dog insists on following the boy when he is leaving the house, even after repeated commands to "Go on back home!" the boy must decide on one of two courses. He must either take the dog back to the house and lock it in the cellar, or, as an alternate course, he can give up the idea of going out himself and stay with the dog. The latter is the better way, especially if the dog is in good voice and given to screaming the house down.

There has always been considerable difference of opinion as to whether or not a dog really thinks. I, personally, have no doubt that distinct mental processes do go on inside the dog's brain, although many times these processes are hardly worthy of the name. I have known dogs, especially puppies, who were almost as stupid as humans in their mental reactions.

The only reason that puppies do not get into more trouble than they do (if there *is* any more trouble than that which puppies get into) is that they are so small. A child, for instance, should not expect to be able to fall as heavily, eat as heartily of shoe leather, or throw up as casually as a puppy does, for there is more bulk to a child and the results of these practices will be more serious in exact proportion to the size and capacity. Whereas, for example, a puppy might be able to eat only the toe of a slipper, a child might well succeed in eating the whole shoe—which, considering the nails and everything, would not be wise.

One of the reasons why dogs are given credit for serious thinking is the formation of their eyebrows. A dog lying in front of a fire and looking up at his master may appear pathetic, disapproving, sage, or amused, according to the angle at which its eyebrows are set by nature.

It is quite possible, and even probable, that nothing at all is going on behind the eyebrows. In fact, one dog who had a great reputation for sagacity once told me in confidence that most of the time when he was supposed to be regarding a human with an age-old philosophical rumination he was really asleep behind his shaggy overhanging brows. "You could have knocked me over with a feather," he said, "when I found out that people were talking about my wisdom and suggesting running me for President."

This, of course, offers a possibility for the future of the child itself. As soon as the boy makes up his mind just what type of man he wants to be, he could buy some crêpe hair and a bottle of spirit gum and make himself a pair of eyebrows to suit the rôle: converging toward the nose if he wants to be a judge or savant; pointing upward from the edge of the eyes if he wants to be a worried-looking man, like a broker; elevated to his forehead if he plans on simulating surprise as a personal characteristic; and in red patches if he intends being a stage Irishman.

In this way he may be able to get away with a great deal, as his pal the dog does.

At any rate, the important thing is to get a dog for the boy and see what each can teach the other. The way things are going now with our Younger Generation, the chances are that before long the dog will be smoking, drinking gin, and wearing a soft hat pulled over one eye.

# "GOOD LUCK"

AND NOW they are trying to take away our superstitions from us. First they tax us until it is cheaper not to earn any money at all, then they force us to drink beer, and now they come along and tell us that we mustn't believe that if your nose itches you are going to have company.

I am not a superstitious man myself, but no Columbia University professor is going to sit there and tell me that if an actor (or anybody) whistles in a dressing room it doesn't mean bad luck for the person nearest the door. That's a scientific fact.

Neither will I be told that I must throw out all the little odds and ends of clothing and currency that I have accumulated during the past quarter of a century, each one of which has been certified by the United States Bureau of Standards as a definite good luck piece. I have proved their worth time after time (chiefly by not having had them with me when I had bad luck). I have an old green tie which I have worn so much that it now looks as if I were being led out to be lynched, and has that ever failed me? Never! I may not have always had good luck with it on, but it was because I forgot to wrap this long end around twice while tying it, or because I didn't have the ends even. The tie itself is sure-fire good luck, and I'll let no crack-brained theorist tell me different.

Not being really superstitious, I can look at the thing calmly. When I was a boy I used to have a silly idea that if I could run upstairs two at a time and reach the first landing before the outside door had shut behind me, everything would be all right. (I don't quite know what I meant by "everything will be all right," but I guess that I meant really *everything*, which was a wild-eyed demand to begin with.) Now that I have reached an age where I am lucky if I barely get inside the outer door before it shuts on me, I see that my youthful idea was sheer superstition. I am under no illusions about superstition when it is superstition.

But some day I am going to put on all my good luck pieces of clothing and carry all my good luck coins and go right out and face the world. And, if I don't get arrested for masquerading as an Indian medicine man, I'll bet I have better luck than that Columbia professor with all his text-book theories.

# "SAFETY SECOND"

IF YOU are one of those people who are constantly getting hurt, falling down or up, crashing into railway trains or tumbling out of people's houses, you have probably wondered why it is. You have probably asked yourself, as soon as you could talk, "Why is it that I seem to be unable to lift a piece of asparagus to my mouth without poking it in my eye, or button my clothes without catching my finger in the buttonhole and tearing the ligament to shreds?" You ask this of yourself, and probably your insurance company asks it too. It almost looks as if there were something fishy about it all.

As it is the insurance companies who really care (the hell with your wrenched ligaments—it costs them *money*) they have put some of their best minds to work on the subject, and a great, big report, all bound in red crocodile (red with embarrassment), has been submitted by the Premium Defaulters' Service Bureau, showing that certain people get hurt oftener than certain others. And for very definite reasons.

Of course, it is no fair to include in this analysis those hearty guys who go around slapping people on sunburned necks or pushing them off rafts. They are going to get hurt *any*way. There is nothing that insurance companies can do for them except kill them before they start out in the morning. I killed seven last year, and am looking forward to a bumper crop this summer. What we are after is the reason why certain people get hurt *in spite of themselves*. Are you one? Are you two?

According to the report issued by the Premium Defaulters' Service Bureau, 30 per cent of the motormen on a well-known trolley-line had 78 per cent of the accidents, or in other words, 30 per cent of the motormen were dumber than the rest. In still other words (we have hundreds more, so don't get worried) there is such a thing as an "accident germ" which makes A more liable to accidents than B. It is the same germ which makes A buy more Peruvian bonds than B, or which makes B walk off more curbings than C. It is just one of Nature's phenomena, that's all.

Take, for example, the safety devices which were placed on certain machines when the "Safety First" campaigns were started, 'way back in 1912. Some of them have never been used since, in spite of the pretty posters. Some of them have been used, but simply to hang jumpers on while the men were changing their clothes. But the cases with which the insurance men have the most trouble are those in which workers get hurt *on the safety devices*. This type of injury calls for special attention. There was one man, in a paper mill in Massachusetts, who was tending a so-called "beater," in which the pulp is taken and thrashed around until it looks something awful. (On Saturdays some of the workers used to bring their wives up for a little going-over, just to save themselves the trouble that night.) A worker, whom we will call Cassidy, because his name was Cassidy, had tended a "beater" for thirty-three years and had never had an accident. The safety device was put on, under the auspices of the State Insurance and Fidelity League, and, the very first day, Cassidy got flustered and dropped one leg of his trousers in the safety device, with the result that he was caught up in the machine and swashed around until all they had to do was to dry him out and they could have printed the Sunday *Times* on him. In fact, that is just what they did do, and it was one of the best editions of the Sunday *Times* that ever was run off the presses. It had human interest.

But the case of Cassidy is still not what we are after in this survey. Cassidy's injury was a special event in Cassidy's life, and there are some workers to whom injury is just an item in the day's work, like lighting a pipe. They get cut, go and have it bandaged, get cut again, go and have it bandaged, get cut again, and by that time it is five-thirty. On their days off, they get cut on the edge of their newspaper. There was one man, for instance, who had been tending a saw for ten years and who had got splinters in his eye regularly five times a week. There was some suspicion that he held his eye out and put it *on* the splinters as they flew off the saw, but he always denied this. Then the Safety First Committee bought goggles for the men, and the very first day he got the goggles caught in his eye and had to have the whole thing readjusted at the nearest drugstore (for which the druggist charged nothing). He collected under the head of "Occupational Disease," but the insurance company was pretty sore about the whole thing and offered to get him a job in a bank. He took it, and within a week had what is known as "eye-penny," caused by flying particles of pennies being caught in the under lid, resulting in great pain. This is what is called an "habitual risk," and is exactly the thing that the insurance companies are trying to stamp out.

Let us say that you start to cross a street. You are trying to look up a word in a dictionary, or are worrying about how you are going to explain to your wife that you haven't got the week's pay envelope. You are obviously in no condition to be crossing a street, but, as everyone can't live on the same side of any one street, you sometimes have to. The traffic-lights are against you, but so is everything else in this world, so what difference can one little traffic-light make? The next thing you know you are halfway into the cylinder head of a motor and someone is saying: "Look in his pockets and see if he has an address-book there." This rather makes you stop short and give pause. Why should *you* have been hit in preference to the three dozen other people who were crossing the street with you against the lights?

The insurance company report says that it is because you were (1) day-dreaming (2) worried over something (3) just a plain damn fool. The day-dreaming part is something that can't very well be regulated. Stop day-dreaming, and you stop Keats and Shelley (although Keats and Shelley stopped themselves pretty successfully, without outside interference). Being just a plain damn fool is another complaint over which modern medicine seems to have no control. Look at the stock market (or, rather, let's *not* look. There is trouble enough in the world as it is). But when investigators come right out and say that one of the big causes of accidents is the fact that people are worried, then a solution presents itself with almost startling clarity. Keep people from being worried.

This would be my scheme: In the center of each town or city have a big pile of money, preferably in one and five dollar bills (it is so hard to get larger denominations changed). Whenever anyone feels a worry coming on, let him walk up to this pile, say "Hello, Joe!" to the keeper, take out whatever amount he needs, and then go on home. I venture to say that in this way accidents resulting from worry could be reduced eighty per cent. I don't suppose the thing could ever be put into practice, however, as in most towns and cities the central square is so full of parked automobiles that there wouldn't be any place for a pile of loose money.

There is one other reason given in this report as to why people get hurt in traffic or at machines or from toppling off doorsteps. It is that the one who is injured is unable to conform to a fixed rhythm. A good dancer, or a good musician, it is said, seldom is a person prone to accidents. Most modern machinery has a certain rhythm to which the man or woman who controls it, or who is subject to its workings, must conform. If he does not conform, he gets hurt. This may be true, but I myself have got just as badly hurt dancing as I have from tripping over high-powered Rolls-Royces, and I venture to say that if you were to put one of the Russian ballet at work at a circular saw, she would get hurt, too. In order for rhythm to help you keep out of trouble, things have got to be going in *your* rhythm, not you in theirs.

My only solution to the problem of habitual accidents (and, so far, nobody has asked me for my solution) is for everyone to stay in bed all day. Even then, there is always the chance that you will fall out.

# TIPTOEING DOWN
# MEMORY LANE

*In the Manner of Our Older Literary Reminiscers*

IN THESE random wanderings down "Memory Lane" (as I call it—and who does not?) I am relying chiefly on a rather faulty faculty for reminiscence, a diary, belonging to somebody else, for 1890 (or rather the first three weeks of 1890, ending with a big blot) and some old bound volumes of *Harper's Round Table* for 1895-7 (1896 missing). For any discrepancies or downright lies, I beg the indulgence due an old man who has already become something of a bore.

Life in literary circles in New York during the late eighteen-nineties and early eighteen-seventies was quite different from literary life today. In the first place, more authors wore large mustaches and beards, which complicated things considerably. One might meet Walt Whitman (if one weren't careful) and think that it was Joachin Miller, except for the fact that Whitman lived in the East and Miller (thank God!) lived in the West. I remember on one occasion that Miller met Whitman in the lobby of the old Fifth Avenue Hotel (then just the plain Fifth Avenue Hotel, without the "old") and Miller said: "For a minute I thought you were Miller!" to which Whitman replied: "For a minute I thought you were Whitman!" It was a contretemps, all right. And not a very good one, either.

All of this made literary contacts very confusing in the old days, whereas today they are so simple that one may avoid them entirely by not going to teas or reading the book notes. I very well remember my first literary contact when I came to New York as a young boy of sixty-five in 1890. I had been out writing a novel, as all young boys were apt to do in those days, and came in, all hot and excited, to find Bret Harte, Frank Norris, Charles Warren Stoddard, and Irving Caesar waiting for me to talk over Mark Twain's latest story about the Drunken Frog of Calvados County. The last part of it hadn't come over the wire yet, so it didn't make much sense as a funny story, but we all laughed hearily at it because it was afterward to become so famous. I shall never forget Charles Dudley Warner's face as he laughed at it. It was terrible.

It was only a few weeks later that Mark Clemens ("Samuel Twain") asked me to lunch at the Century. I was very busy on my new book, and rather hated to leave off work as I hadn't even found my pencil, but my wife said that she thought that I ought to go as it would make such a nice tidbit for my memoirs later. I had also heard that the Century served a very delicious roast-beef hash, browned to a crisp, which was an added attraction. Sometime I must write a book of literary reminiscences about roast-beef hash browned to a crisp.

So I went. And was I bored! The hash was great, but Edmund Clarence Stedman, Henry Fuller, and Richard Watson Gilder all told the Drunken Frog story, and Mark Clemens ("Samuel Langhorne") acted it out, and what with beards and mustaches and jumpings up and down, I finally begged off and went to the Players' to meet J. I. C. Clark, Hamlin Garland, "Buster" West, and Dr. Johnson (who was not really dead at that time but only "playing possum").

I remember that it was on that day that I was an unwilling auditor to one of the most famous interplays of rapier wit which ever devastated a literary memoir. Nat Goodwin took me around to see a rehearsal of "All's Well That Ends All," where I met Sir Beerbohm Tree, who was in this country straightening out a little libel suit (he had accused William Winter of stealing one of his gags and Winter had retaliated with a suit claiming that the gag was no good anyway). Sir Beerbohm (Tree) was engaged at that moment in a controversy with Lester Wallack, so-named after Wallack's Theatre.

The two wits had been discussing something connected with the theatre (otherwise they wouldn't have been able to discuss at all) and Sir Beerbohm had said:

"All right, that's what *you* think!"

Wallack looked about him with a quizzical smile.

"Very well," he said, dryly, "if that's the way you feel about it."

Tree threw back his leonine head and glared.

"I see!" he said, and walked away.

It was a big day for repartee.

Early in January of that year (what year?) Walt Whitman

confided to me that he was doing a play, to be called "Ten Nights in a Broad-brimmed Hat." I told him that it would never go, as there was no adagio dancer in it. He said that he felt that adagio dancing was going out, and that what the public wanted was something good and sexy without people actually throwing each other about. I never liked Whitman, because of his having once worked on a Brooklyn newspaper, but I told him that the only thing to do was to try it out in Newark and see how it went. I never heard anything more of the play—or of Whitman.

In my diary (or the diary that I am using) I find an entry: "Oct. 12th. This is the end! Filkins has gone too far." I am frankly mystified by this entry. So far as I know, there has been no character in our literary history by the name of Filkins (unless it was Ringold Lardner using another name) and I cannot understand just what bearing he has on this matter. If I had my wits about me, I should never include him in this biography. He means nothing.

It was just about this time that Ralph Waldo Emerson had been dead for ten years, so I never knew him. I did know a man named Emerson Cottner, however, which gives me a pretty good loophole for bringing the Sage of Concord (or was that Thoreau?) into these pages. Although I never knew Waldo Emerson (as we used to call him) I thought that he was all right.

During the fall before we went back to Hyannis to live, we were the center of quite a round of literary activity. I say "quite a round of literary activity." I mean that I went to the Century to a dinner given for William Dean Howells. It was a delightful occasion, and I got many names for my list, as well as two new overcoats. Horace Greeley, Richard Watson Gilder, Robert Underwood Johnson, Horace Watson Gilder, Richard Underwood Johnson, Robert Greeley, Otto H. Kahn, Charles Dudley Warner, Thomas Bailey Aldrich, Mrs. S. Standwood Menken (as *Columbia*). Music by the Yacht Club Boys.

I shall never forget an incident which occurred between Horace Watson Aldrich and Mark Twain ("Samuel Langhorne Gibson") during dinner. Twain got up and announced that owing to the limited capacity of the room, most of the people there would have to eat their dinners up in the Children's Room of the Century (for members under sixty). At this, Aldrich (or Gilder, as we used to call him), proposed a toast to "Our Absent Members," which J. A. B. Fuller, having only one leg, took personally, and stamped out of the room in a rage. It was delicious.

At Maybie's quip, a roar went up (which turned out to be from the furnace downstairs), but a great many of us, including Emily Dickinson (who, I thought, had never left Amherst, Mass., but who seemed to get around quite a bit for a recluse) all joined in the laughter, which was negligible. I shall never forget it, at least, not until this book gets proofread and off the presses. I think that my next book will be more in the nature of a serious history where I won't have to remember so many things.

And so we come to the end of the road. What lies beyond, what literary contacts are to be made, all must remain a mystery. (I might make a mystery story out of it, in fact.) There are so many figures in American life which do not come within the scope of this poor outline. But if I can hurry around and get some invitations, I may be able to add a few more names before the next issue. But by the next issue perhaps all my pretty little readers will have flown away. Frankly, I could hardly blame them.

*Sic transit gloria mundi* (as we used to call him).

# WHAT TIME IS IT?

*And What of It?*

BY SECRETLY consulting an old bootleg watch which I hid away (set at Standard Time) under my bed when my native state went daylight-saving, I find that it is a little over a month now since the Cossacks stormed up at the door and forced us to set our clocks an hour ahead. And, at the end of this month, I can give out a definite verdict against daylight-saving. I don't like it. I don't care what the reasons for it are. I don't like it. And beginning tomorrow I, personally, am going back to God's time. My body may belong to the State, but my soul belongs to Standard Time. If necessary, I will carry the case to the Supreme Court.

Time-keeping is a difficult enough maneuver at best, without monkeying around with an extra hour plus or minus. Just the fact that, when it is noon in New York, it is 5 p.m. in Paris has always worried me, and even now I am more or less inclined not to believe it. And when, last New Year's, greetings were radioed from New Zealand which reached here on December 31, I went into a sulk which almost spoiled the holiday for my friends. The whole idea is unpleasant to me.

The thing gets worse the farther west you go. When you cross the 180th meridian in the Pacific (so they try to tell me) you lose a whole day, which I very much doubt. If, at the same time, daylight-saving is in effect just at that time, you lose one day and one hour. I suppose that, if someone were to come along and say so, you lose one day, one hour, and one minute. The thing can easily be made absurd.

If everyone knew the trouble that the Western Union goes to in order to fix Standard Time, there wouldn't be so much tampering with it on the part of irresponsible legislators. From the United States Naval Observatory they select a list of about 150 so-called "clock stars." It is a great honor to be on this list. In order to be on it, a star has to sit very still and not wiggle or whisper, so that its permanent position can be noted in the American Ephemeris or Social Register. The person who told me all this (and who has, for obvious reasons, asked to remain anonymous) says that only stars which cross the meridian within twenty degrees of the zenith are included, "in order that the azimuth error may be small." Just how large an azimuth error has to be before it becomes large I forgot to ask, but I should imagine that six or seven feet would be pretty big for any azimuth error that you or I would be likely to have anything to do with.

Well, sir, after the Western Union has selected its clock stars, it takes a look at them each night through pearl-handled opera glasses, and, according to my informant, in this way finds out what time it is. I am not quite clear on the thing yet, and don't know whether they see the hour marked out *on* these stars or whether the stars, if looked at from the right angle, spell out "E-i-g-h-t-f-o-r-t-y-t-h-r-e-e." However, the experts at the Western Union can tell, and I suppose that is all that matters. If I knew what it was they did, and how they were able to tell time by the stars, I should be an expert at the Western Union. That is, of course, provided that I was socially acceptable to the present experts.

But, on the whole, I think that I shall keep out of any jobs which involve an understanding of clocks and time-keeping. I can't even understand my own clocks. I have an alarm clock, a plain, unattractive piece of mechanism which I bought in a drugstore about eight years ago. This clock will keep perfect time so long as it is tipped over on its face. If I humor it in this whim, however, it is obvious that I am not going to be able to tell what time it is, because I can't see the face. I tried once placing it over on its back, but it raised such a fuss that I had to turn it over instantly into its old position.

I have now solved the problem by having it on a table with a coarse wire net for a top instead of a solid piece of wood. So when I want to see what time it is, I simply get down on my hands and knees and look up through the wire, and there, clear as day, is the face of the clock looking down at me with the correct time. This maneuver also serves a double purpose, as it gets me out of bed much more surely than the mere ringing of an alarm will do.

I have had several letters from friends asking me why I didn't get rid of this clock and get one which would tell time without being coddled; but I have become fond of "Blushing Bennie," as I call it (because it is always hiding its face) and I wouldn't know what to do with a new clock staring directly at me every time I looked at it.

Down in the living room I have a clock which is called a "four-hundred-day" clock, which is supposed to run 400 days without winding. This feat seems to be accomplished by arranging four large cherries on a rotating stem which hangs out of the works of the clock (clearly visible through the glass cover) and they go slowly round one way and then slowly

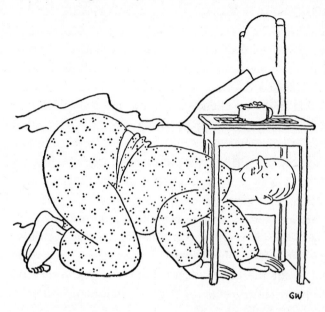

GW

round the other until the person who is watching them has gone mad. I have got myself trained now so that I can lean against the mantel and watch them rotate for six hours without feeling queer, but people who are not used to it should not try watching for more than fifteen minutes at first. If I have any work to do, it is a great comfort to know that I can always keep from doing it by watching these revolving cherries, for after a while I get hypnotized by the sight and am unable to take my eyes away. I have a man who does nothing else but come and lead me away from the clock whenever I have been there too long or when anyone in the room wants to talk to me.

Sometimes a dash of cold water in my face is necessary, and this is apt to irritate me and make me petulant at first, but when I am myself again I realize that it was for the best and reward the man with a warm smile and a "Well done!"

I don't know what we are supposed to do with the clock when the 400 days are up, because the directions distinctly said that under no circumstances was it to be touched once it had been started. I suppose that we shall have to throw it away. I shall want to save the cherries, however, and can perhaps learn to twirl them myself.

All this will perhaps show you how mystified I am by any time-recording device, even the simplest. And when it comes to chronometers of a more complicated nature, I am frankly baffled. This is probably why daylight-saving not only confuses but irritates me, because I wasn't really settled in my mind about the old Standard Time and resent any further attempt to make it more difficult. I understand perfectly the attitude of Holland in the matter of so-called "Zone Time." Or perhaps you don't know what Holland's attitude was.

In 1879 a busybody named Sandford Fleming brought forward a plan for the whole earth which set out twenty-four standard meridians to be fifteen degrees apart in longitude, starting from Greenwich, England. There was to be an hour's difference in time between each two of these.

This was the guy who made all the trouble and made it

possible for people in California who happened to be in the middle of a big party at midnight to call up someone in New York on the telephone and wake him out of a four A. M. slumber to say: "Hello, you big bum, you! Guess who this is!"

Well, all the nations accepted this crazy scheme of time-telling except Holland. Holland couldn't see any reason for messing around with meridians when there was so much trouble in the world as it was (and is). So Holland, although one of the smallest nations, stood out against the whole world and kept its own time, and, as a result, didn't get into the War when it came. And also makes delicious cheeses. And tulip bulbs. So you see?

My plan is to be known as "the Holland of Scarsdale," and to set all my clocks (except the one which cannot be tampered with) back to the old time we loved so well. They may throw me in jail, or they may cut off my electricity, but I am going through with this thing if it takes all summer. I don't like Time, and I never have, and I want to have as little to do with it as possible. If I am bothered much more by it, I shall take all the hands off all the watches and clocks in my house and just drift along, playing the mandolin and humming. I'm too busy a man to be worried by figuring out what time it is.

# DO I HEAR TWENTY THOUSAND?

*The scene is in the "Three Æons for Lunch" Club, made up of the shades of those authors who have "done something" while on earth. Shades of advertising men are admitted because advertising is really a form of belles-lettres and, besides, they keep a club going.* SHELLEY, SWIFT, TENNYSON, POPE, POE, *and others are lounging about the library table preparatory to going in to lunch.*

SHELLEY *picks up a copy of the February issue of* Book News from the Earth *and thumbs its pages over with a badly assumed nonchalance.*

#### SHELLEY

Ho-hum! I wonder what the news is from the old bookmart.

#### SWIFT

If you're looking for the article on the Jerome Kern book auction, it's on page 45. Congratulations.

(*blushing furiously*)
Jerome Kern book-auction? Has there been a—oh, yes, you mean the auction of Jerome Kern's library.
(*Turns unerringly to page 45.*)

SWIFT

Don't be naïve  You read all about it yesterday at that very table. You even copied out the various prices the books brought.

SHELLEY

(*trying to read article as if for first time*)
Honestly, Dean, I wasn't reading—that was this article on Richard Halliburton I was reading—well, I'll be darned—honestly, Dean, this is the first time I knew about this—

POE

What's all the blushing about?
(*to the steward*)
Another round of the same, Waters.

TENNYSON

Not for me, Edgar, thanks. Not in the middle of the day.

POE

Another round of the same, Waters. . . . Come on, Bysshe, what's in the magazine you want us to know about?

**SWIFT**

Oh, they had an auction in New York of Jerome Kern's library and Bysshe was in the Big Money. . . . $68,000, wasn't it, Bysshie?

**SHELLEY**

Well, that's what it seems to say here. I don't understand it.
(*Puts magazine down where it can easily be reached by the others.*)

**POE**

(*picking it up*)
What else was sold?

**SWIFT**

Oh, you didn't come off so badly, Eddie. An old letter of yours about Mrs. Browning was in the money, too.

**POE**

My God! Nineteen thousand five hundred! Say, that's not so bad, is it—for a letter, I mean?

**SWIFT**

Not so *bad!* It's *perfect!* You never earned nineteen thousand five hundred in your whole life. I almost tied you, though. Some sucker paid seventeen thousand for a first edition of *Gulliver.*

**TENNYSON**

(*yawning slightly*)
May I take a look at that, please?

**SHELLEY**

Your *Maud* drew down something like nine thousand.

**SWIFT**

I thought you hadn't read the article, Bysshe.

**SHELLEY**

I just saw that item—it was right there under mine.

**TENNYSON**

(*reading*)

Oh, well, it was just a portion of the manuscript—probably a couple of stanzas. Anyway, I don't like the idea of auctioning off things like that. It sort of takes some of the beauty away.

**SWIFT**

What beauty is that?

**TENNYSON**

You wouldn't understand, Swift.

**LAMB**

I think Alfy is right. It rather cheapens the thing to have a lot of Americans and things bidding for one's work.

**POE**

Well, a lot of Americans and things fell pretty heavily for some old hack-work of yours, Charlie. You ran second to Bysshe with a neat $48,000.

**LAMB**

Who—me? Who—I? Forty-eight thousand? For what?

**POE**

For a mess of stuff you did for *Hone's Weekly*, it says here.

**LAMB**

Well, I'll be darned. Why, I dashed that off in about an hour a week. Was always late with my copy, too. Hone used to get crazy.

**POE**

He'd be crazier if he knew that it was worth forty-eight grand now.

**SWIFT**

You weren't such a big money-maker as a subject, though, Charlie. That thing Bill Wordsworth did about you after you died got only a measly twenty-five hundred.

**LAMB**

You mean "Ode to the Memory of Charles Lamb"?

**SWIFT**

Look—he remembers the title!

**LAMB**

I never cared very much about that myself. It didn't seem to me that Bill did all he might have done with the material.

**WORDSWORTH**

*(putting down his newspaper)*

No? Well, I did all I felt like doing. I had to have something in for the Christmas number and that was all I could think of. They already had a poem scheduled on Milton, which was what I wanted to do.

**LAMB**

I would say that a poem by you on Milton would be worth about seven dollars now—on the original papyrus.

**WORDSWORTH**

*(going back to his newspaper)*

Yeah?

**SHELLEY**

I'm surprised to see that the original manuscript of Keats's "I stood tip-toe upon a little hill" got only $17,000.

*(As the others are talking,* SHELLEY *repeats, a bit louder)*

I'm surprised to see that the original manuscript of Keats's "I stood tip-toe" got only $17,000.

**SWIFT**

I heard you the first time, Bysshe. You're surprised that Keats's "I stood tip-toe" got only $17,000.

**SHELLEY**

Yes. I always rather liked that. Nothing wonderful, of

course, but, if my stuff got $68,000, I should think that Keatsie's would get more than $17,000.

SWIFT

That was just a few lines of Keats, Bysshe, and stuck into an ordinary edition of his works. Yours was the whole, uncut volume of *Queen Mab*—a very fine thing purely from the book-making standpoint, I daresay. Anything that's uncut always gets more money.

POE

By the way, whoever owned that originally didn't think a hell of a lot of it, did he? Not to cut the leaves, I mean.

SHELLEY

It was probably one of those copies the publishers sent me for gifts which I never gave away.

SWIFT

Any time you ever gave away a book.

SHELLEY

(*ignoring him*)

Say, what do you know about this! It says that *Queen Mab* got the highest price ever paid for a book at an auction. That doesn't seem believable, does it? I mean, *Queen Mab* wasn't my best, by a long shot.

SWIFT

The Gutenberg Bible got more.

Yes, but I mean literature.

Oh, the Gutenberg Bible was just a stunt of typesetting, I suppose?

You know very well what I mean, Dean. I think the Bible is a fine book, a great book, but, after all, the big price that it brought was, in a way, due partly to the fact that Gutenberg set it up. You know that.

I've been adding it up, boys, and right here in this room there is represented about $160,000. What about another round?

Not for me, thanks. Not in the middle of the day.

Well, $160,000 is a lot of money. We can't let it pass unnoticed . . . Waters! Another round of the same.

Yes, sir. . . .
(*aside to* POE)
Was that last round yours, Mr. Poe?

(*looking in his wallet*)

Why, er—sure! Sure thing! Just put it on my account, Waters.

(*aside to* POE)

You're posted, Mr. Poe. I'm sorry.

By George, that's right. Well—er— Never mind, then, Waters. Er— Dean, you don't happen to have—er—

Awfully sorry, old boy. You couldn't have struck me at a worse time—just charge it to me, Waters—oh, that's right— I forgot. *I'm* posted right now.

(LAMB *and* WORDSWORTH, *sensing trouble, have slipped quietly away to lunch.*)

I really ought to pay for the whole thing, you know, winning all that money. Next time, I shall insist.

(*A new member who has been looking at the magazines all during the conversation approaches the group.*)

I hope you'll pardon me, gentlemen, but I couldn't help overhearing. I hope you'll allow me to pay for the drinks today. My manuscripts wouldn't bring much in the open market right now, but they didn't do so badly in the original sale . . . Waters, will you please bring another round for us all and charge the whole thing to me—Mr. Hopwood, you know. Mr. Avery Hopwood.

WATERS

Yes, sir. Thank you, Mr. Hopwood.
(*The drinks are brought and the gentlemen carry them in to lunch with them.*)

SHELLEY

(*exiting with the rest*)
I really don't understand it, though, for *Queen Mab* was never one of my favorites.

# IMAGINATION IN THE BATHROOM

O NE of the three hundred and eight (1930 census figures) troubles with American home life today is the alarming spread of Home-Making as an Art. For the past fifteen or twenty years our Little Women have been reading so many articles in the women's magazines warning them against lack of Imagination in the Home that they have let their imaginations get the upper hand and turn them into a lot of Hans Christian Andersens. All that is needed is a band of dwarfs to make any modern home a Rumpelstiltskin's castle which, at the stroke of midnight, turns back into a pumpkin again.

Before Home-Making became an Art, Mother used to feel that she had done pretty well if she and Annie could get the furniture all back into place (and by "into place" is meant "into place *again*") after the spring and fall house-cleaning, with perhaps fresh tidies on the backs of the chairs every so often. Things *had* to go back pretty much where they came from, for the casters had dug little round holes in the carpet, and you wouldn't want to have the place looking like a clam flat.

The only imagination that was necessary in the preparation of the food was to find *enough*; for in the days before dieting set in Daddy and the boys and girls stopped at nothing in the way of loading up, short of foundering with all on board.

But gradually the home-making experts have got their propaganda across, flooding the country with photographs of armchairs planted with geraniums and luncheon tables in pantalets, telling the young wives who are just beginning to worry about that far-away look in George's eyes that the trouble was lack of Imagination in fixing up the Nest. So the young wives have become Imagination-conscious.

On looking back over the past ten years, the arrival of chintz would seem to have been the first indication that things were going imaginative on us. The first designs in chintz curtains and sofa coverings were very mild, perhaps little spatterings of buttercups on a black field, or, in the more radical households, medium-sized poppies; but, compared with the old white lace curtains which used to hang in the bay window back of the rubber plant and were held back in place by a gold ball and chain, they were pretty hot stuff. I remember, back in 1915, a man whose mother came to visit him in his new home (she had never met his wife before) and, after one look at the chintz curtains, she took him upstairs and asked him if he was sure just who his wife's people were. She thought he had married a Chinese girl.

Today those very same chintz curtains would be considered fit only for a mortuary home (or undertaking parlor, as we used to call it: the development of undertaking parlors into mortuary homes would make a story on Home-Making in itself).

As the tide of originality swept on, the poppies began getting larger and larger until the design became one big red poppy with here and there a bit of background which hardly knew that it was a background on the same piece of goods. This obviously would never do, for the next step would have been *all* poppy, or just a good old-fashioned red curtain, which was exactly the thing they were trying to get away from.

You have to look out for that in modern decoration. Beyond a certain point you swing right around back into Grandma's house again.

I have an article before me, written in one of the Home-Making sections of a Sunday paper, which begins as follows:

Color everywhere in the house is the keynote in present-day decorating—from the basement to the attic, from the foyer hall to the back door. Even the kitchen is as gay as a flower garden, for pots and pans have been glorified. Gone are the days of all-white bathrooms. . . .

Is that a terrifying prospect or isn't it? "Gone are the days of all-white bathrooms," are they? Well, not in *my* house. The bathroom is a sacred place, not merely a room where you rush in to wash your hands before a meal. (And, incidentally, a lady member of the party has asked me to inquire why it is that the men-folk always wait until dinner has been announced before rushing up to wash their hands.)

"They have all the time in the world after they get home," says this lady member of the party, "in which to fix up for dinner. But they sit down and read the evening paper, or dawdle around with the radio, or even just smoke a cigarette standing in the middle of the living room, until somebody says, 'Dinner is ready.' Then they say, 'I'll be right down,' tear upstairs into the bathroom, and start splashing about with the soap and guest towels until you would think they were doing the week's wash. In the meantime the soup is stone cold."

*I tried running the bath with my eyes shut*

And I, equally incidentally, would like to ask why, in housekeepers' parlance, everything has to be "stone cold" when it is the man's fault? They are just "cold" when it is anybody else's fault, but when the man is to blame they are "stone cold."

To get back into the bathroom. I like a good warm bathroom, with plenty of light, in which I can sing Old Man River (and, boy, can I take those low notes in Old Man River in a good resonant bathroom! Paul Robeson is a tenor compared with me some mornings); and I like a room in which I can lie in the tub and read until well parboiled, sometimes getting nice big blisters on the pages with wet fingers, or, if very tired, perhaps dropping the whole book into the water; and I don't want to have the feeling, every time I look up, that I am taking part in the first act of the Ziegfeld Follies with Joseph Urban looking on.

I once spent a week-end in a house where the bathroom was so stage-struck that I couldn't even get the cold water to run.

The towels were lavender and the curtains were pink and green and the tub was a brilliant yellow with mottlings of a rather horrid chocolate running through it. I tried running a bath with my eyes shut, but as soon as the water hit the porcelain it began to boil, and even if I had been able to draw a decent bath that a healthy man could get into, I couldn't have kept my eyes on the book for fear that a Chinese dragon would pop out from some of the decorations and get into my slippers.

I finally went back into my room and took a sponge bath from the faucet.

I have dwelt so long on the bathroom end of Home-Making as an Art because the bathroom seems to me to be the last stronghold of the old-fashioned man. If they take our bathrooms away from us we might as well all dress in harlequin costumes and throw confetti all day instead of going to work.

Imagination is all right in the living room, where we can keep our eyes shut. But please, modern home-makers, leave us our white bathrooms, where we can use the towels without feeling that we are wiping our hands on a Michelangelo and look at the walls without going into a pirouette. No wonder so many men live in Turkish baths!

# MUSIC HEAVENLY MAID

SUNDAY afternoons used to be ideal for home-work. No automobile horns outside, no old ladies with hand-organs, no telephone calls, almost, you might say, no home-work. Even in the midst of my furious attack on the Muse on Sunday afternoons I used to catch between forty and forty-five winks.

But with the advent of the Philharmonic concerts on the radio, Sunday afternoon has become one of the noisiest periods of the week. I have nothing against symphonies, and am sure that their being broadcast is a great thing for the public taste in music. All that I am saying is that they are noisy, especially if you happen to be in the next apartment. It may be high-class noise, but it cannot be denied that it is noise, and distracting noise.

The people in the next apartment love symphonies. I also think that they are either deaf or unaware that a radio can be turned down simply by adjusting that little dingus at one side. There are times, during the final movements of a symphony, when I rather expect to see them all come hurtling through the wall, bringing great slabs of plaster with them, so great is the force of the sound waves generated. I often picture them in there, cowering down close to the rugs to escape being blown about the room by the blast which comes out of the loud-speaker.

Today I am embarking on a little piece called "Changing Science," in which I shall attempt to prove that most of the science which was taught in our school days is already so out of date that it seems hardly worth while to teach it to the children today, as in another twenty years it is sure to sound like arguments that the Earth is flat. (Perhaps, in twenty years, it will have been proven that the Earth IS flat.)

The Philharmonic is, at the same moment (4.25 P. M.) embarking on the overture to "Euryanthe," by Weber. I know what it is, because I just heard the announcer say so through the wall. You see, there is nothing that is kept from me. However, I will do my best on "Changing Science."

Most of us remember having been taught about the molecule when we were in school. Practically none of us remembers that the average diameter of gas molecules was said to be about one three-hundred-millionths of an inch . . . Boy, is that kettle-drummer having a good time? Or rather, those kettle-drummers. There must be 50 of them. Go it, you sons-of-guns! Beat their hides off! At-a-boy! I hope your wrists drop off.

Well, whether a molecule is one three-hundred-millionths of an inch or not, along came a lot of things that were smaller. Atoms, electrons, eons, ions, uons and sometimes wons and yons. This made more or less of a bum out of the molecule, but still . . . What's the matter? Have they stopped playing? They shouldn't do that. They shouldn't bang so loud and then stop suddenly. That's worse than keeping it up, for it makes people in the next apartment wonder . . .

Oh, no! There they go again! The brasses! Dear old brasses! Say, they certainly know how to blow, those boys. Hot dickety! It must be fun to have a horn, and, once you are sure of your note, to give it the works like that. You'd have to be pretty sure of your note, though, because if you put your eyeballs and temples and neck-chords into blowing it and it turned out to be the wrong note, you would sound pretty silly. I am not so sure that one of those horns has got it right yet . . . Oh, I guess he'd have to, or he wouldn't be playing in the Philharmonic. It's probably my fault . . .

They've died down again. Quick, now; get a couple of words written!

On glancing through my old Physics book I find . . . Too late! They're at it again! I wonder if I were to go to the door and ask those people in the next apartment if they had ever heard of "loud" and "soft" if they would be offended. I would do it very nicely. I might even go in and show them about turning the dingus, and while I was at the controls I might fix the damn thing so that it would never play again . . . Wait a minute! It sounds like the coda they are going into. The same note twenty-five times usually means that they are nearing the end.

Why is it that a composer never seems able to finish an overture? They act as if they had got going and didn't know how to stop. They come to the end with a series of tremendous bangs—and then go right on with another series of the same bangs. This one now has reached thirty-seven bangs on the same note—now it's forty-two, just while I have been writing. Bang-bang-bang-bang! There! Bangbang! No—one more! Bangbang!

Well, I guess they're through now for a minute, but I've lost interest in "Changing Science." I might as well turn my own radio on and catch "Concertstueck," also by Weber. Perhaps someone in the apartment on my other side is trying to do some work.

# PERRINE'S RETURN

STAR MISSING FOR TWO GENERATIONS RETURNS AS ONE OF
COMET TRIO

CAMBRIDGE, MASS. (A.P.) The spectacle of three comets swinging through the skies is afforded astronomers for the first time in many years. To the two comets, Skjellerup's and Baade's, that have been under observation for weeks, another was added today. The tailed star known as Perrine's, making another visitation to our stellar system after an absence of two generations, has been sighted again.

"Well, if it isn't old Perrine's!" said Skjellerup's. "Come here, you old son-of-a-gun you, and give an account of yourself. Where have you been all these generations?"

"Oh, just flying around," said Perrine's, secretively.

"A likely story!" said Baade's. "Just flying around with what?"

"Say, look here," protested the wanderer, "can't a comet go off by himself once in a while without being ragged all over the place and put through the third degree the minute he gets back?"

"O-ho, touchy, is he? If there's one thing I hate, it's a touchy comet. You must remember, Perry, that if we wanted to, we could find out exactly what you've been doing. All we have to do is look on the records at the Harvard Observatory and there it is in black and white, probably with her name and everything."

"Oh, is that so?" said Perinne's hotly. "Well, since you think you're so smart, it isn't on the records at the Harvard Observatory. I've been out of this solar system entirely. They couldn't have seen me if they had wanted to. And I'll tell you right now that where I've been is the greatest little place in the universe. And cheap! Why, say, I got a room and bath and three meals a day (and, boy, let me tell you they were *some* meals, too. *Hors d'oeuvres,* soup, roast, two kinds of vegetables, salad, dessert and coffee), all for a hundred and twenty-five kronen; that's about—let me see—eleven cents in our money."

Skjellerup's and Baade's looked at each other apprehensively.

"Have a little something to drink," suggested Baade's, more to change the subject than anything else. "It's all right, I can guarantee it. My doctor gave it to me for Christmas."

"Put it up, quick!" whispered Skjellerup's. "They're watching us down there at Harvard."

"I suppose you guys think you know good liquor when you taste it. Well, I could show you a little place where I've been that would make your eyes pop out of your heads."

"And say, let me tell you another thing," he continued. "You all here don't know what climate is. Why, we took a little swirl down the line over there, lasting maybe ten years, and I give you my word that only once in those ten years did we run into anything that you could really call bad weather. And that wasn't anything more than a shower."

The music of the spheres unfortunately cut in at this point, but the following item, when it appears, will explain what finally happened.

### TWO COMETS VANISH FROM AGE-OLD TRIO

CAMBRIDGE, MASS. (A.P.) Astronomers here are mystified at the sudden disappearance of two comets which formerly made up the trio known as "The Jolly Three." Skjellerup's and Baade's are the names of the two missing tailed stars, while Perrine's remains the only one of the group to be visible from the observatory. It is thought that Skjellerup's and Baade's are in hiding somewhere.

·

# BOOKS AND OTHER THINGS

AFTER a series of introspective accounts of the babyhood, childhood, adolescence and inevitably gloomy maturity of countless men and women, it is refreshing to turn to "Bricklaying in Modern Practice," by Stewart Scrimshaw (Macmillan). "Heigh-ho!" one says. "Back to normal again!"

For bricklaying is nothing if not normal, and Mr. Scrimshaw has given just enough of the romantic charm of artistic enthusiasm to make it positively fascinating.

"There was a time when man did not know how to lay bricks," he says in his scholarly introductory chapter on "The Ancient Art," "a time when he did not know how to make bricks. There was a time when fortresses and cathedrals were unknown, and churches and residences were not to be seen on the face of the earth. But to-day we see wonderful architecture, noble and glorious structures, magnificent skyscrapers and pretty home-like bungalows."

To one who has been scouring Westchester County for the past two months looking at the structures which are being offered for sale as homes, "pretty home-like bungalows" comes as *le mot juste*. They certainly are no more than pretty home-like.

One cannot read far in Mr. Scrimshaw's book without blushing for the inadequacy of modern education. We are turned out of our schools as educated young men and women, and yet what college graduate here to-night can tell me when the first brick in America was made? Or even where it was made? . . . I thought not.

Well, it was made in New Haven in 1650. Mr. Scrimshaw does not say what it was made for, but a conjecture would be that it was the handiwork of Yale students for tactical use in the Harvard game. (Oh, I know that Yale wasn't running in 1650, but what difference does that make in an informal little article like this? It is getting so that a man can't make any statement at all without being caught up on it by some busy-body or other.)

But let's get down to the art itself.

Mr. Scrimshaw's first bit of advice is very sound. "The bricklayer should first take a keen glance at the scaffolding upon which he is to work, to see that there is nothing broken or dangerous connected with it. . . . This is essential, because more important than anything else to him is the preservation of his life and limb."

Oh, Mr. Scrimshaw, how true that is! If I were a brick-layer I would devote practically my whole morning to inspecting the scaffolding on which I was to work. Whatever else I shirked, I would put my whole heart and soul into this part of my task. Every rope should be tested, every board examined, and I doubt if even then I would go up on the scaffold. Any bricks that I could not lay with my feet on terra firma (there is a joke there somewhere about terra cotta, but I'm busy now) could be laid by someone else.

But we don't seem to be getting ahead in our instruction in practical bricklaying. Well, all right, take this:

"Pressed bricks, which are buttered, can be laid with a one-eighth-inch joint, although a joint of three-sixteenths of an inch is to be preferred."

Joe, get this gentleman a joint of three-sixteenths of an inch, buttered. Service, that's our motto!

It takes a book like this to make a man realize what he misses in his everyday life. For instance, who would think that right here in New York there were people who specialized in corbeling? Rain or shine, hot or cold, you will find them corbeling around like Trojans. Or when they are not corbeling they may be toothing (I too thought that this might be a misprint for "teething," but it is spelled "toothing" throughout the book, so I guess that Mr. Scrimshaw knows what he is about). Of all departments of bricklaying I should think that it would be more fun to tooth than to do anything else. But it must be tiring work. I suppose that many a bricklayer's wife has said to her neighbor, "I am having a terrible time with my husband this week. He is toothing, and comes home so cross and irritable that nothing suits him."

Another thing that a bricklayer has to be careful of, according to the author (and I have no reason to contest his warning), is the danger of stepping on spawls. If there is one word that I would leave with the young bricklayer about to enter his trade it is "Beware of the spawls, my boy." They are insidious, those spawls are. You think you are all right and then—pouf! Or maybe "crash" would be a better descriptive word. Whatever noise is made by a spawl when stepped on is the one I want. Perhaps "swawk" would do. I'll have to look up "spawl" first, I guess.

Well, anyway, there you have practical bricklaying in a nutshell. Of course there are lots of other points in the book and some dandy pictures and it would pay you to read it. But in case you haven't time, just skim over this résumé again and you will have the gist of it.

# BROWSING THROUGH THE
## PASSPORT

IT WONT be long now before they'll all be coming home—all those Americans who went to Europe this summer. They are hanging on their elbows over the counters in London and Paris steamship offices this very minute, trying to get reservations back to New York, and saying: "The price doesn't matter. Just something on A deck, if you can."

Considering how easy it is to get out of this country, the getting-back-in is made very discouraging. Not only is there the question of passage-money for the return trip (a feat in itself of no mean proportions after you have discovered that those purple Bank of France notes that you had tucked away in the reserve wallet against a rainy day were for 500 francs apiece instead of 1000), but there is also the unpleasant reception you get when you reach the harbor of your native land. It is almost as if the Government didn't want you. Well, I don't want the Government—so we're even.

The thing that makes it confusing is that everyone on board an ocean-liner, bright and early on the morning when she is supposed to dock in New York, gets out on deck all dressed in street clothes, looking very stuffy and strange, just as if it were simply a question of finishing the second cup of breakfast coffee (if you can get the first one down, the second doesn't taste so frightful) and then stepping right off the side of the ship into a taxi. If the thing is supposed to dock at 11, everyone is all set to land at 8 A. M., with umbrellas rolled up and cameras slung over their shoulders, and with nothing to do but walk up and down the deck and fret.

This is all due to the fact that our beloved Government, by way of a welcome home, meets us with little reception committees of doctors and passport tasters, who have come out to the ship in a little boat with what are known as the "delay papers." The idea is simply to delay things. Some of these officials have been in the business of delaying for as much as twenty-five years and have it down to a fine art. They can take a ship which is ready to dock at 9 A. M. and, merely by making little check-marks on a sheet and thumbing passport leaves, with an occasional look under the eyelids of a passenger, hold things up until noon. And not very nicely, either. You would think that they, instead of you, were the ones who had just come from abroad and from seeing the *Winged Victory* in the Louvre and the Rosetta Stone in the British Museum. You would think that the Old World air, which you have paid at least $3000 to acquire, gave you no rights at all.

This hanging around for hours and hours on shipboard between quarantine and the pier can spoil an entire summer of travel for a nervous man. If he has packed his bags and got everything out of his stateroom, donned his straw hat and wrapped his raincoat over his arm (with every indication of the hottest day of the year wafting down the bay from the city) he has nothing to do but pace about and think. He suddenly finds that his shipmates are very dull, at practically the same moment in which they found that he is very dull himself, and there is nothing to talk about. People who have been the life of the ship on the way over, when they get dressed in their landing-suits and come under the influence of the Long Interval, change into flat-footed Babbitts with nothing to say but: "Well, there's Little Old New York." Everyone seems to have produced a dog from somewhere, and there is the constant threat of fighting to keep what little breath of life there is left alive. But there never is a dog-fight, much as it would be welcomed. Even the dogs are let down.

It is at this time, when all one's books and magazines are packed, that one takes out the old passport and reads every word in it just out of sheer boredom. Standing in line waiting for Uncle Sam to look at your tongue or hanging around on dock waiting for the tide to turn, there is nothing like a little red passport to while away the time. And what a bit of reading-matter *that* is!

To start with, there is the unpleasant line on the front page: "In Case of Death or Accident Notify—" Well, unless something happens between quarantine and the pier, you have made a bum out of that. It is nothing to read on the trip across. It brings up too many mental pictures of avalanches or bad fish.

"This passport is a valuable document. Due care should be taken to see that it does not pass into the possession of an unauthorized person." A fine time to be reading that! Practically everybody on the continent of Europe, including bartenders and the young ladies at the Belles Poules, have had a

*Shipmates suddenly seem very dull*

crack at this passport, if only to see how you spell your name. What would "due care" be? What would an "unauthorized person" be? So far as I am concerned, everybody in Europe is unauthorized. I recognize no authority but the Constitution of the United States (some parts of it) and the bouncer at Jack's and Charlie's. And yet my passport has been practically the picture-book of the Continent. More people have read it than have read the Book of Ruth.

Here is a man named "D. Lorinas" or "D. Toinaz" who messed up one whole page under the pretext of getting me into England. I must write him a postcard from America just to show that all Americans aren't rude. Then there is somebody connected with the French government whose name is just nothing but a long line of "m's," written in dandy purple ink. According to the stamp under his name (I translate literally and without any attempt at style) "The present visa does not dispense the porter to conform to dispositions regulating in France the day of strangers." O. K. Monsieur, the porter gets you! No monkey business.

The German one I am not so sure about. It seems to be signed by a man named "Grosvenor" who should, I should think, have signed the British one instead of Mr. Lorinas. Perhaps there was an exchange professorship, with Mr. Grosvenor filling in for Mr. Lorinas at Köln and Mr. Lorinas doing the Dover trick. I'll bet they were both glad to get home and get some real cooking. Mr. Grosvenor, doubtless due to unfamiliarity with German, has filled in a line which, according to my knowledge of the language, would have me traveling backwards, which I certainly never did. I traveled sideways for a couple of days in Paris, but never backwards, especially in Germany. I must check Mr. Grosvenor up on this.

I sincerely hope Mr. Grosvenor will be able to straighten me out on this, because nobody wants to be barging backwards about the continent of Europe, especially when you are unconscious that you are facing in the wrong direction.

The next two pages frankly baffle me. One is headed "Érvényes Magyarországba" and is signed "S. N." I guess that I am supposed to be on very friendly terms with "S. N." and recognize his initials, but, unless it is Sam Northrup, I haven't the slightest idea who it is. And Sam Northrup certainly wouldn't be writing in my book about "Érvényes Magyarországba," not after all we went through together in the old days. Either the same man went right on into the next page of my passport, or it is another language entirely. I wouldn't know. But evidently on the sixteenth of Brez (prijezd odjezo), I rated a paragraph from Str. (name undecipherable) saying that "Plati ve smyslu vynosu nitra ze dne. 31/VII 1925 cis 52858 vyjimeene k jedomu prujezdu pres uzemi csr."

Now I have done some unaccountable things in my travels abroad and have turned up with a lot of little knickknacks that I don't remember buying, but I would swear that, wherever I was on the sixteenth of Brez, I had nothing to do with "vyjimeene k jedomu." I'll bet that the official, Sam Northrup or whoever it was, just was trying to be funny and confuse me. And, if we hadn't been held up so long in the harbor, I never should have seen it. That's the way with those jokes like that. You go to all the trouble of writing them in books, and then the person who is supposed to be the goat never even sees them. I am a little sorry that I looked now.

Perhaps it would be a good idea if the professional joke makers would make it a practice to notify their intended victims well in advance. This would avoid complete confusion as well as doing away with wasted effort. Goodness knows that the life of a jokesmith is full enough of bitter disappointments and disillusionments. We should all do our utmost to make life simpler and sweeter for them.

Of course, this reading over of a passport will not take up all the time between quarantine and the pier. You will still have opportunity to walk around the deck eight or ten times and go back to your stateroom to pick up the things you forgot to pack. But it will help to while away a little of the tedium, and also may make you more reconciled to staying home next summer.

# MEMOIRS

NOW that people have begun writing their memoirs before they are 30 and before they have anything to memoir about I see no reason why I shouldn't do mine and get it over with. I don't remember very much, but then, I haven't got very much space on this page to remember in.

My earliest recollection is that of not liking fireworks, especially those which went "Bang!" This still holds good, so it really isn't any feat of memory to recall it. I don't like any fireworks now, even those which just go "pf-f-f-f-t-t-t!"

This brings me up to the age of 20, when I remember meeting President Taft. I say that I "met" him. I was one of a committee of 50 students who met him at a train in Back Bay, and I remember him saying "How ar-r-re you, boys?" with a distinct Ohio trill on the "r." That was all that he said to me personally, but he later lost the election.

I never met another President of the United States, although I almost taught school at Groton. I say that I "almost taught school." The headmaster of Groton wanted someone from my class in college to teach French, but I didn't know enough French. I talked it over with the headmaster though.

At the age of 33 I had my tonsils taken out, but I do not remember very much about it. I found out later, however, that I was indirectly the cause of a revolution in throat therapeutics. The doctor told my nurse to give me two aspirin tablets and a glass of water and she, being just fresh from Finland, thought that he said "two aspirin tablets in a glass of water," which she prepared and which I gargled with terrific success.

It was from this accident that the aspirin gargle was evolved and hundreds of thousands of tonsil patients relieved. (I am not kidding.) So, at any rate, I can feel that I have done my bit toward the advancement of science. I want, however, to give the nurse equal credit and take this opportunity to do it.

We now come to the age of 40, the most interesting time of a boy's life. I don't remember very much about my 40th year, except that I tried to forget some stocks which I had been told to buy, put away and forget. I haven't forgotten them, even now. They were—but there—I mustn't kiss and tell.

And so the trail winds on and on, into the setting sun, and, as I look back over Memory Lane, sitting in the fire in front of my pipe, I wonder if it has all been worth while, this struggle for Fame and Fortune, this gaining ground and losing it, this petty little work-a-day thing we call life. Who knows?

# LOOKING AT PICTURE
# BOOKS

THE present craving of adults for picture books makes one wonder if all this past business of reading type-matter has perhaps been a pose. Considering how grown-up we are (and lots of us are great big boys and girls now) we do an awful lot of poring over picture books, and we do everything with them that the children do with theirs except drop them on the floor for someone else to pick up. When we drop our picture books, they stay dropped unless we pick them up ourselves. That's why so many of us are so bitter about life.

Within the past year the crop of just plain large picture books has increased to such an extent that the old-fashioned bookcases, built for Dickens and Conrad, are as useless as your first baby sweater. There have been funny picture books, grim picture books, naughty picture books, and now comes "The American Parade," which is simply a plain picture book of American life since the Civil War. And just leave one of them around on your desk or table and see what happens to it when your busy adult gets his talons on it.

154

A man comes into your office, let us say, reeking of insurance. He is a very busy man and can give you but a moment of his time. He may even keep his hat on, he is so busy. All that he wants to do is outline the advantage of a special three-hundred payment endowment policy, and then get away to another client who is taking out twice the amount of insurance that you are considering. (The next man that an insurance agent is going to call on is always doubling your ante.)

He sits down, pulls out a lot of papers from his brief case, and clears his throat. Then his eye lights on the picture book. He opens it casually from where he is sitting and says: "What's this—a collection of pictures of some sort?"

He thumbs the pages aimlessly for a few seconds and then comes across a photograph of Broadway and Pine St. in 1865. "This is very interesting," he says, pulling the book over to get it in better range. Then he turns the page.

"Here's a funny one!" he exclaims. "These girls in 'The Black Crook.' Did you see this one?"

You go and look over his shoulder. "There's another one a few pages on—of the Can-Can," you say. "Here—let me show you!" And you try to take the book away to find the place for him. Taking a juicy bone away from a dog would be simpler.

"I'll come to it in a minute!" he almost snarls, and clutches the volume to his chest. From then on the book is his. Insurance is forgotten, the next client is forgotten, and, if you want to tip-toe out on him and go to lunch, he will never notice that you are gone.

A child confined with measles never was so engrossed in a picture book as this busy man in yours. He turns the pages one after another very slowly, getting his nose right down into

*"I'll come to it in a minute," he almost snarls*

it in order not to miss a detail, and not a sound comes out of him for 15 minutes, except an occasional "Very interesting!"

By having on hand five or six volumes of pictures, left carelessly about on tables and sofas, I have found it possible to do a whole afternoon's work with a roomful of people at my back. It may take 10 or 12 minutes to get them to thumbing, but once they are started, with one holding a book and two others perched on the arms of the chair, there isn't a sign of life in the room except the slow rustle of pages and now and then the wetting of a thumb.

When one group is through with a volume, they swap with another group, and so the afternoon passes until my work is done and I begin to get a little lonesome. Then I go over and look over someone's shoulder, for I am not averse to picture books myself, even ones that I have looked at before.

Aside from the bitterness which arises when someone gets hold of a picture book which you are only half through with, this innocent pastime tends to simplify and sweeten our human relationships. If Man descends to meet, as Emerson said, he certainly unbends to look at picture books. For 15 minutes, at least, everyone in the room is naive and ingenuous. I don't know what particular virtue there is in that, but there must be some.

# OLD DAYS IN NEW
# BOTTLES

*A Glance Backward in the Manner of the
Authors of Theatrical Reminiscences*

FEW, probably, of my readers, will remember the time when the old Forrest Theatre stood where the Central Park Reservoir now is. In those days, Central Park was considered 'way downtown, or "crosstown," as they called it then, and one of the larks of the period was going "down to Central Park to see the turtles." There was a large turtle farm in the Park at that time, run by Anderson M. Ferderber, and it was this turtle farm, expanding and growing as the turtles became more venturesome, which later became the Zoological Exhibit.

I remember very well the night when it was announced at the Forrest Theatre that the building was to be torn down to make way for the New Reservoir. It was as I recall, H. M. Ramus ("Henry" Ramus) who made the announcement. He was playing *Laertes* at the time (*Laertes* was played with the deuces wild and a ten cent limit) when the manager of the theatre (Arthur Semden, who later became Harrison Blashforth) came into the dressing room and said: "Well, boys, it's all over. They're going to build the Reservoir here!" There was a silence for a full minute—probably more, for the manager had come into the wrong dressing room and there was nobody there.

At any rate, "Henry" Ramus was selected to go out and tell the audience. He did it with infinite tact, explaining that there was no need for alarm or panic, as the water could not possibly be let in until the theatre was down and the Reservoir constructed, but the audience was evidently taking no chances on being drowned, for within three minutes from the time Ramus began speaking, everyone in the theatre was outdoors and in a hansom cab. Audience psychology is a queer thing, and possibly this audience knew best. At any rate, the old Forrest Theatre is no more.

Speaking of "Henry" Ramus, an amusing anecdote is told of Whitney Hersh. Hersh was playing with Booth in Philadelphia at the time, and was well known for his ability to catch cold, a characteristic which won him many new friends but lost him several old ones. The theatre where Booth was playing in *The Queen's Quandary, or What's Open Can't Be Shut* was the old Chestnut Street Opera House which stood at the corner of what was then Arch, Chestnut, Spruce, Pine and Curly Maple Streets. This theatre was noted in the profession for its slanting stage, so much so, in fact, that Booth, on hearing that they were to play there, is said to have remarked: "The Chestnut Street, eh?" On being assured that he had heard correctly, Booth simply smiled. He later founded the Players' Club.

Jonathan Henchman, father of Ralph Henchman and Mother of Men, Old Yale ....... MR. MACREADY

Ralph Henchman, father of Jonathan Henchman and a rather wild young chap ... MR. JUNIUS BOOTH

Jack Wyman, M.D., a doctor who has more "patience" than "patients"

MR. EDMUND KEENE

Professor Hawksworth, an irascible old fellow who specializes in bird troubles

MR. HORNBLOW

Professor Hawksworth, an irascible old fellow who specializes in bird troubles

MR. JUNIUS BOOTH

Meeker, a party who lives by his wits and not much of that MR. JONATHAN EDWARDS

Eugenia, daughter of Jonathan Henchman .. MRS. SIDDONS

Mlle. de Bon-Ton, a young lady who is not above drinking a little champagne now and then ...... MISS CUSHMAN

Eliza, maid at the Nortons

BY HERSELF

Hamlet, Prince of Denmark

MR. WILLIAM A. BRADY

MR. BENCHLEY'S FAVORITE SOUVENIR

In *The Queen's Quandary, or What's Open Can't Be Shut,* Hersh had to play the part of *Rodney Ransome*, the father of several people. In the second act there was a scene in which *Rodney* had to say to *Marian*:

"But I thought you said the Duke *had* no moustache!"

To which *Marian* was supposed to reply: "I never was more serious in all my life."

On the night of the opening performance Hersh was, as usual, very nervous. He got through the first act all right, with the aid of several promptings from his mother who was sitting in the balcony. But when the second act came along, it was evident to the other members of the company that Hersh could not be relied upon. This feeling was strengthened by the fact that he was nowhere to be found. They searched high and low for him but, like the sword of Damocles, he had disappeared. At the curtain to the second act, however, he was discovered sitting out front in D-113 applauding loudly and calling out "Hersh! We-want-Hersh!" The only way they could get him back on the stage was a ruse which was not without its pathetic side. The manager of the house stepped out in front of the curtain and asked if any member of the audience would volunteer to come upon the stage and be hypnotized. Hersh, who had always wanted to go on the stage, was one of the first to push his way up. Once behind the footlights again his nervousness left him and he went on with his part right where he had left off. It did not fit in with the rest of the play, but they were all so glad to have him back in the cast again that they said nothing about it to him, and whenever, in later years, he himself mentioned the affair, it was always as "that time in Philadelphia when I was so nervous." . . . And that little girl was Charlotte Cushman.

It was at this time that Stopford's *A New Way With Old Husbands, or The Mysterious Drummer-Boy* was given its first performance at the old Garrick Theatre in New York. The old Garrick Theatre was torn down in 1878 to make way for the new Garrick Theatre, which, in its turn, was torn down in 1880 to make way for the old Garrick again. It is the old, or new, Garrick which now stands at Broadway and Tenth Street on the spot known to passers-by as "Wanamaker's." Thus is the silver cord loosed and the pitcher broken at the well.

*A New Way With Old Husbands, or The Mysterious Drummer-Boy* was written for Ada Rehan, but she was in Fall River at the time; so the part was given to a young woman who had come to the theatre that morning asking if a Mr. Wasserman lived there. On being told that it was not a private dwelling and that there was no one there named Wasserman, she had said:

"Well, then, does anyone here want to subscribe to the *Saturday Evening Post?*"

Those members of the cast who had gathered on the bare stage for rehearsal were so impressed by the young woman's courage that a purse was taken up for her children in case she had any and, in case she had no children, for her next of kin.

"I do not want money," she said, taking it. "All I want is a chance to prove my ability on the stage."

"Can you make the sound of crashing glass?" asked Arthur Reese, the stage manager.

"I think so," replied the young woman without looking up.

Reese looked at Meany, the assistant stage manager. "She is the one we want," he said quietly.

So the young woman was engaged. . . . Some thirty years later the Empire Theatre in New York was aglow with lights on the occasion of the opening of *Call the Doctor*. Gay ladies, bejewelled and bejabbers, were running back and forth in the lobby, holding court, while tall, dark gentlemen in evening dress danced attendance. Those who couldn't dance sat it out. It was the metropolitan season at its height.

Suddenly a man burst excitedly through the crowd and made his way to the box-office.

"This seat is ridiculous," he exclaimed to the Treasurer of

the theatre (Roger M. Wakle, at the time). "I can't even see the stage from it."

"That is not so strange as it may seem to you at first," replied Wakle, "for the curtain is not up yet."

A hush fell over the crowded lobby. This was followed somewhat later by a buzz of excitement. This, in turn, was followed by a detail of mounted police. Men looked at women and at each other. . . . For that young man was Charlotte Cushman.

It was about this time, as I remember it (or maybe later), that the old Augustin Daly Stock Company was at the top of its popularity and everyone was excited over the forth-coming production of *Up and Away*. It had been in rehearsal for several weeks when Tom Nevers asked Daly how much longer they were going to rehearse.

"Oh, about another week," replied Daly, with that old hat which later made him famous.

You can imagine Nevers' feelings!

A glance at the cast assembled for this production might be of interest in the light of subsequent events (the completion of the vehicular tunnel and the Centennial Exposition). So anyway it is at the top of page 160 to look at if you want to.

As it turned out, *Up and Away* was never produced, as it was found to be too much trouble. But the old Augustin Daly Stock Company will not soon be forgotten.

My memories of St. Louis are of the pleasantest. We played there in Dante's *Really Mrs. Warrington*—and *Twelfth Night*. The *St. Louis Post-Dispatch*, on the morning following our opening, said:

"It is quite probable that before the end of the year we shall

163

see the beginning of the end of the work on the McNaffen Dam. The project has been under construction now for three years and while there can be no suspicion thrown on the awarding of the contracts, nevertheless we must say that the work has progressed but slowly."

It was while we were playing in St. Louis that the news came of the capture of J. Wilkes Booth. A performance of *Richelieu* was in progress, in which I was playing *Rafferty*, and Fanny Davenport the *Queen*. In the second act there is a scene in which *Rafferty* says to *La Pouce*:

> *"I can not, tho' my tongue were free,*
> *Repeat the message that my liege inspires,*
> *And tho' you ask it, were it mine,*
> *And hope you'll be my Valentine."*

Following this speech, *Rafferty* falls down and opens up a bad gash in his forehead.

We had come to this scene on the night I mention, when I noticed that the audience was tittering. I could not imagine what the matter was, and naturally thought of all kinds of things—sheep jumping over a fence—anything. But strange as it may seem, the tittering continued, and I have never found out, from that day to this what amused them so. . . . This was in 1878.

And now we come to the final curtain. For, after all, I sometimes think that Life is like a stage itself. The curtain rises on our little scene; we have our exits and our entrances, and each man in his time plays many parts. I must work this simile up sometime.

Life and the Theatre. Who knows? *Selah.*

# THE LURE OF THE ROD

FISHING is one of my favorite sports, and one of these days I expect to catch a fish. I have been at it fourteen years now and have caught everything else, including hell from the wife, a cold in the head, and up on my drinking. Next comes the fish. Immediately after that I'll take up something else.

Along about the time when the first crocuses are getting frozen for having popped out too soon (and, by the way, you might think that after thousands of years of coming up too soon and getting frozen, the crocus family would have had a little sense knocked into it) the old lure of the rubber-boot begins to stir, and Fred and I begin to say, "remember that time—?" From then on the *descensus* is extremely *facilis*, unless you know what I mean.

Out come the rods from the attic, and several evenings are spent in fingering over the cards bearing the remnants of last season's Silver Doctors, Jolly Rogers, Golden Bantams, or whatever they are called. Inveterate fisherman that I am, I have never been able to take seriously the technical names for flies. It is much simpler to refer to them as "this one" and "that one" and is less embarrassing if you happen to be self-conscious. The man who made up the names for flies must have been thwarted in a life-long desire to have children, and at last found that outlet for his suppressed baby-talk.

"Well, I'll tell you," says Fred, "I could get off for about ten days and perhaps we could run up to Rippling Creek, or Bubbling Brook."

"If you can get off as easy as that for ten days to run up to any place," says Mrs. Fred, "you can run up to the attic and put up that partition around the trunk-room. The boards have been lying up there ready since last October."

"Who said I could get off for ten days?" replies Fred, hotly. "I said I *might* be able to get off for a day or two. I don't know. I doubt very much if I could make it."

So Fred doesn't go on the trip.

But there are three or four of us who do, and we start to leave about four weeks before the train is ready. George has to buy some new flannel shirts. These are tricky things to buy, and you have to get them far enough ahead so that if they don't fit right around the neck you can change them. It is important that they fit right around the neck, because you'd hate to have Jo Rapusi, the Pollack who takes care of the shack, see you with a badly-fitted shirt. George buys half a dozen shirts and wears one the whole time he is away.

Eddie needs rubber-boots. His old ones have no feet to them and can be used only as leggings. So we all have to go with Eddie while he tries on a new pair. We sit around in the bootery and watch him galumph up and down the strip of carpet, giving him advice on the various styles which the clerk brings out.

"How are these?" asks Eddie, a little proudly, stepping off

in a pair into which he has not quite got his right foot, with the result that he is thrown heavily to one side as it buckles under his weight.

"They're fine, Eddie," we say, "only watch out for that right one. It's got a nasty canter."

"The fish will hear you coming in those, Eddie," is another hot one. "You ought to wear them on your hands."

This sort of thing takes quite a time, because it has to be done well if you are doing it at all. There is just enough time left to go and see about the liquid bait which Mac is taking in three portable cases, and to sample it, and then it is almost midnight, and we are due to leave on the trip in four days.

These days are spent in making enemies among our friends by talking about what we are going to do.

"Well, you poor sons-of-guns can think of us a week from today, wading down the stream after a nice big baby with round blue eyes," we say. "And when we get him all nice and slit up and fried in butter, we'll stop and think of you before we eat him and maybe drink a silent toast to the goofs at home."

"'At's fine!" say our friends. And then they start a petition around among the other members of the club to have us locked up in the steam-room until August.

The day for the Big Departure comes around and Eddie finds that, at the last minute, he can't make the grade. He uses his new rubber-boots to plant bay-trees in, one at each corner of his driveway. The rest of us get started, loaded down with rods and baskets, blankets and flasks, and seven knives

*Eddie stepped up and down the strip of carpet*

to cut fish with. (On reaching the camp next day, it is found that no one in the party has a knife.)

There is a great deal of singing on the way up. The line-up consists of five tenors and one voice to carry the air. This gives a rich, fruity effect which necessitates each song's being sung through twenty-five times, exclusive of the number of times we sing it after we have returned to town, to remind one another of what a good time we had singing it on the trip.

There is also considerable talk about what we are going to do with the extra fish. Roberts is going to send his home to his brother's family. They love fish. It turns out, oddly enough, that Mac's father (who lives in Wisconsin) also loves fish, and Mac is going to send his surplus to him. He has always sent his father fish, every Spring, and it seems to be the only thing that has kept the old man alive. Mac says that he has never known such a grand old man as his father, eighty-nine and reads the papers every Sunday, especially the funnies. If anyone takes the funnies out of the paper before his father gets them, he raises a terrible row. At this, Mac starts to cry slightly, just at the thought of his poor old father's having to go without his funnies, even for one Sunday.

Skinner, to whom Mac is confiding, also starts to cry a little, but he never lets on that it is at the thought of his own father, thirty years dead, that he is crying. Skinner is too much of a man for that. He lets Mac think that he is affected by the tragedy of Old Mr. Mac. This brings the two men together to a touching degree and they decide not to go on with the fishing trip at all, but to stop at the next town they go through and start in business together for themselves, and when they have made enough money they will have Mac's father come and live with them. The conversation ends in a disgusting fight between Mac and Skinner over the kind of business they are going into.

Once in a while someone catches a fish. As I said in the beginning, I, personally, never have, but that is because once I get out in the open air I get so sleepy that I don't move off my cot, except to eat, from one day to the next.

# GOOD LUCK, AND TRY
# AND GET IT

YOU may think that you are not superstitious, but would you walk under a burning building? Would you hold a hammer in your left hand and bring it down on your right? Would you light three bank-notes with one match? Probably not. But do you know why?

Most of the superstitions which we have today date back to the Middle Ages, when Superstition *was* something. In the Middle Ages they were superstition-poor they had so much. For several centuries there a man couldn't stoop over to lace up his shoon (middle-aged word for "shoes") in the morning without first throwing salt over his shoulder and wetting his finger in a distillation of wolfsbane. For every single thing they did in those days they had to do three other things first, and, by the end of the day, you know that runs into time. Often they never could get started on the real business at hand because they were so occupied in warding off the Evil Eye; and a man who really took care of himself and ran no chances might very well starve to death before he got through his warding-off exercises.

For instance, there was a thing called a "mandrake root"

which was considered practically infallible for keeping naughty spirits at bay, but you had to go out and dig your own mandrake root. You couldn't say to your little boy while you were dressing: "Run out into the garden and pull up Daddy's mandrake root for him this morning." You had to go and dig it yourself. Furthermore, you had to dig it at midnight, or under just the right conditions of the moon, or it was no good. And, just to make things harder, you had to be deaf, otherwise you would hear the mandrake root shriek when you pulled it up, and, if you once heard that, you would fall down dead. People used to tie the root to a dog and then whistle from a safe distance where they couldn't hear the root complain. The dog would pull up the root in answering the whistle (as dirty a trick as ever was played on Man's Best Friend), hear the deadly scream and fall down dead in his tracks. Then the mandrake digger would rush up, grab the root, and tear off to the office. But, by this time, his office was probably in the hands of the sheriff or the water had overflowed the tub and dripped down into the room below, and there he was stuck with a mandrake root and a bill for $115.00.

Of course, today we know that there is no such thing as Bad Luck, but, just the same, there is no sense in making a fool of yourself. If, simply by walking around a ladder, you can humor some little gnome into not dogging your footsteps all day with a red-hot pea-shooter, then why be narrow-minded? Walk around the ladder, even though you laughingly say to yourself that you are spoiling that little gnome by being so indulgent. What harm can come from walking around the ladder, unless possibly you slip off into the gutter and sprain your ankle?

The reason why we feel an instinctive urge not to walk under a ladder is fairly interesting (only fairly), and perhaps it would be just as well if I told it to you. If you are superstitious about hearing stories about how superstitions arose, wet your right thumb and turn this page over once.

It seems that when William the Conqueror (or Lief the Unlucky, as he was known in the Greek version of the fable) first landed in England (you know the date as well as I do—1215 Magna Carta) he was very nervous for fear that a Certain Party had followed him from Normandy (his real reason for leaving). Every night he used to take a walk around the ramparts of his castle "just to get a breath of fresh air" as he said, but, as he had had nothing but fresh air all day, he fooled nobody. What he really was doing was taking a look to make sure that this Certain Party was not snooping around trying to find a way into the castle to get some evidence on him. One night he came upon a ladder placed up against the wall and, thinking to trap the intruder, he stood under this ladder, very close up against the stone work, to see if he could hear without being seen. It wasn't a ladder at all (he was pretty unfamiliar with the layout of the castle, having just come from Normandy) but a part of the drawbridge mechanism, and, just at that moment, the man in charge opened up the portcullis and pulled up the bridge to let in one of the menials who had been in town to a dance, and William the Conqueror was catapulted over backwards into the moat (from which all the water had been drawn that very evening to make room for fresh) and wrenched his back very badly. From that day on he gave orders for his bodyguard never to let him walk under a ladder *unless he was sure it was a ladder*. Gradually this last provision was dropped from the command and it became known as "William's Folly" to walk under *any* ladder. Gradually the "William's Folly" was dropped, and it became just a sap thing to do anyway. But we do not realize that the *original* form of this superstition was "Don't walk under a ladder unless you are sure that it *is* a ladder!" So, you see, we have just been overcautious all these years.

The practice among athletic teams of carrying along monkeys or owls as mascots comes from a very old custom of monkeys and owls carrying along athletic teams as mascots. The word "mascot" comes from the French *mascotte*, meaning little witch, but practically nobody today carries around a little witch to bring him good luck. In fact, a little witch would be a liability today, for it would mean just one more mouth to feed and one more railroad ticket to buy, even though you could probably get her on for half-fare.

But other things, usually inanimate, have taken the place of the little witch, and a great many people have odds and ends of crockery and bric-a-brac which they would not be without on any venture involving luck. (Name three ventures which do *not* involve luck.) These are sometimes called amulets, and range anywhere from a "lucky penny" (any penny at all is pretty lucky these days) to a small bust of some famous man. I once heard of a man who was carrying a trunk down stairs when a messenger boy came up to him and gave him a note saying that he had won a raffle. From that day on he considered the trunk his "lucky piece" and was afraid to go anywhere without it. This caused him no end of inconvenience and people stopped asking him to parties, but he still persisted in dragging the trunk with him wherever he went, always looking for another messenger boy to come up with another message of good-cheer. He finally hurt himself quite seriously, so that he couldn't take the trunk with him any more, and then he just stayed at home with the trunk. The last I heard he had not had any more good luck, but he laid it to the Depression.

Thus we see that, even in this enlightened day and age, the old medieval superstitions still persist in some form or other. Some of us go on feeling that if we sign our name on a little piece of paper, or cheque, we can get money from it. Others are perfectly convinced that if they go into a polling booth and push down a button they are having a part in running the government. If it isn't one sort of superstition it is another, and sometimes it is both.

# THE LETTER BOX

ONE of the unhappy results of living in an age like this, with the world resting uneasily on one elbow and twitching nervously, is that most of the letters written in to the newspapers deal with international problems. Nobody seems to care any more about the twippet, or the derivation of the word "squeam." At least, not enough to write in letters about them.

That department in newspapers known flippantly as "The Letter Box" or "Communications to the Editor" is now practically unreadable, owing to "Audax," "Perplexed," and "Old Subscriber" having given themselves over to solutions of the problem and the Menace of Inflation. There is nothing too big for "Constant Reader" to tackle these days, whereas there used to be nothing too small to fascinate him, not even merples' eggs.

Once in a while the first robin gets a paragraph or two in the Letter Box and an occasional snooper breaks out with a discovery that, if you read the last ten lines of "Love's Labor Lost" backward, you will find that Marlowe really wrote it, but, day in and day out, the best we get from correspondents is problems, problems, problems and solutions, solutions, solutions.

The English letter-writers seem to keep their heads better in a crisis. In all the confusion of war, revolution and financial collapse the tiny twippet has never been forgotten and controversy still rages over the methods of salting fish among the ancient Druids. If you think that I am letting my imagination run wild in these subjects, just glance over the controversial matter which agitated the readers of the London Sunday Times last month, a pretty hot month, as months go, in world affairs:

A. M. Goodhart wrote in as follows, under the heading: "Hurtleberries."

"Sir: With reference to the hurtleberries, or windberries, the description quoted from Gwillim's 'Display of Heraldry' 1638, ends thus:" (He then follows with a quotation from Gwillim, which puts an end to any monkey business on the other side.)

Under the heading "Did the Greeks Have Cats?" we read the following from J. F. Clayton, of Clapton E.

"Is there not an apparent reference to the domestic cat in the first book of Batrachomyomachia, where Psycarpex tells the Frog King about the various enemies by whom the noble race of mice are afflicted?" (I give you my word I am not making this up.)

Mr. Clayton, of Clapton E. evidently has quite a lot of time on his hands, besides a deal of erudition, for in the same issue he also has a letter stating that "Mein Lieber August" dates back to 1799. Things can't be very much upset in Clapton E.

John A. Buckley, of East Wittering, Sussex, writes in to deplore the weed threat of Hickling Broad, and L. E. Steele wants to know, with considerable apprehension, if there is any foundation for the statement that Robert Bruce, Henry the Fourth of England and Louis the Fourteenth were lepers. C. R. Haines of Petersfield wants it distinctly understood that swifts do not fly faster than about sixty miles an hour and that a hobby can outfly and take them. He gives no proof, however.

And so it goes, gold standard or no gold standard, twippets and merples' eggs take first place. Can't something be done to keep "Audax" and "Veritas" from fussing around with odds and ends of international crises and to make them settle down to something worth while writing-in about?

(Signed)<br>"AUDAX"

# HOW TO TRAVEL IN PEACE

*The Uncommercial Traveler and His Problems*

THE conversational voltage in the smoking rooms of the trans-Atlantic greyhounds (ocean liners) is so high between June and September that it has been figured out (right here on this page) that if it were possible to harness this jaw motion, the engines could be shut down, and the boats run on talk-power. There is something in the sea air which seems to bring a sort of kelp to the surface even in the most reticent of passengers, and before the ship has passed Fire Island you will have heard as much dull talk as you would get at a dozen Kiwanis meetings at home. And the chances are that you, yourself, will have done nothing that you can be particularly proud of as a raconteur. They tell me that there is something that comes up from the bilge which makes people like that on shipboard.

I myself solved the problem of shipboard conversation by traveling alone and pretending to be a deaf-mute. I recommend this ruse to other irritable souls.

There is no sense in trying to effect it if you have the

family along. There is no sense in trying to effect *anything* if you have the family along. I needn't go into that. But there is something about a family man which seems to attract prospective talkers. Either the Little Woman scrapes up acquaintances who have to have their chairs moved next to yours and tell you all about how rainy it was all spring in Montclair, or the children stop people on the deck and drag them up to you to have you show them how to make four squares out of six matches, and once you have established these contacts you might as well stay in your stateroom for the rest of the voyage.

It is agreed then that you must be a Lone Traveler if you hope to avoid having your good ear talked off. If, by any chance, you find yourself on board ship *with* the family, it is a very easy matter to take them up on the boat deck after dark and push them overboard under the pretext of having them peer over the side at the phosphorus. It is pitiful how unsuspectingly they will peer over the side to look at the phosphorus.

Once you are alone, you can then start in on the deaf-mute game. When you go down to dinner, write out your order to the steward and pretty soon the rest of the people at your table will catch on to the fact that something is wrong. You can do a few pleasant passes of sign language if the thing seems to be getting over too slowly. As a matter of fact, once you have taken your seat without remarking on the condition of the ocean to your righthand neighbor, you will have established yourself as sufficiently queer to be known as "that man at our table who can't talk." Then you probably will be left severely alone.

Once you are out on deck, stand against the rail and look off at the horizon. This is an invitation which few ocean-talkers can resist. Once they see anyone who looks as if he wanted to be alone, they immediately are rarin' to go. One of them will come up to you and look at the horizon with you for a minute, and then will say:

"Isn't that a porpoise off there?"

If you are not very careful you will slip and say: "Where?" This is fatal. What you should do is turn and smile very sweetly and nod your head as if to say: "Don't waste your time, neighbor. I can't hear a word you say." Of course, there is no porpoise and the man never thought there was; so he will immediately drop that subject and ask you if you are deaf. Here is where you may pull another boner. You may answer: "Yes, very." That will get you nowhere, for if he thinks that he can make you hear by shouting, he will shout. It doesn't make any difference to him what he has to do to engage you in conversation. He will do it. He would spell words out to you with alphabet blocks if he thought he could get you to pay any attention to his story of why he left Dallas and what he is going to do when he gets to Paris.

So keep your wits about you and be just the deafest man that ever stepped foot on a ship. Pretty soon he will get discouraged and will pass on to the next person he sees leaning over the rail and ask *him* if that isn't a "porpoise 'way off there." You will hear the poor sucker say, "Where?" and then the dam will break. As they walk off together you will hear them telling each other how many miles they get to a gallon and checking up on the comparative sizes of the big department stores in their respective towns.

After a tour of the smoking room and writing room making deaf-and-dumb signs to the various stewards, you will have pretty well advertised yourself as a hopeless prospect conversationally. You may then do very much as you like.

Perhaps not quite as you like. There may be one or two slight disadvantages to this plan. There may be one or two people on board to whom you *want* to speak. Suppose, for instance, that you are sitting at one of those chummy writing desks where you look right into the eyes of the person using the other half. And suppose that those eyes turn out to be something elegant; suppose they turn out to be very elegant indeed. What price being dumb then?

Your first inclination, of course, is to lean across the top of the desk and say: "I beg your pardon, but is this your pen that I am using?" or even more exciting: "I beg your pardon, but is this your letter that I am writing?" Having been posing as a deaf-mute up until now, this recourse is denied you, and you will have to use some other artifice.

There is always the old Roman method of writing notes. If you decide on this, just scribble out the following on a bit of ship's stationery: "I may be deaf and I may be dumb, but if you think that makes any difference in the long run, you're crazy." This is sure to attract the lady's attention and give her some indication that you are favorably impressed with her. She may write a note back to you. She may even write a note to the management of the steamship line.

Another good way to call yourself to her attention would be to upset the writing desk. In the general laughter and confusion which would follow, you could grab her and carry her up on deck where you could tell her confidentially that you

*Ostentatiously making deaf-and-dumb signs to stewards*

really were not deaf and dumb but that you were just pretending to be that way in order to avoid talking to people who did not interest you. The fact that you were talking to her, you could point out, was a sure sign that she, alone, among all the people on the ship, *did* interest you; a rather pretty compliment to her, in a way. You could then say that, as it was essential that none of the other passengers should know that you could talk, it would be necessary for her to hold conversations with you clandestinely, up on the boat deck, or better yet, in one of the boats. The excitement of this would be sure to appeal to her, and you would unquestionably become fast friends.

There is one other method by which you could catch her favor as you sat looking at her over the top of the desk, a method which is the right of every man whether he be deaf, dumb or bow-legged. You might wink one eye very slowly at her. It wouldn't be long then before you could tell whether or not it would be worth your while to talk.

However it worked out, you would have had a comparatively peaceful voyage, and no price is too high to pay for escaping the horrors that usually attend commuting across the Atlantic Ocean.

# DOWN IN FRONT

FOR years and years the audience has been the worst feature of the theatre. Many a good play has failed, and many a frightful one succeeded, simply because the audiences in this broad and fertile (it certainly is fertile, you can't deny that) land of ours, if all assembled in one large field, would average in a mentality test something approximating one-half of one per cent, or three grammes penny-weight, which is the standard set for the chipmunks before they can become squirrels. If it weren't for the audiences, the drama would be miles ahead of where it is now.

Among the many reforms which must be instituted before the theatre can progress is the ostentatious and horribly painful execution of all people who come in late.

What chance has Ibsen if, just as Helma or Tholwig, or whoever the girl is, begins to explain why she finds herself at the age of thirteen with three husbands, you have to stand up and clutch your overcoat upside down and drop your program to allow a theatre-party of five to scrape past you on their way to the "fourth-fifth-sixth-seventh-and-eighth seats in, please"? How can you keep your mind on the *nuances* of

Ben-Ami's performance if your shirtfront is constantly being scratched by the jet beads or the Masonic fob of some tardy dowager or bon vivant crushing in front of you?

A lot of good it does for them to say "So sorry!" as they grind the gloss from your pump. Slight return is a muttered "I beg your pardon" for the obstructed vision of Delysia kissing the young Prince. If they are so polite as all that, they should begin the good work by starting dinner earlier when they are going to the theatre, or going without the demi-tasse, or standing up back until the act is over. Or better yet, hiring the actors to come to their house and give them a private performance.

So much for them! Lead them away!

We next come to the bronchial buster, or the man (it is usually a man) who, being in the throes of a terrific throat and tube trouble chooses that night for theatre-going on which the crisis is expected. If he can cough his way back to life on that night, the doctor has said that he will pull through, and so he decides that a good show is what he needs to keep him entertained between paroxysms.

He will soon learn to pick his pauses with finesse. It does no good to cough while there is a great deal of noise going on on the stage. No one can hear. The time is just as the star is about to do a little low speaking to her dying lover or when the hero, alone in his garret, goes silently over to the fireplace and tears up the letter. Then for a good rousing bark, my hearty, followed by a series of short, sharp ones like those of a coxswain! If possible the appearance of apoplexy should be simulated. This will cause consternation among those around you—consternation for fear that you may come out of it alive.

Before the current has been turned off, let us offer the chair to the person who applauds long after everyone else has settled down to go on with the show. His offense is born of enthusiasm, it is true, and he thinks that he is doing both actors and audience a favor, but that won't get him anywhere if the reform I have in mind is ever instituted. He will look just the same as the late birds and the cougher when they are all stretched, cold and silent, in the tumbril on its return trip.

This one appears to be under the delusion that he is an occupant of the royal box, and that, if he likes a song, all he has to do is clap his palms together and the song shall be repeated until he has had his imperial fill. When his favorite actor or actress comes on, the show needs must stop while he lets them know that he is right with them every minute of the time. This is especially satisfying encouragement if the favorite actor's entrance happens to be one in pursuit of a fleeing policeman or a sudden discovery of his wife saying "hello" to the man who came to fix the bell. In the midst of such trying scenes, the favored actor must either stop in his pursuit to bow in acknowledgment, or stand stock still, in awkward tableau, waiting for the applause to die down so that he may cry: "So this is how matters stand, is it?"

It may be claimed that the actors themselves like this, and if they don't mind, who am I to object? Well, I'll tell you who I am. I'm the guy that some night is going to get right up and go across the aisle and untie the necktie of the inordinate clapper and, if he says anything back to me, I will tie it up again so that it looks simply terrible. That's who I am.

There isn't much to be said about the reform which must be brought about in the line at the box office. Everyone recognizes that, but, as most of the victims will have to be women,

*The man who applauds long after everyone has settled down to go on with the show*

we men are rather hesitant about proceeding. Even nowadays a man can't step up and kill a woman without feeling just a bit unchivalrous.

But sooner or later it has got to come if the women don't learn how to buy tickets. It makes no difference how good a mother a woman may be, or how lovely in her own home, if she is going to stand at the head of a line of twenty people who are waiting to buy tickets and ask the theatre-treasurer to show her a picture of the stage from the seats he is trying to sell her, and change her mind about the Wednesday and Saturday matinees, and lose her money, and demand to be told if that isn't a picture of E. S. Willard hanging in the lobby, if she is going to do these things, then she must be killed. There are no two ways about it.

And then, when we have made a start with these few drags on the progress of the drama, it will be time enough to pay some attention to the plays themselves.

# CONFESSION

PRETENDING to swoon at grand opera when it really bores you, or pretending to crave Château Neuf du Pape 1921 when you honestly can't tell the difference between it and cooking sherry 1931, is a form of pretense which is universally recognized. We all practice it in one form or another.

But we also pretend to dislike a lot of things because we know that we should dislike them—that is, if we want to have any standing at all among connoisseurs—when secretly they are exactly our dish.

Feeling rather low today, and wondering just how long I can hold onto any standards at all, I would like to break down and admit some of the things that I have been pretending to ridicule all my life, or that I have been ashamed to admit liking before.

Of course, even in this form of self-exposure, there is a chance for hypocrisy. I could pretend humility in admitting that I prefer cold canned corn eaten out of the ice-box to the best brand of Russian caviar, but that wouldn't be humility. I would merely be currying popular favor, for no one that I have ever heard of, rich or poor, high or low brow, has ever looked down on the practice of picking at cold canned corn in the ice-box. There is certainly nothing to be ashamed of in it, even in the face of a congress of gourmets.

What I hope to do is really to abase myself in the eyes of the world of experts, and to confess that, after years of quipping and sneering at them, I really enjoy the following despised items in the connoisseur's code. Let us get the unpleasant business over with as soon as possible. I really like:

Edgar A. Guest.

The music to "Trees." (I'm a little tired of it, perhaps, but, given a respite, I shall like it again.)

The odor of onions on people, and living-rooms which reek of cooking cauliflower from the kitchen.

Paintings which "tell a story," like "The Doctor."

Portraits which look so much like the subjects as to be "photographic."

Salvation Army music.

Westerns.

Parsley.

"In the Baggage Coach Ahead," and similar ballads.

Pansies.

Lunch-cart food.

The old "While Strolling Through the Park One Day," dance routine, even when being burlesqued."

Honest whimsey.

The aroma of fish-houses, the stronger the better.

"My Rosary" and "Among My Souvenirs."

The idea of "Service" in business.

There are dozens more that I could add to this list, but I can't think of them now.

I have tried to be honest. I have not put down anything that I did not like for itself alone, and nothing, as "In the Baggage Coach Ahead" might have been, that I like as a humorous example of the sentiment of an elder day. I am genuinely moved by "The Baggage Coach Ahead," in just the way that its authors intended, and I am spiritually stirred by Salvation Army music. I have done no slumming in this list.

So I guess I'll just get my hat and coat and go, thank you.

# ON SAYING LITTLE AT
# GREAT LENGTH

*With Special Reference to That Master of the Art,*
*Robert Louis Stevenson*

B EING simply a person who writes little articles spo-
radically, and with no distinction, I am always forced
to have something in mind about which to write. That
is to say, I cannot sit down with nothing to say and
then say it to the extent of two thousand words, so that an
editor will buy it. Editors always demand a little subject matter in my stuff.

And, even if I could sell an article about nothing in particular, I wouldn't feel quite right in doing it.

I am funny that way.

When I write a thing, I do it because I have something
fairly vital burning within me which I feel it is only my simple obligation to the State to express, and, if I were less susceptible to the voice of the "Stern Daughter" (quotation from
W. Wordsworth, an English poet, in his Ode to Duty, in
which poem he refers,—and quite rightly, too,—to Duty as

the "Stern Daughter of the Voice of God"), I should, by preference, devote all of my time to my insurance work.

And yet think of all the famous writers who have done volumes and volumes about nothing at all! . . . After three consecutive minutes of thinking, the only author I can think of who has done this is Robert Louis Stevenson, but as it was Stevenson that I had in mind, anyway, he will do.

Nothing was too trivial for Stevenson to wind up in a beautiful drapery of literary style and send out as an octavo-420 pp.-$1.75 net-volume. He could go from the kitchen to the ice-box and, by keeping a diary on the way, get out something nice in limp leather for the holiday trade. Thus, under the title, "Random Rambles to the Ice-Box," with a preface by Fannie V. deG. Stevenson, showing how this book came to be written and what the prevailing winds were at the time and what Stevenson said on the occasion of Sydney Colvin's offering him a match, we might read this:

"It was already hard upon four o'clock before I was ready to set forth, and, in our back entry, the dark falls swiftly, though not without a touch of Lesbian sureness. I was determined, if not to have a light, at least to have the means of a light in my possession, for there is nothing more harassing to the easy mind than the necessity of feeling about in an ice-box, even one's own ice-box, in the dark, and the reflected glow from the neighboring apartment is not always to be reckoned sure by those who trudge on foot at late afternoon.

"A traveler of my sort was considered not without his eccentricities by those in the front room. I was looked upon with doubt, as one who should project a journey to Algeciras, but, yet with respectful interest, like one setting forth for an inclement antipode.

"It will be readily conceived that I was in a high state of expectancy at the prospect of my unusual, not to say extremely unusual, expedition. Going from the kitchen to the ice-box is a successive progression of steps, no matter from what angle you look at it, and a successive progression of steps has always, even since my boyhood in Ardnamurchan, possessed a strange, impalpable fascination for me. In them you are always moving, always advancing, with the ecstatic swishing of the wind in your ears and the song of the heath in your heart—and when you are progressing, even if it be only toward the ice-box, there is always the comforting certainty which moth cannot corrupt, that you are, at least, not retrogressing.

"I had with me, to cheer my declining spirits and, incidentally, to make another paragraph: a pocket handkerchief, —not one of your tremendous linen affairs, but a formidable expanse of silk,—and hemstitched, too, if you please, by no less a personage than our old family hemstitcher, Janet Mac-Mac; a bunch of keys, which jangled as I walked, like so many keys jangling,—which, indeed, they were; a pen-knife to be worn closed,—not open, for your life, else you receive an ugly jab in the groin unawares; two cancelled theatre-checks for Row H, seats 111-112 at the Adelphi Theatre; a rubber eraser, such as boys use to erase black marks which they have, in unscholarly fashion, made in their copy-books; and, in conclusion, but not, let us hope, in refutation, the unadaptable end of a match.

"Thus equipped, I felt myself ready to start. I was, in a sense, free to go my own way, and yet, withal, constrained to modulate my motions to the temporal necessity of walking warily across the kitchen-floor, for it was at that time in the satisfying, yet undeniably slippery, process of being washed with soap and water by an enormous female in seersucker regimentals, who crouched, as one about to leap at some unseen adversary, directly in my path.

"For those who are restricted to silence in the presence of menials, I can only offer the sympathy of an absolutely democratic and articulate citizen of the world. I dare say that I am not without reserve, and yet, when confronted by an individual of a certain susceptibility to literary reproduction, I become voluble to the point of volubility. Of such a mould was this Woman of the Kitchen Floor. Honest soul! Long may she continue to swosh about in the certainty of a rich reward, happy yet care-free, washing, yet, beyond cavil, *insouciante*.

"It was to her that I spoke as my path intersected the field of her purging operations.

" 'I beg your pardon,' I said, as I walked to one side to avoid stepping into her pail, or, what were ten times more gruesome, on the woman herself.

"Thus ended my first adventure by the way. As I raised my eyes from the surface of the floor I beheld the kitchen threshold, and there beyond, in the pleasant cool of the evening, nestling in the back-hall, like an enraged mother bear at bay, stood the ice-box. Was it Destiny, or Fate, or the clean-cut song of the pines? Who shall say? But because of it, we go the lighter about our business, and feel peace and pleasure in our hearts."

Not only in paid contributions does this concession to padding hold true. When it comes to writing letters, you simply *have* to be famous or else have something to say. If you are one of the hewers of wood and drawers of small weekly paychecks, your letters will have to contain some few items of news or they will be accounted dry stuff. You can't string along for six pages on reasons why you haven't written before and reasons why you must close now. But if you happen to be of a literary turn of mind, or are, in any way, likely to become famous, you may settle down to an afternoon of letter-writing on nothing more sprightly in the way of news than the shifting of the wind from south to south-east.

Here again, Stevenson was a master at utilizing style to fill whatever space might be left over when he had said all there was to say. Especially in his boyhood letters did he give promise of writing at space-rates. To judge from his early letters, one might expect from him something like this, written, let us say, at the age of four:

*Ardnaclochenburn*
*Thursday*

My dear Mrs. Babington Churchill:—

To what extremes of heat and cold does the yearly planetary revolution bring us! Now we are suffused by the delicate warmth of genial, let us say, May; now chattering in the equally indelicate rigours of, for instance, November. Before we have first glimpsed the soft luxury of Ceres,—pouf!—and we are confronted with the downy carpet which heralds the advance of the winter solstice.

So it is here with us. Each day is more like the others than the one before it, and I find myself wondering, my dear Mrs. Babington Churchill, if it is not better so, after all. For just so often as the thrush sings,—nay more—just so often as the linnet warbles, so often do I think of you all in Old House, Ashley Heath, Cheetles Cheshire, and wonder what, in the immutable turnings and strugglings of events, you are doing.

You will remember those lines of Stanchfield's on the coming of age of his grocer:

> *Noo lyart leaves blaw ower the green,*
> *Whilk noo, wi' frosts ohint her.*

These words are often brought home to me by the febrile, even openhearted, attempts of my man-servant to brush my waistcoat, and I feel that I am no longer capable of judging such things.

You will doubtless deem me a churlish fellow for not having replied to your last epistle long ere this, and, indeed, such I am. But you must know, in your *coeur des coeurs* that I am inseparably bound up with my work here.

Yesterday I saw a man on a bicycle. He was pedalling along, hands on the handle-bars, feet in their proper places, eyes on the road, for all the world like Prometheus on the rocks, and, although I incur your verdict of sentimentalist, I must tell you that I whistled at him as he went by. It is little incidents such as this that make life here what it is.

And now comes the twilight, and with it the consciousness of approaching darkness. Will you not write at an early date, and tell me all about your good self? Do plan to favor this province with a visit before the Equinox. We have artichokes every day. What more can I say?

Believe me, my dear Mrs. Babington Churchill,

Yours, etc., etc.,

R. L. S.

But I won't be able to sell this article myself if I run on so, even in imitation of Stevenson. Editors simply won't take padded stuff from an unknown writer.

# THE DYING THESAURUS

O N TOP of everything else comes the announcement in the newspapers that, unless $10,000.00
is forthcoming within a month, the great thesaurus
of the Latin tongue will have to be abandoned!
And yet the war was fought ostensibly for Democracy!

In case there are a few scattered illiterates who have never
heard of the great thesaurus of the Latin tongue, let it be explained that it has been under way for twenty years, that five
volumes of it have already been published (even if the whole
thing were to collapse now, we still would have those five
volumes; so don't take on so), and that the general scheme
of the thing was to give the history of every word in the Latin
tongue from the earliest times to the Middle Ages. And now,
for the lack of a mere $10,000.00, the Thesaurus Commission,
through Dean West of Princeton, stands in the doorway looking up the road toward the setting sun and murmurs sadly:
"Well, Dean, we might as well face it now as later. We
can't go on. We've—got—to—stop—(*glup*)—the—old—thesaurus."

It hardly seems possible that, in a land of plenty like ours,
a project like this can be allowed to fail. Just think what it

would mean to have a complete history of every word in the Latin tongue from earliest times right plumb up to the Middle Ages. You may think perhaps that the history that you have is complete enough, but does it bring the thing up to the Middle Ages? Suppose, for instance, that a dispute were to arise some night at dinner over the history of the word *agricola*.

"I'll bet you two seats to the *Follies*," you might say to your brother-in-law, "that the word *agricola* used to be practically interchangeable with the masculine demonstrative pronoun *hic*. *Agricola* means 'farmer,' and so does *hic*, or, as it has come down to us in English, 'hick.' "

One word would lead to another, or perhaps to something worse, and the upshot of the whole thing would be a hurried reaching for your vest-pocket history of Latin words and phrases. And what would be your chagrin to find that the volume began with the First Punic War and gave absolutely nothing previous to that period that you could rely upon!

We are a thorough people and we demand that our history of the Latin tongue shall be thorough. As the popular song-hit has it: "If our thesaurus ain't a real thesaurus, we don't want no thesaurus at all." That's the way the rank and file of Americans feel about it. Home life is the basis of all our national institutions and there is nothing that contributes to its stability like a good book for reading aloud.

"What shall it be tonight, kiddies?" says the father, drawing up his chair before the fireplace in which stands a vase of hydrangeas, "the story of how *mensa* came to have its feminine ending?" "Oh, no, Daddy," lisps little Hazel, "read us about the root verbs which are traceable to the Etruscan influence on the early Latin language. You know, Daddy, the one about the great big prefix, the middle-sized prefix, and the little baby prefix which went '*huius, huius, huius*' all the way home."

And so the father read the old, old story of how the good fairy came and told *ad, ante, con, in, inter, ob, post, prae, pro, sub*, and *super* that some day they would grow up and govern the accusative and how it all worked out just as the good fairy had said. And all the little children fell asleep with smiles and post-toasties on their faces.

And for the lack of ten thousand dollars shall this dream of American home life fade away?

# BRAIN-FAG

I T HAS been figured out by somebody who likes to figure out things that students in institutions for the feeble-minded die much earlier than people on the outside. This is because, according to the figurer-out, their brains do not function normally.

Several feeble-minded people have disputed this, claiming that their brains are the only ones which do function normally, and I have no way of proving that they are wrong, except that they are in the minority. I also have no way of proving that they are in the minority.

But the point seems to be that it is all a question of using up energy, and that idiots use it up quicker than anybody else—idiots and people who run around the Reservoir every morning. When a feeble-minded person starts thinking, he goes at it hammer and tongs, and thinks so hard and so fast that he wears himself out. This should certainly be a lesson to all of us not to think too much. I, myself, haven't had much trouble in this line since I gave up worrying over transmigration of souls. I worried over that perhaps 15 minutes once.

But a man named Friedenthal (never heard of him) went to work and made things harder by figuring out a ratio of brain-weight, body-weight and longevity, which he called "the cephalization factor." (Possibly he heard it wrong and meant "civilization factor," but the result is the same in the end.)

The "cephalization factor" is expressed by the formula "brain-weight over body-weight multiplied by two-thirds." The "two-thirds" is just put in there to give the thing a scientific look, I guess.

Personally, I would be inclined to multiply by seven-eighths, and I'll bet that no one could tell me why I shouldn't. Crazed with success, I might even go ahead and multiply by 12 apples and a man swimming a mile down-stream with a current running four miles an hour. Give up?

Now, as the cephalization factor rises, so does the natural length of life. In other, and worse, words—"the larger the brain in proportion to the protoplasmic mass it controls the longer the animal lives." That's something to think over.

I haven't any idea how much my brain weighs. Some days (shall we say today?) it feels like an old-fashioned Remington Invisible sitting up there in my cranium, and other days it is off somewhere up in the corner of the ceiling lying in wait for butterflies. And as for "the protoplasmic mass which it controls," I would rather not think about it. I know what it weighs, all right, but I won't tell.

So I guess that I'll just have to wait and see how long I live, without having recourse to the cephalization factor. But, what I don't understand is, if feeble-minded people die earlier because they wear their brains out with too concentrated thinking on subjects which are beyond their grasp, wherein do they differ from Mr. Friedenthal, who certainly worried a lot about the cephalization factor?

Granted that Mr. Friedenthal had a better mental equipment to wear out, why didn't he wear it out just the same? You can't tell me that all that formula-business came easy to him, especially that deciding to multiply by two-thirds.

My inclination would be to avoid thinking entirely, whether it be with feeble-minded people or Mr. Friedenthal, and just see what happens. I'll bet I outlive them both.

# PLANS FOR ECLIPSE DAY

*What To Do When It Gets Dark*

IF YOU really want to figure out just when and where there will be a complete eclipse of the sun, it is a pretty simple matter. All you have to do is think of a number. The only specification is that it has to be a number of twelve digits. You must know lots of good numbers of twelve digits. When you have found one, you write it on a piece of paper and hand it to an usher. Then you take the circumference of the earth and draw a line from it parallel to the sun's orbit. (You may have a little trouble in finding the sun's orbit, but don't be discouraged. Look everywhere.) Now this line represents the earth's shadow. It isn't a very good representation, it is true, but it will do, unless you are an artist and can draw a good shadow.

Now put a calendar under this piece of paper (what piece of paper?) and trace the line representing the earth's shadow onto the calendar. When you take off the tracing sheet you will find that the line points to the exact day of the month when the next eclipse will take place. And in some strange way, as yet unexplained by science, you will also find written in a clear, round hand, the exact hour and locations from which the eclipse will be visible. This is the most interesting phase of the whole thing. Where does that writing come from? And yet there are people who deny that there are supernatural forces at work in the world! I forgot to add that if you want to know how long the eclipse will last, you must add seven to the total, one for each of the days in the week.

Now that we have found out that there is surely going to be an eclipse, the next thing to do is to plan how to take advantage of it. It isn't often that right in the middle of the day you get complete darkness, and there is no sense in just sitting around looking blank while the thing is going on. At such times there is a man's work to be done, and "England expects every man," etc.

In the first place, you can count on practically everyone else being out in the street gaping up at the sky or paying fifty cents to look through a telescope at nothing. You will have the run of the town. This is no small advantage. The only thing is that you will have to work fast, for the eclipse lasts only a few minutes. This will make it necessary for you to decide just what it is you want to do, map out your route, and be ready to start the second that darkness sets in.

For instance, supposing that for years you have been repressing a wild desire to insult somebody—the president of your local board of aldermen, your wife's father—anybody. Find out where he is going to be at the time of the eclipse, station yourself within ten feet of him, and just as soon as it gets good and dark, rush up and pull his hat down over his ears, untie his necktie and then run. By the time the lights are on, or the sun is out again, you can be back at your desk, breathing heavily but very happy.

Perhaps you have always wanted to violate the law against smoking in the Art Museum. Very well, now is your chance. Get your pipe or cigarette all lighted and, at the proper moment, rush into the *verboten* territory, take a dozen good drags, and fill the place with smoke. You might even knock a lot of ashes on the floor. You won't have to run after this, for when it grows light you can hide the apparatus and help the authorities look for the culprit.

Another good game would be to hire some accomplices and change all the street signs. This would be more in the nature of a prank and would call for the release of no malicious repressions. It would be a lot of fun that afternoon to stand on the corner and watch the confusion of traffic, with people and cars going up the wrong streets, family men rushing about trying to find their homes (giving up after two or three minutes and staying downtown all night), postmen crying softly to themselves and roaming through Elizabeth Street looking for 114 South Division Street with a lot of undelivered mail, and the whole town in general facing a complete tie-up. It might be necessary to re-district the whole city or perhaps build an entire new one ten miles up the river. Then, a few years later, at the Board of Commerce dinner, you could get up and tell everybody of the joke you played and get a good laugh.

Personally, I intend to devote myself to a more harmless experiment. For years I have wanted to wear a silk hat, a bat-wing collar, and a spotted bow tie. I tried it once and was told that I looked terrible. It wasn't just a few friends who told

*Perfect strangers wrote letters to the papers about it*

me. Perfect strangers wrote letters to the papers about it and said that it was a disgrace to the city that such things should be allowed. A lot of people got up a round robin and sent it to me, reminding me of my wife and children. The thing created such a stir that I bowed to public opinion and put the hat away in a box on the top shelf of my closet and went back to the old fedora. But in my heart I knew that I was in the right and resolved to wear that outfit once more before the Grim Reaper got in his dirty work—in the daytime, too.

So on January twenty-fourth, I will stay at home in the morning and have a simple breakfast of fruit and one dropped egg on toast. Then I will put on my Appellate Division coat, with perhaps a gardenia in the buttonhole, a pair of trousers with a modest stripe, patent-leather shoes and gray spats, a white waistcoat, and a batwing collar with a spotted bow tie. Then I will have my man ready at the door to hand me my silk hat and stick when the time comes. At the very first sign of darkness, I will start out on a brisk trot up the street, covering the block bounded by Madison Avenue, Forty-fourth Street, Fifth Avenue, and Forty-fifth Street. If I see that things are working out all right and that I have plenty of time, I may slow down to a walk, or even saunter, swinging my stick when I get on Fifth Avenue. I have paced the distance out in my regular clothes and find that I can do it in about five minutes, or under, if the track is fast. This will bring me back to the house just in time to escape the full light of day and yet I guess enough people will see me to give the thing that spice which danger lends to an exploit of this kind. I don't care about the elevator man. He is paid to take people up and down in the elevator and it is none of his business what they look like. He's used to masqueraders anyhow.

The only trouble with these plans for Eclipse Day is that it may not be entirely dark during the event. I can't find anyone who knows exactly about that. It may work out to be merely like a very cloudy day. And in some sections of the country, of course, there won't be a complete eclipse visible at all. This would make it rather difficult to get away with anything spectacular, like kissing Peggy Hopkins Joyce. And, at any rate, the very fact that there is an eclipse going on at all, will give you an excuse for knocking off work for a few minutes.

# IN THE BEGINNING

*Thoughts on Starting Up the Furnace*

ALONG about now is the time when there falls upon the ears of the Old Man one of the most ominous of all household phrases: "Well, Sam, I guess we'll have to get the furnace-fire started today."

No matter what Daddy is doing at the moment, no matter how light-hearted he may be, gathering autumn leaves or romping on the terrace, at the sound of these words a shadow passes across his handsome face and into his eyes there comes that far-away look of a man who is about to go down into the Valley. He drops his golf-clubs or balloon or whatever it is he is playing with when the news comes, and protests softly: "The paper says warmer tomorrow."

But in his heart he knows that it is no use. The family has been talking it over behind his back and has decided that it is time to have the furnace started, and he might as well tell the back wall of the Michigan Central Terminal that the paper says it will be warmer tomorrow and expect it to soften up. So there is nothing for him to do but get ready to build a fire.

Building the furnace-fire for the first time of the season is a ritual which demands considerable prayer and fasting in preparation. I would suggest that the thing be considered far enough in advance to get it done right, and to this end have outlined a course of preliminary training.

For a man who is about to build a furnace-fire, good physical condition and mental poise are absolutely essential. I knew a man once who had been up late every night during the week preceding his ordeal in the cellar and as a result was tired and nervous when the day came. Furthermore, he had neglected his diet in the matter of proteins, so that his system was in rather poor shape. When confronted with the strain of getting the kindling going and putting the coal on, he simply went all to pieces and when they found him he was kicking and screaming, and trying to burrow his way through the pile of pea-coal in the corner of the cellar. They caught him just in time; otherwise he might have succeeded and would probably never have been found.

It would be wise, therefore, along about the first of September, for the prospective father of the bouncing fire to pack up and leave home for a few weeks, taking a complete rest in the wilds somewhere and eating nothing but the plainest and most healthful foods. Ten hours' sleep a night would not be too much, and during the day he should be careful to let his mind dwell on nothing but the most peaceful thoughts. He should say to himself every afternoon at three o'clock: "I am Love. Love is All. I reflect no disturbance. I am Being." For exercise, he should go out and chop down several good-sized trees. This will help him when the time comes to break up the kindling.

After several weeks of this kind of training he will be in fair shape to face what he has to face. If it is possible, he should stay in his retreat until it is time to build the fire, coming home on the day of the event. If this cannot be arranged, he should be most careful not to lose the good effect of his rest, and should refuse all invitations for the week previous. Above all, he should take no alcohol into his system. (An alternative to this prescription would be to take all the alcohol that he can get just before going down cellar, so that he is in a state of extreme intoxication during the procedure, thereby deadening the unpleasant features of what he has to do and lending a certain gaiety and enthusiasm to the affair which could not possibly be stimulated otherwise. The danger of this method is, of course, that he might become so interested and excited in what he was doing that he would set the house on fire, too.)

At last the day comes. Kissing his family all around and leaving his papers and insurance documents where they can easily be found in case of the worst, he descends into the cellar. It is better to have no one accompanying him to witness his shame, or to hear what he has to say. At times like these, a man should be alone with his own soul.

There will be no kindling ready. This is a certainty. This means that he will have to break up some boxes. It will be found that these boxes, while seemingly constructed of wood like other boxes, are in reality made of a sort of marble composition which was originally put together to resist the blows of an axe. (In case there is no axe in the cellar, which is more than likely, the shaker to the furnace will do nicely. Place the box or board against the wall and strike it heavily with the iron shaker, saying, "You .... .... .... ....!" at each blow. Your chances are at least even that it will not bounce under the blow and fly up and strike you in some vital spot. If it doesn't do this, it may split.)

After breaking up a sufficient number of sticks, you will take them over to the furnace. The furnace has been standing there all this time, laughing.

A quantity of newspaper is necessary, and while crumpling it up preparatory to filling the bottom of the fire-box with it, you will probably discover several old funny sections which you have never seen before and will have to sit down and read over. This will rest you after the chopping and will take your mind off the furnace. If your wife inquires from the top of the cellar stairs how the fire is coming on, you can reply that you are waiting for it to catch.

The papers once placed in the fire-box, the time has come to pile the sticks in on top of it. Now is also the time to discover that the sticks are too long and won't fit. Back to the axe or the furnace-shaker and a little more fun, smashing and talking to yourself. And now for the big moment!

Placing the wood on the paper, you apply the match. The first match. Follow thirty other matches. Then discover that the draughts aren't open. A good joke on you, at which you laugh heartily.

And now a merry blaze! Up goes the paper in a burst of flame and you feel that the job is about done. After all, not such a hard task, once the wood is split. You shut the door, in order to give the wood a better chance to catch, and hear the cheery roar as the flames rush up the flue. Gradually the roar dies down and you strain your ears to catch the sound of crackling wood. Now the roar is gone, but there is no crackle.

Carefully you open the door, afraid to learn the worst, and there, in a nice, black fire-box, is your wood, safe and sound, with one or two pink wisps of paper blowing coyly underneath. The rest is silence.

Pick the wood out carefully, piece by piece, and start again. Oh, the joy of starting again! Think of what it means, this glorious privilege which Nature gives us of making a fresh start after each one of our little failures! In with more paper! In with more wood! Now the match! And again the roar! Is it not splendid, Little Father? This time certain sections of the wood catch and flicker sadly.

The wood started, we now come to the real test of the fire-builder. Sneak quietly to the bin and get a shovelful of coal. Stand with it by the door of the fire-box, behind which the wood is blazing. Quick! Open door! Quicker! In with the coal! Back for another shovelful! In with it! That's right! It may look for a minute as if you were smothering the bright blaze with the black coal, but don't waver. Another shovelful to cover the last tongue of flame from the burning wood. Hurrah! Hurrah! The fire is out!

The next thing to do is go upstairs and telephone for Jimmie the Italian who makes a business of starting furnace-fires and keeping them going throughout the winter. This requires no more practice than knowing how to use the telephone. And it is the only sure way of getting your furnace going.

# ARE YOU AN OLD MASTER?

WHAT won't they do with infra-red rays next? Or first—what *have* they done with infra-red rays? Or, better yet—what *are* infra-red rays? (Mercy me—is this man's curiosity insatiable? The latest thing that they have announced as being susceptible to infra-red ray treatment is fake painting. Take the Old Master, called "Old Woman With Dour Expression" that has been hanging around in your house for years, and treat it with infra-red rays, and you can tell whether or not it is a fake. If it is, just raise the merry dickens. If it isn't, put it back on the wall and forget it again.

What the infra-red rays do to a painting is to show what's underneath. Lots of so-called old masters have been painted on top of other paintings, and probably lots of other paintings have been painted on top of old masters, although the idea is not a very pleasant one.

How would you like to have an infra-red photograph taken of you in your immaculate evening clothes and, when the proofs are sent around, see that you were just a whited sepulchre, covered from head to foot with tattooings of serpents and the collier "Fleetwood," with "From Annie to Phil" written across your collarbone? Not very much, I fancy!

The old-fashioned X-ray was bad enough. That showed what things you had swallowed, in the line of trinkets and nails. It also disclosed any little oddments of armament that you might have in your pockets, and brought out your garters into pretty sharp relief.

But now we have got to face inquiring photographers with infra-red cameras who want to see whether we are genuine old masters or not. That suit of long underwear that you sneak on when the weather gets cold, that electric health belt that you thought might throw a little more pep into your stride, those built-up shoulders that lend the military air to your carriage—all these will be an open book to the Paul Prys of science.

There is one comfort. The infra-red people will take a long time to get around to us with their cameras. They aren't interested in Poor Little You and Poor Little Me. We could go about painted a bright red underneath and nobody would ever know the difference, provided we lead the kind of lives we're supposed to live.

All the time I am reading of new discoveries of science: emanations from tinfoil which are going to show up subconscious thoughts, invisible smoke from silver nitrate which is going to revolutionize crime detection, rays from rotting apples which are going to make it possible to make anyone invisible except for his belt-buckle, and all kinds of awful disruptions of what I like to think of as my daily life.

But they never seem to impinge on me in the end. I plod along unnoticed, and no scientist will even talk to me, much less work his miracles on me. I never even get an offer to pose for a hay-fever cure. I don't expect ever to have an infra-red photographer so much as ask me to take my hat off.

This is O. K. with me. I don't want to be subjected to anything more than I am subjected to already. If I am not a genuine old master, I don't even want to know about it. It's too late to do anything about it now.

# BIRD LORE

I AM not much of a boy for birds. They frighten me just a little. Out in the trees they are all right, as I seldom get up into a tree myself unless I am very nervous; but a bird at close range has got me completely cowed.

So I was never one of those children who went in for bird-calls. A ruby-throated grosbeak sounded to me just about the same as an owl, and I was perfectly willing to let all the birds in the world chirp their throats off so long as they stayed out of my hair. "Live and let live" has always been my motto with birds.

But out here in California where I am writing this, the birds go too far. Like the Native-Sons, they pride themselves on just being birds.

"Boy, am I a bird!" they seem to be saying. "Just get a load of this!" And then they go into a long number like the two Dodge Sisters, who used to make vaudeville what it was in its declining days.

Last night I had one of my most unpleasant experiences with birds—or, rather, with a bird. I am convinced that it was only one bird, for it was sitting on a bush just outside my window and there were no other birds about.

I had decided to go to bed early and see how that would work, having tried everything else to catch up on my sleep,

*I leaned far out into the bushes and gave a terrific whistle*

and had just put the light out when the thing began. The night was very still outside, and I was wishing that the old Sixth Avenue Elevated would rumble by just once, when a shrill warble sounded in the shrubbery below my window-sill.

"Steady, Bob, old man!" I said to myself, as I leaped out of bed in a cold sweat. "It's only a bird. Pull yourself together!"

Reassured by these words of my own, I clambered back under the blankets (adv. Los Angeles Chamber of Commerce) and listened. In a few seconds it came again, but an entirely different call.

I would say that that bird gave off a noise of some sort every five seconds during the night and each one was different! Not just different in note, but in volume and personality. Once it would be a small bird with a high voice. "A thrush!" I said to myself. Then, in five seconds, it was a great big, burly bird with a long black beard. "An eagle!"

I finally got up and put on the light. "This thing has got to be faced!" I said.

So I went over to the window and leaned far out into the bushes. Collecting all the breath that I could muster, I gave a terrific whistle between my teeth and lips. It was a corker.

"If you want to whistle, whistle that!" I fairly screamed. And back at me came my whistle, only just a bit louder.

I think that I must have fainted, for, when I woke, the sun (adv. Los Angeles Chamber of Commerce) was streaming through the window and I was alone. The Bird to End All Birds had flown.

I am moving today to the top floor of the tallest hotel in town, and to an inside room. From now on, if any birds want to work out on me, they will have to ask at the desk downstairs.

# THE UNITED STATES
# SENATE CHAMBER

*How M. T. Cicero Would Fare at the
Hands of Our Senators at Washington*

THEATRICAL seasons may vary in quality from year to year.

But there is one organization which always runs true to form, regardless of changes in the cast or revisions in the book. Why withhold its name any longer simply to heighten the rhetorical suspense?

In so many words, I refer to the Congress of the United States.

Yes, you can always find something merry going on in the dual bill at the National Capital. In the House—for lovers of the big, noisy type of extravaganza, with smoking allowed in the first twenty-five rows; and in the Senate—for those who like their comedy neat, and produced in an intimate, fratty style by a small cast of consistent comedians.

To one who is steeped in the classic,—as is the average

business man of to-day,—there can not help but arise the question of whether or not the ancient Roman Senate was better, or worse than our own. And, once this question has arisen in one's mind, it is impossible to down it. I have known men of affairs, busy captains (and first lieutenants) of industry, who have gone about, day after day, muttering to themselves, "I wonder if the Roman Senators were anything like as funny as the bunch at Washington?" until they were mere shadows of their former selves.

This question is, therefore, a very vital one at this time, so vital that I feel justified in devoting a fair amount of space to it. I shall try to work up a little nugget of satire in this article, and show, in a vivid manner, just what chance an ancient Roman orator would stand if he started in to deliver one of his classic speeches in the Senate chamber at Washington—in the face of its daily program.

I can think of no safer Roman orator to pick out, for this experiment, than old Dr. Cicero, and no more fitting speech than his little heart-to-heart talk in favor of the proposed Manilian Law, which, as we all remember—by referring to the encyclopedia volume entitled "Cal to Cle"—was a bit of legislation designed to make Lieut. Col. Pompey a Generalissimo and speed up the war program against Mithridatic Kultur.

Let us consider, then, that the Hon. M. T. Cicero, senior Senator from Rome, has announced that, on Tuesday afternoon, he will address the Senate of the United States on the Manilian Law.

Let us go even further, and consider that it is Tuesday afternoon.

As Mr. Cicero begins, there are four Senators in the Senate Chamber at Washington. Three are of Mr. Cicero's party and are seated behind him, matching quarters. The other is an opposition Senator who sits across the room with his feet on his desk, reading a newspaper and eating a cigar. A dozen page-boys are engaged in shooting pennies, behind the President's desk, laughing merrily. The Presiding Officer is on the point of beating himself at Canfield, whistling softly through his teeth the while.

This performance continues throughout Cicero's entire peroration. In the meantime, additional Senators have been pushing their way through the swinging doors, some taking their seats and opening their mail, others congregating in juntas in the aisles and telling each other the one about the two Irishmen who were walking down the street and met a beautiful girl with very low skirts.

The fine points of the opening paragraphs, including exhortations (vocative-plural) to, "O Romans! O Senators," are thus completely lost. For the sake of getting on with this story, however, we shall have to consider that some of the Senators have taken their seats and are paying attention.

To continue, then, in the rowdy manner of that leading American funny paper, the *Congressional Record*:

### MR. CICERO

Thus, O Romans, you perceive what the case is. Now, consider what you ought to do. It seems to me that I ought to speak, in the first place, of the sort (kind of) of war that exists; in the second place, of its importance, and lastly, of the selection of a general. It is—

Mr. President—

Does the Senator from Rome yield to the Senator from Nebraska?

Sure.

I should like to ask the Senator, simply for my own information, if he is referring to the present war, or to the Second Punic War.

I was going on to explain, although I thought that I had made myself clear on that point. The kind of war in which we are now engaged is such as ought, above all others, to incite your minds to a determination to persevere in it. It is a war in which the glory of the Roman people is at stake. It is—

Mr. President—

Does the Senator from Rome yield to the Senator from North Dakota?

You've said it.

The learned Senator from Rome has said that this is a war in which the glory of the Roman people is at stake. I agree with him heartily. But I question the advisability of making such a statement at the present time. Will it not create a feeling of despondency in the public mind to say that our glory is in such desperate straits as to be "at stake"? Would it not be better to say that our glory is "directly concerned" or "certainly a factor"? This is no time for hysteria.

### MR. CICERO

I do not agree with the Senator, but I thank him for his suggestion.

### MR. GISH

I need not assure the competent Senator from Rome that I thank him for thanking me for my suggestion.

### MR. CICERO

Certainly not. . . . If I may be permitted, however, I will continue. It is a war in which the glory of the Roman people is, to say the least, one of the things to be considered. Our glory has been handed down to you from your ancestors, great indeed in everything, but most especially in military affairs. It is—

### MR. WEENIX

Mr. President—

Does the Senator from Rome yield to the Senator from Massachusetts?

Go to it, Senator.

As the witty Senator has just said, or should have said, it is indeed gratifying that party lines have been, so to speak, cast aside in this debate. In all my years in the Senate I have never seen such absence of partisan feeling. But I would like to ask the Senator from Rome, since he has seen fit to take up the cudgel in defense of the Administration, by referring to military affairs, if he can explain the shortage of war-chariots of the so-called "Victoria" type, which I am informed, exists to a shocking degree in our national equipment to-day. I base my information on a clipping from the Utica (N. Y.) "Union-Standard-News-Republican," which states that, whereas the present situation calls for 4,000,000 Victoria chariots, we have produced, so far as the "Union-Standard-News-Republican" can find out, just seven chariots of this type. This is no time for lulling the people into a sense of false security. I—

I should like to ask the intelligent Senator if he will explain to the Senate the difference between the so-called "Victoria" type of chariot and the "surrey" type, of which we hear so much.

227

I am not a technical man myself, but this is the way I understand it. A "surrey" chariot has the whip-socket on the right hand side of the dash-board, while the "Victoria"—

### MR. WINTERHALTER

If I may be allowed to correct the intuitive Senator, the difference between the two types of chariots, according to the best information which I can get from several of my constituents who are in the chariot business, is that the "Victoria" chariot is a little worse than the "surrey" chariot, but that both are decidedly inferior to that made by the Appian Way Chariot & General Vehicle Co. This model (so my informant tells me, and he is a member of that firm and ought to know) was turned down by the Government at the beginning of the war, simply because it was found that *the wheels would not stay on,* —a fault which could have been remedied in a very short time. In a crisis like this, when, as the distinguished Senator has so well said, the very glory of the Roman people is at stake, it seems disgraceful, nay more, it seems too bad, that this great country of ours should give itself over to a commercialism in which a perfectly loyal chariot manufacturer is not given a chance to get a government contract when he comes all the way on to Washington to arrange for it. Why, I could tell you of instances—

### MR. WEENIX

If I may be allowed to interrupt the clever Senator, I would like to say that my experience, and the experience of several of my constituents, bears out directly the point he has just made. It is high time that the people knew the truth in this matter. I am not versed in technical matters myself, but I understand from the newspapers (I have a clipping here from the Lima, Ohio, "Bee-Chronicle-News" which substantiates this statement) that not only have we no "surrey" chariots (whatever they may or may not be does not affect the situation), but, gentlemen, *we have no whip-sockets to go in them!* Think of that,—no whip-sockets!

### MR. MC NEE

May I say that I understand that whip-sockets are not used in "surrey" chariots; that the whip is carried in the driver's teeth. This would account for none being built.

### MR. WEENIX

I am exceedingly sorry that the Senator has seen fit to inject a partisan tone into the proceedings by attempting to defend the whip-socket situation. But, since he has started it, I can only say that the whole thing is a terrible fiasco and that the country should know who is to blame.

### MR. CICERO

If I may be allowed to proceed, I have a few more remarks to address to this body on the subject of the Manilian Law which is under discussion. . . . Wherefore, if on account of their allies, though they themselves had not been aroused by any injuries, your ancestors waged war against Antiochus, against Philip, against the Aetolians, and against the Carthaginians—

Mr. President—

THE PRESIDING OFFICER

Does the Senator from Rome yield to the Senator from Alabama?

MR. CICERO

Right-o.

MR. WINKLE

May I ask if the ingenious Senator refers to the inhabitants of Carthage?

MR. CICERO

Yes.

MR. WINKLE

I do not believe that the Senator understands my question. By "Carthaginians" does he mean "inhabitants of Carthage?"

MR. CICERO

Yes.

MR. WINKLE

Let me make myself clear. What is the place of residence of these Carthaginians? I ask for my own information, as I am not a technical man myself.

MR. CICERO

These people live in Carthage.

##### MR. WINKLE

Thank you. That is all that I wanted to know.

##### MR. CICERO

To continue. . . . With how much earnestness ought you, when you have been provoked to such—

##### MR. LAMKIN

Mr. President—

##### THE PRESIDING OFFICER

Does the Senator from Rome yield the floor to the Senator from South Dakota?

##### MR. CICERO

Like Hell I do. And, what is more, I am going to ask to have the remainder of my remarks on the Manilian Law inserted in the *Record*, and take up what is left of my time with a little song and some dance steps. Then, when I come to the chorus, everybody up and join in to your hearts' content. Now is the time for co-operation. Cast party feeling to the winds, and let us all sing the first stanza of "Intiger Vitae," number 264, in the song-book—now, altogether!

The motion was agreed to, and (at 5 o'clock and 20 minutes P.M.) the Senate took a recess until tomorrow, Wednesday, May 26, 1918, at 12 o'clock meridian.

Yes, thinking it over, if the Roman Senate was organized and managed in exactly the same manner as we have organized the Senate at Washington, we have certainly got to hand it to Cicero.

# THE FIRST PIGEON
# OF SPRING

*To the Bird Editor:*

I AM a city boy, forty-four years old, and living in Forty-fourth Street, but taking a forty-five-year-old suit. I have always been interested in birds, but never could seem to get them interested in me. Most of my friends are men.

This was not what I wrote in to say, however. I have read in your columns where various people have seen "the first robin" or "the first thrush" while walking in the country, and they seem very proud of it. I thought that you might like to know that this morning I saw a pigeon right on my window sill. I do not know what the season for pigeons is, in the city, but I am sure that this was one of the first. The first today, anyway.

There couldn't have been many ahead of it, because it was 5 o'clock in the morning when I saw it and it was just getting light. I had been out gathering mushrooms for breakfast and had just tumbled into bed, a little nervous after my experience. (I didn't tell you what my experience was, as this is a letter about birds and I don't suppose you would be interested. Maybe some other time.)

I had just dozed off into a stupor when I heard what I

thought was myself talking to myself. I didn't pay much attention to it, as I knew practically everything I would have to say to myself, and wasn't particularly interested.

The mumbling increased, however, and what was more, seemed to be coming from the window. As I was in the bed across the room I didn't like the look of things.

First, I tried to make out what the matter was, without opening my eyes. (Everything being equal, I would much rather not open my eyes—ever.) But it was no go. I couldn't seem to get the right angle on the situation without taking at least one peek. This I did, and what do you think I saw? Oh, well, I guess you already know what it was, for, like a fool, I gave it away in the beginning of my letter when I told you I had seen the first pigeon of Spring. I could bite my tongue off.

Anyway, there was a big bull-pigeon walking about on the window ledge and giving me an occasional leer with its red eyes, all the while rumbling in a deep, bass voice and giving every indication of immediate attack. Quick as a wink I shut my eyes and lay still. There is no love wasted between pigeons and me, and I wanted to pass the matter off as quietly as possible.

I passed it off so quietly that I didn't get around to opening my eyes again until around noon, and by then the pigeon had given up trying to intimidate me and had flown, or waddled elsewhere to try his bullying tactics on some man of less stern stuff.

But I am sure that it was a pigeon, and if any of your readers are interested in the sighting of early birds I am sure that they have been interested in this account. If they are not interested they have nothing on me.

# VOX POPULI

I AM very sympathetic to marches for causes, provided I know what the cause is. Any group of people who will march through the snow and slush shouting slogans, must have something on their side. All I ask is that I can make out what they are shouting.

As I write this, a long line of people are marching under my office window, three abreast, shouting something in unison, or what they think is unison. There are a lot of them, and they look as if they were in earnest. They also carry signs.

My office is on the tenth floor, and my eyesight is not what it used to be. I have gone to the window eight times now and tried to spell out what the signs say, but the best I can make of it is "xxx xxxx BLOTTERS." Now, they can't be marching for blotters. That's obvious.

I have strained my ears to try and catch the battle cry. This is what I get: "Five . . . Ten . . . Four and twenty! Five . . . Ten . . . four and twenty!" I still think that the nub of the argument has eluded me. Much as I would like to be with them, I can't whip up any enthusiasm over "Five . . . Ten . . . Four and twenty!" and signs reading "xxx xxxx BLOTTERS."

As a matter of fact, I am almost losing my sympathetic

frame of mind. In another fifteen minutes (they are going 'round and 'round the block, so that the thing is continuous) I shall be definitely anti. Or crazy.

You may think that you don't care what people are shouting if it is unintelligible. But just try and sit at a typewriter and compose one sentence in English with "Five . . . Ten . . . Four and twenty!" ringing through the street, especially when you know that it *isn't* "Five . . . Ten . . . Four and twenty!" that is being shouted.

I can't even be sure that it is a parade of strikers. The last time one of those demonstrations took place under my window it was something about Dolfuss. For all I know, this may be a demonstration against the King of Greece, in whom I have only an academic interest, to say the least.

For all I know, it may be the Revolution—and here I sit!

# "WHY I AM PALE"

ONE of the reasons (in case you give a darn) for that unreasonable pallor of mine in mid-Summer, is that I can seem to find no comfortable position in which to lie in the sun. A couple of minutes on my elbows, a couple of minutes on my back, and then the cramping sets in and I have to scramble to my feet. And you can't get very tanned in four minutes.

I see other people, especially women (who must be made of rubber), taking books to the beach or up on the roof for a whole day of lolling about in the sun in various attitudes of relaxation, hardly moving from one position over a period of hours. I have even tried it myself.

But after arranging myself in what I take, for the moment, to be a comfortable posture, with vast areas of my skin exposed to the actinic rays and the book in a shadow so that I do not blind myself, I find that my elbows are beginning to dig their way into the sand, or that they are acquiring "sheet-burns" from the mattress; that the small of my back is sinking in as far as my abdomen will allow, and that both knees are bending backward, with considerable tugging at the ligaments.

*Often I have to be assisted to my feet*

This is obviously not the way for me to lie. So I roll over on my back, holding the book up in the air between my eyes and the sun. I am not even deluding myself by this maneuver. I know that it won't work for long. So, as soon as paralysis of the arms set in, I drop the book on my chest (without having read more than three consecutive words), thinking that perhaps I may catch a little doze.

But sun shining on closed eyelids (on *my* closed eyelids) soon induces large purple azaleas whirling against a yellow background, and the sand at the back of my neck starts crawling. (I can be stark naked and still have something at the back of my neck for sand to get in under.) So it is a matter of perhaps a minute and a half before I am over on my stomach again with a grunt, this time with the sand in my lips.

There are several positions in which I may arrange my arms, all of them wrong. Under my head, to keep the sand or mattress out of my mouth; down straight at my sides, or stretched out like a cross; no matter which, they soon develop unmistakable symptoms of arthritis and have to be shifted, also with grunting.

Lying on one hip, with one elbow supporting the head, is no better, as both joints soon start swelling and aching, with every indication of becoming infected, and often I have to be assisted to my feet from this position.

Once on my feet, I try to bask standing up in various postures, but this results only in a sunburn on the top of my forehead and the entire surface of my nose, with occasional painful blisters on the tops of my shoulders. So gradually, trying to look as if I were just ambling aimlessly about, I edge my way toward the clubhouse, where a good comfortable chair and a long, cooling drink soon put an end to all this monkey-business.

I am afraid that I am more the pale type, and should definitely give up trying to look rugged.

# MY OWN ARRANGEMENT

THE fact that more leaders of radio orchestras and bands are not murdered in their sleep by song writers is a great tribute to the mild manners of the song writers. I, in my tempestuous Mexican way, would have knifed several of them long ago if they had taken one of my tunes and "arranged" it in the current radio manner.

As every radio listener knows, when an orchestra leader announces "my own arrangement," or "my own impression" of a song, the fun comes in trying to discover two successive passages of the original song. This cannot be so much fun for the composer of that song, if he happens to be listening in.

Suppose you had written a nice little waltz number, called, let us say, "Even the Daisies Are Blabbing, What I Can't Confide in You." And some night you hear over the radio an orchestra leader say: "And now, folks, I will play you my own interpretation of that delightful new number, 'Even the Daisies Are Blabbing.'" Forthwith there comes a red-hot fox-trot, with one sustained note on the cornet and a series of trombone retchings, accompanied by an off-beat swishing of a fly-swatter on a drum. It isn't even a waltz, much less your waltz. Would you burn up, or wouldn't you?

I do not know whether Mr. Handy has ever heard what they have been doing to his "St. Louis Blues" all these years with their "special arrangements." If he has, and isn't stark, staring mad, then he is a great deal more phlegmatic than one would suppose the composer of that masterpiece to be. The "St. Louis Blues" has been ripped apart and sewed together again, kicked around and beaten, more than any one song in the history of music, and I am not forgetting "The Beautiful Blue Danube" either. It has got so that any one who can play one long note on the cornet can play the "St. Louis Blues."

And now the pack has turned on Mr. Arlen's "Stormy Weather," easily the top number in its class, and a number especially dependent on its original orchestration for much of its effect. "Stormy Weather" hadn't been on the market a week before it had been "arranged" to a point where no one bar of it could recognize another, and Mr. Arlen himself couldn't recognize even the tempo. If there were a penalty for music-murder, there would be lots less "arranging" done over the radio.

And, while we are on the subject of the popular game of "Hide the Melody," let us devote a word or two to those radio harmonizers who sing their version of a number in which the only thing that can be heard is the tenor or alto. They may be two sisters, or they may be four roustabouts, but when it comes time to get into the chorus, they are all tenors.

I used to play in a mandolin club when I was a boy (too big a boy to be playing in a mandolin club, I may say), but, as I was not quite strong enough on my tremolo, I always played

*My mother felt I wasn't getting along in my music*

second-mandolin. Being conscientious, if not expert, I used to practice the second-mandolin part at home alone. If you have ever heard a second-mandolin part being played alone without the air, you will understand why my mother felt that I wasn't getting along in my music as fast as I might. She thought I was always playing the same tune. What my mother went through is no more than what radio-listeners are asked to go through when the close-harmony boys and girls get their heads together.

If a tune is good enough to play or sing, let's hear it.

# HEY, WAITER!

MR. PETERS usually had his lunch sent in to his office, since it consisted of a glass of milk and perhaps a wisp of chicken. It seemed hardly worth while to check one's coat and hat at a restaurant for just that, to say nothing of unfolding a napkin and telling a waiter about it. And besides, Mr. Peters was still a little self-conscious in restaurants. Something left over from his boyhood still haunted him with the feeling that he had got into the wrong dining-room. For, in spite of his long list of murder victims, Mr. Peters was at heart a timid and retiring citizen.

On certain occasions, however, he had to go out to lunch, as, for instance, when some out-of-town representative wanted to talk business. Out-of-town representatives can always talk business better when munching on a roll, and tablecloths are notoriously better scratch pads than office stationery, possibly because they cannot be saved and held against the scratcher. So on this particular day (you have no reason to know on *what* particular day yet, but you will have in just a minute) Mr. Peters found himself headed for the Belvidere grill with Mr. Hertz of the Oldtown Drop Forge and Tool company, to settle several unimportant things over a curry of lamb.

Mr. Hertz was no stranger to Mr. Peters, but he was not what you would call a "crony." He was a rather disagreeable man, who always wore a stiff white shirt and a bow tie with a batwing collar, having decided early in his business career that an important man should dress in an important manner. In fact, his dress was one of the few ways that Mr. Hertz had of showing that he *was* an important man. His dress and his attitude toward underlings. In his attitude toward underlings he acted as Mussolini looks. (Come to think of it, when Mussolini is not dressed up as a *carabinieri* or a *bersaglieri* he also seems to be wearing a stiff white shirt and a batwing collar. This is probably just a coincidence.)

As they checked their hats and coats, Mr. Hertz began his campaign to show the employés of the establishment that he was not going to be imposed upon.

"Hang that coat somewhere where you can find it, now," he said to the girl. "I don't want to have to stand around all night waiting when I come out." And then he added to Mr. Peters: "You have to watch these girls. They're a dumb bunch."

The girl, who was a friend of Mr. Peters, said she would do her best to put the coat where she could remember it. Mr. Peters slipped her a wink and a quarter in advance. It wouldn't be such a great loss, he thought to himself, if Mr. Hertz *did* lose that coat. It was like something you take along on a camping trip in case the nights get cold.

The head waiter, who was also a friend of Mr. Peters, led them to a table by the window, usually considered a choice location by those who like to see what they are eating, especially if it is bluefish. But Mr. Hertz took it as a personal affront.

"What are you trying to do; freeze us to death?" he growled at the head waiter.

His tone implied that the man was a member of a gang in conspiracy to get this guy Hertz at any cost. He even went to the window and examined the casing.

"There's a draft here that would blow you out of your chair," he said. "Give us another table!"

"I thought—" began the head waiter.

"Never mind what *you* thought," snapped Mr. Hertz. "It's what *I* think. I'm paying for this lunch."

And he picked out a table that pleased him better and sat down. It happened to be a table whose occupants had just left.

"And get some of this stuff cleared off, too," he said, adding sarcastically, "unless you are just being paid to wear a dress suit in the daytime."

Mr. Peters laughed apologetically, trying to make the head waiter think that Mr. Hertz was just an old joker. The head waiter laughed, too, but without spirit. Mr. Hertz didn't laugh at all.

"These captains think they own the world," he said to Mr. Peters. "They'd kill you if they could." And Mr. Peters thought that maybe it wasn't a bad idea.

"Now let's see," muttered Mr. Hertz, picking up the menu and turning to the waiter who stood by, "what's here that's fit to eat? Anything?"

"The chicken hash is very nice today, sir," said the waiter.

"You *would* suggest that," snapped Mr. Hertz. "I never sat down at a table that the waiter didn't try to make me take the chicken hash. What do you get, a rakeoff on all the chicken hash you sell?"

The waiter smiled uneasily.

"Good *night!*" said Mr. Hertz. "What a layout. Why don't you have something that people can eat once in a while? What's that you've got on your shirt front? That looks good."

The waiter looked in embarrassed fashion at his shirt front, but couldn't think up a good answer. There was a spot there, but he didn't know what it was. So he said nothing.

"A surly boy, eh?" said Mr. Hertz. "Well, that takes a quarter off your tip." And then, with a knowing nod to Mr. Peters, "*That's* the only language these wops understand."

"Eric is a Swede, aren't you, Eric?" asked Mr. Peters with forced geniality, trying to get the conversation out of its nasty tone.

"Swedes are the worst of all," said Mr. Hertz. "Well, Swede, have you got any mussels?"

"Not this time of year," said the waiter. "The clams are very good, sir."

"O, not this time of year eh? Well, that's the first time I ever knew that mussels had to have a certain time of year. What do they do, just come out in the summer? Why don't you just say that you haven't got 'em? Nobody asked you their habits."

"I'll have some chicken hash," put in Mr. Peters. He really didn't want it, but he wanted to do something to discredit Mr. Hertz.

"Well, you're easier than I am," said Mr. Hertz. "I can't

eat any of this truck on here. Broil me a small steak and make it snappy. And have it well done on the edges, too. Don't bring it to me half cooked."

"Any potatoes, sir?" asked the waiter, in evident relief that the first stage of the ordeal was over.

"I *said* potatoes! Are you deaf? *Hashed in cream potatoes!* Do you want me to write it out for you? And some new peas, too, if you think you can remember all that."

The waiter disappeared, perspiring from every pore.

"These waiters give me a pain in the eye," said Mr. Hertz. "They never listen and then when they get out in the kitchen they match to see what they'll bring you. In my traveling around the country I've found that the only way is to treat 'em rough if you want to get any service at all."

"That's one way," replied Mr. Peters, snapping a piece of roll at the saltcellar.

Mr. Hertz drew out of his pocket a neat packet of letters, from which he extracted one. It proved to be something written in connection with the Oldtown Drop Forge and Tool company, and it interested Mr. Peters only slightly more than it would interest you if I were to tell you about it. Mr. Peters would not have been interested in the private correspondence of Lucretia Borgia if offered to him by Mr. Hertz. In fact, Mr. Hertz was in a precarious position, if he only knew it.

A detailed résumé of this document consumed perhaps four minutes, at the end of which Mr. Hertz looked around the room and then banged heavily on the table, frightening Mr. Peters out of his rather sinister musings and attracting the attention of the head waiter.

"Come here!" he shouted.

The head waiter came over.

"What are they doing—fishing for that food out in the river? We've been waiting half an hour."

"I'm sorry, sir," said the head waiter. "You ordered something that took a little extra time to prepare. I'll see where it is."

"Extra time! How long does it take you to put a steak on the fire and broil it? It's been three-quarters of an hour now. I could slap a cow to death and get a steak out of it in the time you've taken."

Unfortunately, the waiter put in an appearance at this moment, bearing Mr. Peters' chicken hash.

"Well, here you are!" snarled Mr. Hertz. "What do you do out there in the kitchen—play chess?"

"I'm sorry, sir," said the waiter. "Your steak took a few minutes—"

"*You're* sorry? What do you think *I* am? I'm *hungry!* My God, I've seen rotten service in my time, but never anything that could beat this. Where's my steak?"

"I'm getting it right now, sir," said the waiter.

Mr. Hertz's voice was now raised to a pitch in which most men speak over a long distance telephone.

"Where's the manager?" he bellowed. "I've stood all of this I'm going to!" And he pushed his chair back like a man about to go and look for a manager.

Now, as any friend of Mr. Peters knows, there is one thing which upsets him probably more than anything else, and that is to be made conspicuous in a public place. And Mr. Hertz was rapidly attaining a conspicuousness usually reserved for men with sidewalk fits. As he turned to project his venom more fully on the members of the restaurant staff, Mr. Peters reached over and dropped something in his glass. And Mr. Hertz, to refresh himself after his tirade, immediately obliged by drinking it.

The waiter came rushing up with the steak, but Mr. Peters was alone at the table.

"The gentleman has left the room, Eric," he said. "I don't think he'll be back for his steak. I'll take the check—and here's something for yourself." And, taking one more bite of his chicken hash, Mr. Peters put his napkin on the table and walked out.

As he passed through the anteroom he sensed a commotion in the gentlemen's lavatory, but, as two hospital attendants seemed to be headed in that direction, he decided to go back to his office.

"You can give Mr. Hertz's overcoat to some good horse," he said to the coatroom girl as he passed. "He won't need it where he's going."

# HOW TO GET THINGS
# DONE

A GREAT many people have come up to me and asked me how I manage to get so much work done and still keep looking so dissipated. My answer is "Don't you wish you knew?" and a pretty good answer it is, too, when you consider that nine times out of ten I didn't hear the original question.

But the fact remains that hundreds of thousands of people throughout the country are wondering how I have time to do all my painting, engineering, writing and philanthropic work when, according to the rotogravure sections and society notes, I spend all my time riding to hounds, going to fancy-dress balls disguised as Louis XIV or spelling out GREETINGS TO CALIFORNIA in formation with three thousand Los Angeles school children. "All work and all play," they say.

The secret of my incredible energy and efficiency in getting work done is a simple one. I have based it very deliberately on a well-known psychological principle and have refined it so that it is now almost too refined. I shall have to begin coarsening it up again pretty soon.

The psychological principle in this: anyone can do any amount of work, provided it isn't the work he is supposed to be doing at that moment.

Let us see how this works out in practice. Let us say that I have five things which have to be done before the end of the week: (1) a basketful of letters to be answered, some of them dating from October, 1928 (2) some bookshelves to be put up and arranged with books (3) a hair-cut to get (4) a pile of scientific magazines to go through and clip (I am collecting all references to tropical fish that I can find, with the idea of some day buying myself one) and (5) an article to write for this paper.

*Now.* With these five tasks staring me in the face on Monday morning, it is little wonder that I go right back to bed as soon as I have had breakfast, in order to store up health and strength for the almost superhuman expenditure of energy that is to come. *Mens sana in corpore sano* is my motto, and, not even to be funny, am I going to make believe that I don't know what the Latin means. I feel that the least that I can do is to treat my body right when it has to supply fuel for an insatiable mind like mine.

As I lie in bed on Monday morning storing up strength, I make out a schedule. "What do I have to do first?" I ask myself. Well, those letters really should be answered and the pile of scientific magazines should be clipped. And here is where my secret process comes in. Instead of putting them first on the list of things which have to be done, I put them last. I practice a little deception on myself and say: "First you must write that article for the newspaper." I even say this out loud (being careful that nobody hears me, otherwise they would *keep* me in bed) and try to fool myself into really believing that I must do the article that day and that the other things can wait. I sometimes go so far in this self-deception as to make out a list in pencil, with "No. 1. Newspaper article" underlined in red. (The underlining in red is rather difficult, as there is never a red pencil on the table beside the bed, unless I have taken one to bed with me on Sunday night.)

Then, when everything is lined up, I bound out of bed and have lunch. I find that a good, heavy lunch, with some sort of glutinous dessert, is good preparation for the day's work as it keeps one from getting nervous and excitable. We workers must keep cool and calm, otherwise we would just throw away our time in jumping about and fidgeting.

I then seat myself at my desk with my typewriter before me and sharpen five pencils. (The sharp pencils are for poking holes in the desk-blotter, and a pencil has to be pretty sharp to do that. I find that I can't get more than six holes out of one pencil.) Following this I say to myself (again out loud, if it is practical) "Now, old man! Get at this article!"

Gradually the scheme begins to work. My eye catches the pile of magazines, which I have artfully placed on a near-by table beforehand. I write my name and address at the top of the sheet of paper in the typewriter and then sink back. The magazines being within reach (also part of the plot) I look to see if anyone is watching me and get one off the top of the pile. Hello, what's this! In the very first one is an article by Dr. William Beebe, illustrated by horrifying photographs! Pushing my chair away from my desk, I am soon hard at work clipping.

One of the interesting things about the Argyopelius, or

"Silver Hatchet" fish, I find, is that it has eyes in its wrists. I would have been sufficiently surprised just to find out that a fish had wrists, but to learn that it has eyes in them is a discovery so astounding that I am hardly able to cut out the picture. What a lot one learns simply by thumbing through the illustrated weeklies! It is hard work, though, and many a weaker spirit would give it up half-done, but when there is something else of "more importance" to be finished (you see, I still keep up the deception, letting myself go on thinking that the newspaper article is of more importance) no work is too hard or too onerous to keep one busy.

Thus, before the afternoon is half over, I have gone through the scientific magazines and have a neat pile of clippings (including one of a Viper Fish which I wish you could see. You would die laughing). Then it is back to the grind of the newspaper article.

This time I get as far as the title, which I write down with considerable satisfaction until I find that I have misspelled one word terribly, so that the whole sheet of paper has to come out and a fresh one be inserted. As I am doing this, my eye catches the basket of letters.

Now, if there is one thing that I hate to do (and there is, you may be sure) it is to write letters. But somehow, with the magazine article before me waiting to be done, I am seized with an epistolary fervor which amounts to a craving, and I slyly sneak the first of the unanswered letters out of the basket. I figure out in my mind that I will get more into the swing of writing the article if I practice a little on a few letters. This first one, anyway, I really must answer. True, it is from a friend in Antwerp asking me to look him up when I am in Europe in the summer of 1929, so he can't actually be watching the incoming boats for an answer, but I owe something to politeness after all. So instead of putting a fresh sheet of copy-paper into the typewriter, I slip in one of my handsome bits of personal stationary and dash off a note to my friend in Antwerp. Then, being well in the letter-writing mood, I clean up the entire batch. I feel a little guilty about the article, but the pile of freshly stamped envelopes and the neat bundle of clippings on tropical fish do much to salve my conscience. Tomorrow I will do the article, and no fooling this time either.

When tomorrow comes I am up with one of the older and more sluggish larks. A fresh sheet of copy-paper in the machine, and my name and address neatly printed at the top, and all before eleven A. M.! "A human dynamo" is the name I think up for myself. I have decided to write something about snake-charming and am already more than satisfied with the title "These Snake-Charming People." But, in order to write about snake-charming, one has to know a little about its history, and where should one go to find history but to a book? Maybe in that pile of books in the corner is one on snake-charming! Nobody could point the finger of scorn at me if I went over to those books for the avowed purpose of research work for the matter at hand. No writer could be supposed to carry all that information in his head.

So, with a perfectly clear conscience, I leave my desk for a few minutes and begin glancing over the titles of the books. Of course, it is difficult to find any book, much less one on snake-charming, in a pile which has been standing in the corner for weeks. What really is needed is for them to be on a

*I push back my chair and start clipping*

shelf where their titles will be visible at a glance. And there is the shelf, standing beside the pile of books! It seems almost like a divine command written in the sky: "If you want to finish that article, first put up the shelf and arrange the books on it!" Nothing could be clearer or more logical.

In order to put up the shelf, the laws of physics have decreed that there must be nails, a hammer and some sort of brackets to hold it up on the wall. You can't just wet a shelf with your tongue and stick it up. And, as there are no nails or brackets in the house (or, if there are, they are probably hidden somewhere) the next thing to do is to put on my hat and go out to buy them. Much as it disturbs me to put off the actual start of the article, I feel that I am doing only what is in the line of duty to put on my hat and go out to buy nails and brackets. And, as I put on my hat, I realize to my chagrin that I need a hair-cut badly. I can kill two birds with one stone, or at least with two, and stop in at the barber's on the way back. I will feel all the more like writing after a turn in the fresh air. Any doctor would tell me that.

So in a few hours I return, spick and span and smelling of lilac, bearing nails, brackets, the evening papers and some crackers and peanut butter. Then it's ho! for a quick snack and a glance through the evening papers (there might be something in them which would alter what I was going to write about snake-charming) and in no time at all the shelf is up, slightly crooked but up, and the books are arranged in a neat row in alphabetical order and all ready for almost instantaneous reference. There does not happen to be one on snake-charming among them, but there is a very interesting one containing some Hogarth prints and one which will bear even closer inspection dealing with the growth of the Motion Picture, illustrated with "stills" from famous productions. A really remarkable industry, the motion-pictures. I might want to write an article on it sometime. Not today, probably, for it is six o'clock and there is still the one on snake-charming to finish up first. Tomorrow morning sharp! *Yes, sir!*

And so, you see, in two days I have done four of the things I had to do, simply by making believe that it was the fifth that I *must* do. And the next day, I fix up something else, like taking down the bookshelf and putting it somewhere else, that I *have* to do, and then I get the fifth one done.

The only trouble is that, at this rate, I will soon run out of things to do, and will be forced to get at that newspaper article the first thing Monday morning.

# MORALE IN BANKING

THERE has always been a slight feeling of strain in my personal relations with banks, owing doubtless to my never having had quite enough money on deposit in them. I may be hypersensitive about the matter, but I have had a suspicion that they weren't very crazy about me for this reason. Once in a while they have even spoken to me about it, and that has just made my inferiority the worse.

But, with the beginning of the New Deal, I see no reason why we shouldn't clear the whole horrid mess up and try to understand each other better. The banks themselves, during the past year, have known what it was to be the underdog, and possibly the experience has chastened them a little. Maybe they will realize that, when I draw out a check for just a teeny-weenty bit more than I happen to have at that moment on deposit, I am not doing it from any vicious motives but simply because I don't subtract as well as some people, or possibly because I don't subtract at all if I happen to be in a non-subtracting mood. That's all it is.

Now I have been broadmindedness itself about the banks' little troubles since last March, and have said to any number of people: "Oh, banks are all right! Just a little irresponsible, that's all. Let them alone and don't scold, and everything will turn out all right." And everything is turning out all right, I am sure. But I do think that the banks ought to take my attitude into account and give me credit for it. Only about fifty dollars credit is all it would take at any one time. Well, let's say a hundred and be on the safe side.

What is needed most in the personal relations between a bank and its depositors is a sense of fun. If I, in a happy-go-lucky vein, happen to sign a check "Peter Rabbit" (as I did once, in a playful mood), the bank ought to know that I wasn't trying to forge Peter Rabbit's name. And, if the amount of the check doesn't happen to be in my account at that particular moment, they should cash it in the spirit that it was written, and perhaps drop me a kidding line in return, saying:

Dear Peter Rabbit: Your check received and was sure glad to get it. We knew that it was yours by the handwriting and only wish we had been there that night to see the fun. Drop in whenever you are in the neighborhood and add perhaps twenty-eight dollars and fifty cents to your account, just to make the thing legal. Yours for fun—The Molly Cottontail Trust Company.

Now a note like that would put me at my ease and would make me want to do all that I could to cooperate with them by getting the $28.50 into the vaults as soon as possible. There wouldn't be any of this friction that the old system engendered, and, if the time ever came when I could do the bank a favor in return, you may be sure that I would do it with the same idea of genial burlesque and make a joke of the whole thing.

This surely isn't too much to ask, with all the readjustment that is going on in the business affairs of the nation. All that would be necessary to change would be the tone of things. We could still keep up the old overdrawing on my part and the same notification of my delinquency on theirs. We would simply be doing it as a lark, that's all. And there wouldn't be this constant feeling that I am doing something wrong, a feeling which, sooner or later, could drive a fellow into melancholia. Money isn't everything, you know.

# THE QUESTIONNAIRE
# CRAZE

PROFESSORS in our universities are getting awfully nosy of late. They are always asking questions or sending out questionnaires inquiring into your private life.

I can remember the day when all that a professor was supposed to do was to mark "C minus" on students' examination-papers and then go home to tea. Nowadays they seem to feel that they must know just how much we (outside the university) eat, what we do with our spare time, and how we like our eggs. I, for one, am inclined not to tell any more. I have already filled in enough stuff on questionnaires to get myself divorced or thrown into jail.

A particularly searching series of questions has just come from an up-state university trying to find out about my sleeping habits. The director of the psychological laboratory wants to know a lot of things which, if I were to give them out, would practically put me in the position of sleeping in John Wanamaker's window. I would have no more privacy than Irvin Cobb.

The first question is a simple one: "How many hours do you sleep each night, on the average?"

Well, professor, that would be hard to say. I might add "—and what's it *to* you?" but I suppose there must be some reason for wanting to know. I can't imagine any subject of less general interest than the number of hours I sleep each night on the average. No one has ever given a darn before, and I must say that I am rather touched at this sudden display of interest on the part of a stranger. Perhaps if I were to tell him that I hardly sleep at all he would come down and read to me.

But I would like to bet that the professor gets a raft of answers. If there is one thing that people like to talk about it is their sleeping habits. Just get a group started telling how much or how little they sleep each night and you will get a series of personal anecdotes which will put the most restless member of the party to sleep in no time.

"Well, it's a funny thing about me," one will say. "I get to bed, we'll say at eleven-thirty, and I go to sleep the minute my head hits the pillow and sleep right through until seven-thirty."

He will be interrupted at this point by someone who insists on having it known that the night before he heard the clock strike two, three and four. (People always seem to take a great deal of pride in having heard the clock strike two, three and four. You will very seldom find one who admits to having slept soundly all through the night. Just as a man will never admit that the suit he has on is new, so is he loath to confess that he is a good sleeper. I don't understand it but, as I am getting pretty old now, I don't much care.)

You will be very lucky if, in an experience-meeting of this kind, you don't start someone off telling the dream he had a few nights ago. "It was the darndest thing," someone will say, as the rest pay no attention but try to think up dreams they themselves have had recently, "it was the darndest thing. I seemed to be in a sort of big hall, only it wasn't exactly a hall either, it was more of a rink or schoolhouse. It seemed that

Harry was there and all of a sudden instead of Harry it was Lindbergh. Well, so we all were going to a football game or something and I had on my old gray suit, except that it had wheels on it——"

By this time everybody is engaged in lighting cigarettes or looking at newspapers or even talking to someone else in a low tone of voice, and the narrator of the dream has practically no one to listen to him except the unfortunate who happens to be sitting next. But he doesn't seem to care and goes right on, until he has finished. There is a polite murmur of "What had you been eating?" or "That certainly was a corker," and then someone else starts. The professor who sent this questionnaire will have to watch out for this sort of thing or he will be swamped.

The whole list is just a temptation to garrulousness. Question No. 3, for example, is likely to get people started on an hour's personal disclosure. "Do you notice ill effects the day after sleeping on a train?" is the way it is worded.

Well, now take me, for example, I'm glad you asked that, professor. I *do* notice ill effects the day after sleeping on a train. I notice, in the first place, that I haven't got my under-things buttoned correctly. Dressing in a Pullman berth is, at best, a temporary form of arraying oneself, but if I happen to have to go right from the train to my engagement without going first to a hotel and doing the whole thing over again, I find, during the day, that I have buttoned the top button of my running-drawers into the bottom buttonhole of my waist-coat and that one whole side of my shirt is clamped, by some mysterious process, half way up my back. This, as the day wears on, exerts a pull on the parts affected until there is grave danger of the whole body becoming twisted to the right, or left, as the case may be. This, in turn, leads to an awkward gait in walking and is likely to cause comment. Of course, if it is a strange town, people may think that you walk that way naturally and, out of politeness, say nothing about it, but among friends you are pretty sure to be accused of affectation, or even worse.

Another ill effect, Professor, which I feel after having slept on a Pullman (leaving aside the inevitable cold in the head

*This leads to an awkward gait in walking*

acquired from sleeping with a light brown blanket piled high on one hip) is the strange appearance I present when I take my hat off. As I am usually the last man in the washroom, I am constantly being harried by the porter who keeps coming to the door and telling me that the train is pulling out into the yards in three minutes. (It is always three minutes, never less and never, by any chance, more.) Now, with this un-

pleasant threat hanging over me, I am in no state of mind to make my customary exquisite toilet. I brush my teeth and possibly shave one half of my face, but almost invariably forget to brush my hair. It is all right going through the station with my hat on, but later in the day, when I come to my business appointments, I notice that I am the object of considerable curious attention from people who do not know me, owing to my hair standing on end during an entire conference or even a luncheon. It is usually laid to my being a writer and of an artistic temperament, but it doesn't help me in a business way.

Now you will see what you got yourself into by merely asking me that one question, Professor. I could go on like this for hours, telling about the ill effects I feel the day after sleeping in a Pullman, but maybe you aren't interested any longer. I am afraid that I have bored you already.

The next question, however, is likely to start me off again. "Do you usually sleep through the night without awakening?"

It is funny that you should have asked that. I was just about to tell you anyway. Some nights I do, and some nights I don't. I can't be any more explicit than that. When my little boys were small, I really can't say that I did. Not that they meant to be mean about it, or did it deliberately, but, as I look back on it, it seems that there was always something. A glass of water was usually the ostensible excuse, but a great many times it turned out to be just a desire on their parts to be chummy and have someone to cry with. I would say that, during the infancy of my bairn, my average was something like ten complete arisings from bed during the night and fifteen incomplete ones. By "incomplete" I mean those little starts out of a sound sleep, where one leg is thrust out from under the bed-clothes while one waits to see if maybe the disturbance will not die down of its own accord. These abortive arisings are really just as disturbing to the sleep as the complete ones, and should count as much in any scientific survey. (I do not want to convey the impression that I did *all* the hopping up during the night. The mother of the boys did her share, but it was a good two-man job on which turns had to be taken. It also depended a lot on which one could best simulate sleep at the time of the alarm.)

Now that the boys are old enough to get up and get *Daddy* water when he wants it, things are a little different, but I find that the amount of undisturbed sleep that I get in one night's rest is dependent on so many outside factors that it is almost impossible to make up any statistics on the subject. A great deal of it depends on the neighbors and how much fun they happen to be having. Then there is the question of what tunes I happen to have been hearing during the day. One good, monotonous tune firmly imbedded in my consciousness will make going to bed merely a mockery. Two nights ago I retired early for a good rest (my first since 1921) but unfortunately spent seven out of my possible eight hours trying to get "What Is This Thing Called Love?" out of my mind. If I had only known some more of the words it wouldn't have been quite so bad, but one can't go on, hour after hour, mentally singing "What is this thing called love—what is this thing called love—what is this thing called love—what is this thing called love" without suffering some sort of nervous breakdown. It would have been much better for me to have been walking the streets than lying there in bed plugging a song for nobody in particular.

It is this sort of thing which makes it difficult to answer Question No. 4. One night I am one way—the next night I am another way. The only means that I can think of for the professor to employ to get an accurate check-up on my sleeping habits would be for him to come down to my place and sleep on an army-cot at the foot of my bed himself. He would have to bring his own blankets, though, as I have hardly enough for myself as it is.

# HOME SWEET HOME

IN THESE days when one is forced to stay at home more, on account of the expense of going out, it is discouraging to learn that the home is one of the most dangerous places to stay if you don't want to get hurt. The National Safety Congress in London has recently announced that 1,800 British women are killed annually just sticking around their homes. Nobody knows how many British men are killed, what with the British women and everything.

According to Miss Bondfield, former Minister of Labor in the British Cabinet, these 1,800 housewives met their deaths falling down stairs, tripping over buckets and broom-handles and in other domestic pursuits. "But falling over a bucket or broom-handle," said Miss Bondfield, "or even falling down stairs, is a human failing." This is very broadminded of Miss Bondfield, but it doesn't make the situation any the less grim.

The argument advanced by the congress was that too many houses nowadays are filled with unnecessary sharp edges and corners or cluttered up with too many sharp-edged tables and other pieces of furniture. This is all very well, but it doesn't take care of the stair-problem, nor does it explain just how corners are to be done away with unless everybody can live in a rotunda. And it doesn't seem to me that it exhausts the sources of death and destruction which lurk in every household, whether well-ordered or not.

What, for example, is to be done about cellar-stairs with too low a ceiling? A man may take care of a furnace for

GW

twenty-five years and still forget to duck his head when he starts going down the cellar-stairs. And, even if he never quite kills himself with one bump, the constant banging at his forehead, year after year, night after night, is going eventually to result in a general concussion or softening of the brain, with an early and unpleasant death as a result.

What of bureau-drawers which stick until the puller has got himself quite off balance, and then throw him over backward against his rowing-machine? What of slipping in the shower-bath or getting out of the tub and crashing into unresisting porcelain? And, while on the subject of showers, what of those which stop for a second in the middle of a warm bath and then give forth a gush of scalding hot water? What of sectional book-cases which topple over on top of one while trying to get a volume from the top stratum?

It would seem that, in doing away with stairs (a dangerous experiment in the first place, what with the jumping it would entail) and eliminating corners and mop handles, the work of making the home safe has only just begun. Perhaps it would be better if we all just went out and lived in fields.

But even there, certain people are going to be always falling down on rocks. Things look pretty black.

# LITERARY NOTES

THIS being the centenary of the death of Mrs. Felicia Hemans, perhaps we ought to give a thought to the Boy Who Stood on the Burning Deck, and possibly, if time remains, to the Breaking Waves Which Dashed High. Those who do not wish to join in this sport will find falcons and shuttlecocks in the Great Hall. Ask Enoch to give them to you.

Everyone knows how Mrs. Heman's famous poem begins:

> The boy stood on the burning deck,
> Whence all but him had fled;
> And this was odd, because it was
> The middle of the night.

The question is: How does it go from there? Darned if I know.

How typical this slipshod knowledge of great literary works is! How often do we find ourselves able to recite the first four lines of a poem, and then unable to keep our eyes open any longer!

Not many people know that the name of the boy in the poem was *Giacomo*, and that his father's name was *Louis*, and that the ship was the *Orient*. Or possibly it was the other way 'round. Anyhow, there they were!

So things went on like this for quite a while, and then Mrs. Hemans wrote a poem about it and called it *Casabianca,* because if she hadn't used the name in the title she couldn't have jammed it into the poem itself in the meter she had picked out. If she had wanted to use the name *Casabianca* in the poem she would have had to do it in this meter:

> Casabianca, through the woods
> To grandmother's house we go.

Then she couldn't have got in about the burning deck. She was in a pretty tough spot all around.

We don't hear much about Mr. Hemans, probably because he and Mrs. Hemans separated in 1818. (See—I know everything!) The *Casabiancas* went right ahead, however, and only last month one of their descendants helped launch the new French submarine *Casabianca* at Saint-Nazaire, which only goes to show how those things work out. This 1935 *Casabianca,* however, is the last remaining member of the family, whereas there are two Hemans listed in the Minneapolis telephone directory alone.

A lot of people claim that it does no good to cram one's head with facts, but I hope that this little essay has proved that facts may be very fascinating things if properly assembled. I am holding out one or two facts (for example, that Mrs. Hemans was the original *Egeria* in Maria Jane Jewsbury's *Three Histories*), because I didn't want to make this too rich a mixture.

I will say, however, that the French poets, Lebrun and

Chenier, both wrote poems about the boy *Casabianca*, neither of which I know. As soon as I find out something about Lebrun and Chenier I will tip you off. In the meantime, you might run over this centenary sketch again, just to get it fixed in your mind.

Now you may come in, kiddies!

# THE CORRESPONDENT-
# SCHOOL LINGUIST

*(Showing How a Few Words of Foreign Extraction
Will Help Along a Border Story)*

IT WAS dark when we reached Chihuahua and the *cab-ronassos* were stretched along the dusty *cartoucheras* like so many *paneros.*

It had been a long day. We had marched from Bena-vides and were hot and thirsty. As El Nino, the filthy little *rurale* who carried our *balassos,* remarked in his quaint patois, *"Oyga, Senor, Quien sabe?"*

And we all agreed that he was right. It *wasn't* much like Bryant Park. And, after all, why should it be? Weren't these men fighting for their rights and their *pendicos?*

Suddenly the heavy air was rent with a sound like the rending of heavy air. We rested on the shift-keys of our typewriters, and looked at one another. There was really nothing else that we could do.

I was the first to speak. The rest had, by that time, gone to see what was the matter.

I later found out that it was a practice battle between the *Bandilleros* and the *Caballeros*, and that the noise was caused by General Ostorzo refusing to make a more picturesque fall from his horse for the moving-picture men. Considering the fact that the old general had done the fall four times already, it was hardly to be *sorolla*. (The American Public does not realize, as I do, what the "Watchful Waiting" policy of the administration has brought about in Mexico; and the end is not yet.)

As we turned the corner of the *cabecillos* I stumbled over the form of an old *carrai*. He was stretched out on the hot sand with his waistcoat entirely unbuttoned and no links in his cuffs. It was like an old clerk I had once seen when I was a very little boy, only much more terrible.

Now and then he raised his head and muttered to his press-agent, *"Quien sabe? Quien sabe?"* And when the press-agent, who was intoxicated too, did not answer, the poor wretch would fall back into his native Connecticut dialect and dig his nails into the grass.

We passed by, and on into the night. But none of us talked much after that. We had looked into the bleeding heart of a *viejos* country and it was not a pretty sight.

. . . . .

I was sitting on the *cabron* of the old *colorado*. The sun was setting for the first time that day. Dark faced *centavos* straggled by, crooning their peculiar *viejas*. Suddenly there was a cry of *"Viva, viva! Quien sabe?"* and out from the garage came General Ostronoco, leader of the Bonanzaists.

There was a whirring of moving-picture machines and the

sharp *toscadillos* of the *bambettas*, and the man who repudiated Wilson made his way up the escalator.

He is a heavy man; not too heavy, mind you, just *todas*. In fact, the Ostronoco that I knew looked very much like his photographs. Only the photographs do not show the man's remarkable vitality, which he always carries with him.

On seeing me he leaped impulsively forward and embraced me as many times as his secretary would allow.

"*Mi amigo! Mi bambino,*" he exclaimed. "*Quien sabe?*"

I told him that I was.

Then he passed on his way into the hotel bar. It was the last that I saw of him, for the next moment we were surrounded by *muyjas*.

# LEARN TO WRITE

THERE are a lot of schools advertising today that they can teach people how to write for a living. (They don't explain why anybody should want to, however.) "How Do You Know You Can't Write?" they ask. And "What Makes Writing Ability Grow?"

The biggest obstacle to professional writing today is the necessity for changing a typewriter ribbon. Any school that can teach me how to do this can triple my earning capacity overnight (making it three dollars). Anybody can write, but it takes a man with snake-charmer's blood to change a ribbon.

I have never known it to fail, once I get ensconced on a train, or a boat, or up in the country, anywhere far away from that nice man in the typewriter store who fixes my machine for me when it gets full of nut-meats, that my ribbon, new as it may have been when I started, did not suddenly develop pernicious anemia or break out with a rash of holes. As soon as I begin to see those "M's" come out dark at the bottom and light at the top, I know that the jig is up, the entire page is going to look as if had been written with an old pin, and the ribbon itself is going to stop at the end of the line and refuse to turn. There is no more sickening feeling for a writer of my mechanical ingenuity than to realize that his ribbon has gone bad.

Obviously, if any of the family is going to eat (I don't ask that all of us eat, just the little ones who need food for bone and sinew), the ribbon has got to be changed. First the top has got to be taken off the machine. This is easy. (We can worry about getting it back on when the time comes.) Then those two spinnets, or spindles, or whatever they are, have got to be lifted off and the old ribbon yanked out of their grip and unwound. This isn't so bad, either, for you can throw it across the room and haul it in as you would a fish-line. It doesn't make much difference how you treat the old ribbon. Look how it treated you.

Getting the new ribbon into the spinnets, or spindles, and woven through those two little needle eyes, there's the trick! You may either put the typewriter on the floor and lie on it, or lie on your back and let the typewriter rest on your chest. Or, you may bury both hands in the keys and work upwards or wind the ribbon around your fists and work inwards, threading in and out among all the openings you can see. Nothing does any good. Eventually you are going crazy, and you might as well face it. You are going crazy and scream and tug at the ribbon until it breaks, or you are going quietly crazy and bite your under lip off and end by pulling the ribbon through slowly with one hand while you type even more slowly with the other. And, in any event, just for the fun of it, go and look at your face and hands! You look like both Moran and Mack, and don't you wish you were?

That is why I smile grimly when I see schools offering to teach people how to write. What we writers need is not a school, but a good loom operative.

# KNOWING THE FLOWERS

**A**LITTLE learning may be a dangerous thing, but a lot of learning may turn out to be even worse. I have tried to know absolutely nothing about a great many things, and, if I do say so myself, have succeeded fairly well. And to my avoidance of the responsibilities which go with knowledge I lay my good digestion today. I am never upset when I find that I know nothing about some given subject, because I am never surprised.

The names of birds and flowers, for example, give me practically no worry whatever, for I never set out to learn them in the first place. I am familiar with several kinds of birds and flowers by sight, and could, if cornered, designate a carnation or a robin as such. But beyond that I just let the whole thing slide and never torture myself with trying to remember what the name of that bird with the yellow ear is or how many varieties of gentians there are. (By the way, what ever became of gentians? Are they used only for models in elementary school drawing classes?)

People who specialize in knowing the names of birds and flowers are always in a ferment, because they are always running up against some variety which stumps them. Show an ornithologist a bird that he can't name and he is miserable for a week. He goes home and looks up reference books, writes letters to the papers asking if someone can help him, and tosses and turns at night, hoping that his subconscious will solve the problem for him. He develops an inferiority and, unless closely watched, may actually do away with himself out of sheer frustration. It isn't worth it.

I once had a heart-breaking experience with a flower-namer. He was one of those men who began when they were boys spotting the different types of wild-flower, and, at a hundred yards, could detect a purple wolf's cup (or "Lehman's dropsy") and could tell you, simply by feeling a flower in the dark, which variety of "bishop's ulster" it was. There was practically no wild-flower of North America that he didn't know to speak to, and he took a little more pride in his knowledge than was really justified. At least, so it seemed to me.

I found myself on a walking trip through Cornwall with this man one summer, for, when he wasn't spying on wild-flowers, he was very good company. On account of the weather, we spent the first five days of our walking trip in the tap-room of an inn at a place appropriately named Fowey (pronounced Pfui), and on the first sunny day set out with our knapsacks on our backs and a good song ringing clear. Looking back on it now, I don't see what ever got into me to be doing so much walking.

Along about noon we came to a large field which was completely covered with multi-colored wild-flowers. There must have been a thousand different varieties, or, at any rate, a hundred. I saw what was coming and winced. I was going to be a party to a botany exam. Little did I realize that I was also to be a party to a tragedy.

My companion went over to the edge of the field and examined a red flower by the roadside. His face took on a worried look. He didn't recognize the species! He looked at a blue flower next to it. He didn't recognize that, either! He gave a hurried survey of the five square feet surrounding him and blanched. He said nothing, but I could tell from his staring eyes and damp brow that there was not one variety of flower that he could name.

He ran into the field, stooping over and straightening up like a mad man, turning round and round in circles and looking wildly about him, as a dog looks when 10 people start whistling at him at once. Here was not only one flower that he had never heard of before, but a whole field full—hundreds and hundreds of unknown blossoms, all different and all staring up at him waiting to be named.

A chameleon is supposed to go insane when placed on a plaid. This man was in danger of going raving crazy from pure chagrin.

I tried to get him to leave the field and continue our little march, but he hardly heard what I was saying. He would pick a flower, examine it, shake his head, mop his brow, pick another, wipe the perspiration from his eyes, and then throw them both to the ground. Once he found something that he thought was a poppy and his joy was pitiful to see. But the stamen or something was wrong, and he burst into tears.

There was nothing that I could do or say, so I just sat by the roadside with my back turned and let him fight it out with himself. He finally agreed to leave his Waterloo, but the trip was ruined for him. He didn't speak all that day, and that night, after we had gone to bed, I heard him throwing him-

*I saw what was coming and winced*

self about the bed in an agony of despair. He has never mentioned wild-flowers since.

I cite this little instance to show that being an expert in any one line is a tremendous responsibility. For, if an expert suddenly finds out that he isn't entirely expert, he just isn't anything at all. And that sort of thing gets a man down.

# A WARNING NOTE IN THE
# MATTER OF PREPAREDNESS

*Some Revelations in
Our Modern Educational System*

AT THIS time, when we have suddenly become so
woefully unprepared in everything pertaining to
the defense of the integrity of our firesides and our
national honor (whatever that may be), it seems
to me that we ought to awake to the shocking inadequacy of
several other of our national institutions. Each man of us
should take himself into his jam closet, shut his eyes very
tight, and ask himself "In what department of our daily life,
as a nation, are we so lamentably weak that I could make a
campaign issue out of it?"

But, feeling as I do that I owe it to my district and my
many loyal friends to get elected to the School Committee
this fall, it is naturally incumbent upon me to scrape up some
issue to represent. And, after talking it over with the family,
I have come to the conclusion that there is nothing, always

excepting our National Defense, in which we are so shockingly deficient as we are in the matter of the education of our own, or someone else's, children.

Now, here is an issue which is too big for any one man to settle, which relieves me of any responsibility, and yet no possible odium can fall on me for stirring it up, as everyone, when he tries to remember how to prove all that about the square on the hypothenuse or to conjugate "amo," realizes that there was something radically wrong in the way in which he was educated. So, taken all in all, what could be more suitable for a campaign issue than "Our Educational Unpreparedness"? Absolutely nothing.

To begin with, I shall launch forth on a biting denunciation of our elementary educational system, the so-called "kindergarten" (insidious in its very etymology). At the age of five I was hauled in from a healthy sand-pile, washed within an inch of my life, and sent to "kinder-garten." On the first day, a big girl pushed me over backwards in my chair and I hit my head on a desk and had to be led home. From that event has sprung a feverish dislike for women which has made me the hypochondriac I am today. The second day of my education I went as far as the school door and then, as the automobile blue-books have it, turned "a sharp left and continued along down good macadam road to watering trough by four-corners" and there spent the morning in gleeful contemplation of my sins. This, I shall always feel, was the beginning of my insensate disregard for the Law which has nearly been my undoing in numberless encounters with the authorities.

Thus it may fairly be said that my first two days of the march toward the light inculcated such vicious principles in my spirit that I have never fully recovered from them. As for the rest of that year's work, I learned the fine points of sewing worsted lambs on cards, and the names, but *not* the musical equivalents, of the notes in the scale—arts which, while I have been comforted in the knowledge of their possession, have never stood by me in any of the big crises of my life. So much for the elementary training that our boys and girls are receiving to fit them for the struggle for a career.

Appalling as this revelation of affairs is, there is a still more unbelievable condition existing in the so-called "secondary schools" of our country! Here, for instance, our young people are taken and taught that the tibia and fibula are personal assets, but no word of how to use them in an emergency. Why have a tibia about you anyway, rather than an inner-tube, for example, if you don't know how to utilize its peculiar function at a time when nothing except that peculiar function will answer the purpose? Just as a test of the inadequacy of our educational system I came suddenly upon my young nephew, who has just skipped the fourth grade because he was so bright, and said to him quickly, "Horace, what would you do with your fibula if an attacking force were to appear in the vestibule?" And what did he do? He began to cry and ran and told his mother that I was picking on him. Could anything be more disheartening? Absolutely nothing.

Or, to take another case, the boy learns that if he draws two lines from a point to the extremities of a straight line, their sum will be greater than the sum of two other lines similarly drawn but included by them. Now in all the years of my life since I was let in on that secret I have had many desires. I have yearned to compose immortal lyrics like Gil-

*Ran and told his mother I was picking on him*

bert's; I have longed to decimate scientifically the man across the court who plays Schubert's Serenade on his pianola as if he were participating in a six-day bicycle race,—yet all these things have been beyond the reach of my powers. But I have never yet desired to draw two lines from a point to the extremities of a straight line, even though I knew in my heart for a dead certainty that their sum would be greater than the sum of two other lines similarly drawn *but* included *by* them. It just simply isn't in my nature to want to do this, and consequently here I am, saddled with that power for which I care nothing, while I watch other men doing things which I would sell my vote to be able to perform. Such is the wretched lack of adaptability of our present system.

In the other fields we find much the same lack of attention to essentials. What though your boy know a verse beginning,

> First William the Norman, then William his son,
> Then Henry, then Stephen, di-dum-didi-dum—

indicating the succession of English kings? Does that help him to figure out for himself why there should *be* any English kings *anyway*, or why the present English King's mother didn't make him stand up straight when he was a little boy so that he wouldn't look quite so useless when he has his picture taken alongside Lord Kitchener?

What boots it if he knows how to find interest on $256 at 3 per cent. for ten days if he doesn't know how to get and keep $256 for ten days? These are sobering questions. They have sobered me, and I can prove it.

I remember giving up a good time when I should have been playing tennis to memorizing, by setting it to a tune, that "aus, auser, bei, mit, nach, seit, von, and zu" take the dative and that "Mädchen," in spite of appearances, is neuter. These facts I tucked away so tightly that the only time I have ever forgotten them was when questions were asked on them in the examination. And yet, one afternoon when I happened to be in Germany, I was shocked to hear no reference made to the dative. In fact, they had no more use for the dative, as such, than they have for treaties, as such, because, when you get a regular German sentence well-mouthed up it doesn't make any difference what constructions you have used so long as you keep your health. And there I had practically broken my spirit learning that stuff for a German master named Kennedy.

I have hesitated to make these disclosures at this time, for it would seem that our country has enough troubles to handle without my bringing any pressure to bear. But when you consider the tremendous interests that are at stake, I feel that I have done only my duty, unpleasant as it may be. And though I have no particular remedy to suggest, I can promise my constituents, if I am elected to the School Committee, a strictly "business administration." I am in the hands of my friends.

# MY SUBCONSCIOUS

ONE of the many reasons for my suspecting that I am headed for the last break-up is my Subconscious is getting to be a better man than I am. In fact, I am thinking of resigning and letting my Subconscious take over the business.

I go through the day in my bungling way, making mistakes, forgetting names, going north when I mean to go south and, in general, messing things up pretty thoroughly. I can get affidavits to this effect from five hundred disinterested observers. My average of direct hits is getting smaller and smaller each day and I am afraid that, before long, I shall have to hire somebody to go about with me just to keep me from hurting myself on sharp corners.

But once I get to sleep and my little old Subconscious gets started working, things begin to pick up. It does everything but sing to me. Dates and names that I have been unable to remember during the day are flashed before my closed eyelids; ideas which have kept coyly hidden behind a barricade when I wanted them suddenly trip out and say: "Here I am, Daddy!" Solutions to problems which had me beating my head and heels on the carpet when I was awake offer themselves with startling simplicity, and if I could only train my Subconscious to make notes during the night, I could get through the next day with flying colors.

Last week, while wallowing with some friends in onion sandwiches and Limberger, one of the less-highly educated members of the party asked what the German word for "onion" was. Quick as a flash I volunteered the information that it was "zweibel." There being no Germans in the group, I got

away with it, and even asked if there were any other German words they wanted to know about.

But I had scarcely got to sleep that night when my Subconscious started in on me. "A fine mess you made of that word for 'onion,'" it said to me crossly. "You know as well as I do that it is 'zwiebel' and not 'zweibel.' Now you wake right up and telephone that guy that you made a horrible mistake, and tell him what the right word is. That all reflects on me, you know."

I tried to argue that the next day would be time enough, but my Subconscious would stand for no dilly-dallying, so I woke up and did the handsome thing. The fact that it was three in the morning made my retraction a little less impressive than it might have been in the daylight, but, at any rate, I squared myself with my Subconscious. This sort of thing could get to be a nuisance in time, I am afraid, at any rate to my friends.

The trouble is that it has now reached a point where I don't know whether my Subconscious or I am on the job. If I happen to be reading in bed and doze off in the middle of a paragraph, my Subconscious finishes the paragraph on its own hook, sometimes in a rather fancy fashion. Then I come to and go on reading, and have a little difficulty in tying up the two versions, the written one and my Subconscious's.

The worst of it is that my Subconscious's version makes just enough sense for me to believe that I have actually read it, and makes me liable to assert the next day that I saw in "Time" where Ambassador Bullitt had blown up the Kremlin. This is bad for "Time," Ambassador Bullitt and me, especially for me, as I cannot find the paragraph to prove it.

However, on the whole, my Subconscious makes a much better job of things than I do, and a little flightiness in current events shouldn't be held against it. If I could somehow manage to get my Subconscious at the controls during the daytime and take over the reins myself when I am asleep, I am sure there wouldn't be all this criticism.

# PROFESSIONAL PRIDE

I SUPPOSE that it is a very good thing for the Nation's business to have people take pride in their work, and I am sure, from certain hints dropped here and there, that it would be a lot better for me if I took more pains with my own.

It probably is because I am always in a hurry when I get my hair cut that it seems to me that barbers, as a class, have made too much of a religion of the mere snipping and shaving of hair. Granted that hair-cutting is a delicate operation, the bungling of which can send a man, or a woman, blushing into the seclusion of a hill-side dugout for two weeks.

But once my hair is cut or my face shaved with all the artistry that he wants to bestow upon the job, couldn't he just dust me off and let me out of the chair without taking as long on the "finishing touches" as Gutzon Borglum on the mountain carving of George Washington's head?

The curator of the Luxembourg Museum never took so long in dusting off a Rodin as most barbers take in flicking a few hairs away from my neck. It is bad enough that they insert dry towels into your ears, causing a squeak which is practically death-dealing to a man of my temperament. But surely five minutes is too long to stand flicking, like an artist, in front of a canvas, just to get me ready for the street.

Granted that after shaving some sort of cooling lotion is grateful, even though you have to avoid your more virile friends for hours after. But why five different lotions?

Then, just as it seems as if it were all over, and you could make your appointment, the hair brushing begins. This involves a free scalp massage, which, in the old days, would have

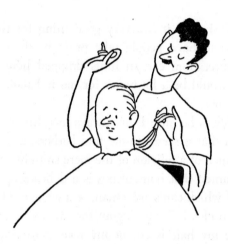

cost you forty cents. A great deal of professional pride goes into this scalp-massaging and it sometimes runs into fifteen or twenty minutes, what with rubbing and finger-waving.

A nice, gentle rub is a highly pleasant experience for any scalp, but I have had barbers who put real venom into the thing, evidently with some idea of getting the fingers through the scalp and well into the anterior lobe of the brain.

Now, all of this comes under the head of hair-cutting and shaving and doesn't cost you a cent, and I am sure that the barber does it because he wants to give you your money's worth. This is very laudable of him. But if I am in a hurry, as I always am in a barber's chair, it is all a little irritating.

This conscientiousness is not confined to barbers alone, although I seem so to have confined it. There are elevator operators who are so careful about stopping the car exactly flush to an eighth of an inch with the landing that you are sometimes kept within calling distance of a business date for ten minutes. There are waiters who—

But there! Why complain, really? Suppose I am a little late getting somewhere? What would I have done if I had been on time?

# A WRITERS' CODE

THERE has been a lot of criticism of the Government (on my part) for not asking the employers of writing labor to submit a code for the regulation of hours and wages of their help. Are we writers to be the only workers left shackled to a medieval machine?

Working on the piece-system as we do (so much per word or per piece—or perhaps) it should be fairly easy to set a minimum wage and keep to it. The only difficulty comes in counting the words. I can't count words on a page without getting dizzy after eight lines. You try it.

You begin "one-two-three-four-five-six-seven-eight" (I wish I were getting paid by the word for *this* one)—"one-two-three-four-five-six," using a pencil-point as a guide. The idea, in general, is to see how many words there are in perhaps six or seven typical lines, strike an average, and then count the number of lines. This, I may say, gets you nowhere. Before you have got very far down the page, the lines begin unravelling on you, forming designs like jack-straws and sometimes actually wriggling out of position and moving upward vertically. This confuses anyone but the most phlegmatic line-counter.

I have evolved, therefore, a system of wordage-reckoning

called "the guess-system." Instead of actually counting and giving myself vertigo, I *guess* at the number of words and let it go at that. That this is not the ideal measure can be seen by glancing at the space between the end of this column and and the bottom of the page. There is something wrong somewhere.

Some editors, descendants of Simon Legree, adopt sweat-shop tactics in such cases and call for "about two hundred more words to fill." Now is that any way to talk to an artist? After completing a little gem of English composition, with every word carefully chiseled and polished, so that just enough has been said without saying too much, how would you like to be told to write "about two hundred more words to fill"? Two hundred more words of life's-blood would come easier. I usually compromise, in such emergencies, by writing an extra introductory paragraph saying exactly what has been said in the original introductory paragraph only in more general terms, and inserting an anecdote in the middle beginning "I once heard of a man who—," illustrating some point that has already been made.

I once heard of a man who, when asked to fill out a column with a few words, made up an anecdote about a man who made up an anecdote in order to fill a column, and was later sued for libel by another author who claimed that he was unmistakably the one referred to and that his professional standing with editors had been irreparably damaged. Both writers were fired and later married each other. (One of the writers was a woman.)

As for the regulation of hours for writers, the code would have to be pretty fairly elastic. You couldn't say "no writer shall be made to work more than six hours a day or less than four," because there would be some days when the salmon had been bad the night before or a couple of people from the next apartment (or even the same apartment) dropped in, and even four minutes' work would be out of the question. This might even go on for weeks.

My own hours of work depend a great deal on how the rest of the world has been going. If I read something in the papers which upsets me, like the failure of a conference or something unpleasant in Germany, I am no good for the rest of the day. I am also easily affected by the prevalence of divorce items and the Lost and Found columns. I may be all set for a good day's work and then, on glancing at my newspaper for ideas, read that a Michigan postmaster has reached the appalling age of a hundred and three, and—piff—there goes my day! The only thing left to do is to spend my time looking at pictures in the London illustrated weeklies, of which I have an inexhaustible supply. They are constantly making remarkable discoveries in the Etruscan-tomb belt, and photographs of these have sometimes taken the place of work in my schedule for five or six days.

So it will be seen that any attempt to regulate hours or wages among writers must meet with a certain amount of confusion, but I see no reason why it should be impossible. My idea would be to simplify the problem by paying a minimum weekly wage or, say, five hundred dollars to all writers and more or less leave the hours of work up to them.

# DOING YOUR BIT IN THE GARDEN

*Preferably a Very Little Bit,*
*If You Are To Be Advised*

D URING the past month almost every paper, with the exception of the agricultural journals, has installed an agricultural department, containing short articles by Lord Northcliffe, or someone else in the office who had an unoccupied typewriter, telling the American citizen how to start and hold the interest of a small garden. The seed catalog has become the catechism of the patriot, and, if you don't like to read the brusque, prosy directions on planting as given there, you may find the same thing done in verse in your favorite poetry magazine, or a special department in *The Plumbing Age* under the heading "The Plumber's Garden: How and When to Plant."

But all of these editorial suggestions appear to be conducted by professionals for the benefit of the layman, which seems to me to be a rather one-sided way of going about the thing.

Obviously the suggestions should come from a layman himself, in the nature of warnings to others.

I am qualified to put forth such an article because of two weeks' service in my own back yard, doing my bit for Peter Henderson and planting all sort of things in the ground without the slightest expectation of ever seeing anything of any of them again. If, by any chance, a sprout should show itself, unmistakably the result of one of my plantings, I would be willing to be quoted as saying that Nature *is* wonderful. In fact, I would take it as a personal favor, and would feel that anything that I could do in the future for Nature would be little enough in return for the special work she went to all the trouble of doing for me. But all of this is on condition that something of mine grows into manhood. Otherwise, Nature can go her way and I'll go mine, just as we have gone up till now.

However, although I am an amateur, I shall have to adopt, in my writing, the tone of a professional, or I shall never get any one to believe what I say. If, therefore, from now on I sound a bit cold and unfriendly, you will realize that a professional agricultural writer has to have *some* dignity about his stuff, and that beneath my rough exterior I am a pleasant enough sort of person to meet socially.

### Preparing the Ground for the Garden

This is one of the most important things that the young gardener is called upon to do. In fact, a great many young gardeners never do anything further. Some inherited weakness, something they never realized they had before, may crop out during this process: weak back, tendency of shoulderblades to ossification, misplacement of several important vertebrae, all are apt to be discovered for the first time during the course of one day's digging. If, on the morning following the first attempt to prepare the ground for planting, you are able to walk in a semi-erect position as far as the bath-tub (and, without outside assistance, lift one foot into the water), you may flatter yourself that you are, joint for joint, in as perfect condition as the man in the rubber-heels advertisements.

Authorities differ as to the best way of digging. All agree that it is impossible to avoid walking about during the following week as if you were impersonating an old colored waiter with lumbago; but there are two schools, each with its own theory, as to the less painful method. One advocates bending over, without once raising up, until the whole row is dug. The others, of whom I must confess that I am one, feel that it is better to draw the body to a more or less erect position after each shovelful. In support of this contention, Greitz, the well-known authority on the muscles of the back, says on page 233 of his "Untersuchungen uber Sittlichkeitsdelikte und Gesellschaftsbiologie":

"The constant tightening and relaxing of the *latissimus dorsi* effected in raising the body as the earth is tossed aside, has a tendency to relieve the strain by distributing it equally among the *serratus posticus inferior* and the corner of Thirty-fourth Street." He then goes on to say practically what I have said above.

The necessity for work of such a strenuous nature in the mere preliminaries of the process of planting a garden is due to the fact that the average back-yard has, up till the present time, been behaving less like a garden than anything else in the world. You might think that a back-yard, possessed of an ordinary amount of decency and civic-pride would, at some time during its career, have said to itself:

"Now look here! I may some day be called upon to be a garden, and the least I can do is to get myself into some sort of shape, so that, when the time comes, I will be fairly ready to receive a seed or two."

But no! Year in and year out they have been drifting along in a fools' paradise, accumulating stones and queer, indistinguishable cans and things, until they were prepared to become anything, quarries, iron-mines, notion-counters—anything but gardens.

I have saved in a box all the things that I have dug from my back-yard, and, when I have them assembled, all I will need will be a good engine to make them into a pretty fairly decent runabout—nothing elaborate, mind you, but good enough to run the family out in on Sunday afternoons.

And then there are lots of other things that wouldn't even fit into the runabout. Queer-looking objects, they are; things that perhaps in their hey-day were rather stunning, but which have now assumed an air of indifference, as if to say, "Oh, call me anything, old fellow, Ice-pick, Mainspring, Cigar-lighter, anything, I don't care." I tell you, it's enough to make a man stop and think. But there, I mustn't get sentimental.

## Preparing the Ground for the Garden

In preparing the soil for planting, you will need several tools. Dynamite would be a beautiful thing to use, but it would have a tendency to get the dirt into the front-hall and track up the stairs. This not being practicable, there is no other way but for you to get at it with a fork (oh, don't be silly), a spade, and a rake. If you have an empty and detached furnace boiler, you might bring that along to fill with the stones you will dig up. If it is a small garden, you ought not to have to empty the boiler more than three or four times. Any neighbor who is building a stone house will be glad to contract with you for the stones, and those that are left over after he has got his house built can be sold to another neighbor who is building another stone house. Your market is limited only by the number of neighbors who are building stone houses.

## Preparing the Ground for the Garden

On the first day, when you find yourself confronted by a stretch of untouched ground which is to be turned over (technical phrase, meaning to "turn over"), you may be somewhat at a loss to know where to begin. Such indecision is only natural, and should cause no worry on the part of the young gardener. It is something we all have to go through with. You may feel that it would be futile and unsystematic to go about digging up a forkful here and a shovelful there, tossing the earth at random, in the hope that in due time you will get the place dug up. And so it would.

The thing to do is to decide just where you want your garden, and what its dimensions are to be. This will have necessitated a previous drawing up of a chart, showing just what is to be planted and where. As this chart will be the cause of considerable hard feeling in the family circle, usually precipitating a fist-fight over the number of rows of onions to be set out, I will not touch on that in this article. There are some things too intimate for even a professional agriculturist to write of. I will say, however, that those in the family who are standing out for onions might much better save their time and feelings by pretending to give in, and then, later in the day, sneaking out and slipping the sprouts in by themselves in some spot where they will know where to find them again.

## Preparing the Ground for the Garden

Having decided on the general plan and dimensions of the plot, gather the family about as if for a corner-stone dedication, and then make a rather impressive ceremony of driving in the first stake by getting your little boy to sing the first twelve words of some patriotic air. (If he doesn't know the first twelve, any twelve will do. The idea is to keep the music going during the driving of the stake.)

The stake is to be driven at an imaginary corner of what is to be your garden, and a string stretched to another stake at another imaginary corner, and there you have a line along which to dig. This will be a big comfort. You will feel that at last you have something tangible. Now all that remains is to turn the ground over, harrow it, smooth it up nice and neat, plant your seeds, cultivate them, thin out your plants and pick the crops.

It may seem that I have spent most of my time in advice on preparing the ground for planting. Such may well be the case, as that was as far as I got. I then found a man who likes to do those things and whose doctor has told him that he ought to be out of doors all the time. He is an Italian, and charges really very little when you consider what he accomplishes. Any further advice on starting and keeping up a garden, I shall have to get him to write for you. I've done my bit, and I'll leave it for him, as the Oxford chaps say, to "carry on."

# PICKING FRENCH PASTRY;
## A HARDER GAME
## THAN CHESS

MOST people, if asked offhand what national pastime requires the greatest degree of concentration and involves the deepest pondering, would say, equally offhand, "The game of chess." Without carrying the argument further, let us say that they are wrong.

Chess is all right in its way as a thought provoker. It undoubtedly is diverting. But compared with the task of selecting a piece of French pastry from a tray held by an impatient waiter a move in chess is like reaching for a salary check in its demand on the contemplative faculties. It is comparatively a matter of touch and go.

Many a man has gone out to get a quick bite to eat between contracts and has been led back at four-forty in the afternoon by a passer-by who has found him, a gibbering moron, muttering to himself: "If I take the little one with the inflamed joint it may be stuffed with library paste, while if I take the lemon meringue pin-wheel, I may find that the meringue stops at the limbo and that the whole inside is flaked confetti, while if I take the—jobble, jobble, jobble." After seventy cases of this kind had been reported at the State Hospital in one day, an investigation was begun, and it was found out that they were due to over-application to the choice of French pastry.

And it is rather a pathetic fact that the man who orders French pastry does so to avoid choosing anything more definite from the list of other desserts. After deciding which of to-day's ready dishes among the entrées to have, he is so depleted that, rather than run his finger down the price-list of desserts, he mutters "French pastry" simply to get the waiter out of the way. And what is the result? A quandary of ten times the proportions of the one he has just evaded.

For he is confronted with a tray which looks like a concentration camp, with rows upon rows of varied types of pastry, from which he is to choose two which he thinks will do him the least harm. If he could take it to his room and give a little constructive thought to the thing it might not be so bad, but there is the waiter holding it and giving every indication of breaking into tears if the choice is not made soon; and so it is little wonder that the player, after feverish meditation for as long as he dares, makes a wild dab at the nearest pastry and says, "I'll take that," knowing the while that, of all the things in the exhibition, it is the one that he wants least.

The ordeal has assumed such proportions during the last two or three years that it is being seriously considered making a pleasure of it by making it into a game. It would be played similarly to the present game of chess, there being two contestants to each tray of pastry. Each man would have to eat immediately the piece he chose, and the object of the game would be so to choose that the more deadly ones would be left until the end, when the contestant could finish on his nerve. If, for instance, one of the players chose an arsenic-lined cuff in the third round, the other man would obviously win out.

# THE PERFECT AUDIENCE

BEFORE we do a thing, we must get one point straight; so please pay attention and don't go woolgathering out the window.

When, in the following *jeu d'esprit*, I refer to "movie audiences," I do not mean those members of the general public who go *to* the movies, but audiences whom we see taking part *in* the movies themselves. . . . Oh dear, I am afraid that we never shall get this clear!

Let's get at it from another angle. Let us say that we are watching a movie in which there is supposed to be a performance of a musical comedy. The scene is inside a theatre. (*Now* we're getting it!) The audience, made up of extra men and women, is in its seats, and we are shown a long shot, first from the back of the imitation theatre looking toward the stage, and then from the stage showing how the theatre looks to the actors. *That* is what I will mean from now on when I say "movie audiences." . . . Whew! I almost wish that I had never started this.

The audiences (remember now!) which one sees in pictures appear to be recruited from a class of people considerably more naïve than those one sees in real theatres. If each and every face were not visible (the house lights always seem to be on during the performance, showing up every nook and cranny of the house and the features of everyone in the audience), one might think that most of them were children who had never been to the theatre before. In fact, the nearest approximation in real life to the behavior of an "audience" in the movies is that at a children's matinée of "Beauty and the Beast."

There is a constant stirring sense of repressed motion, of excitement, of intense personal interest in the goings-on on the stage. Everyone seems acquainted with everyone else, and there is a running buzz of nervous conversation which sometimes rises to a roar. One would not be surprised to see frequent and tearful departures toward the exits and rest-rooms of the more temperamental spectators who just couldn't stand the strain of another minute.

But they make ideal audiences, these movie extras. Not only do they fill every seat in the auditorium but they *keep* their seats. And they all wear impeccable evening dress. There is none of this sneaking-in-late of newspaper critics dressed in sport togs, and no thumping down the aisle of theatre parties at nine-twenty. The entire opening chorus is watched by a sea of excited eyes, registering vital emotion, and there is not a seat left empty or a face left blank. It must be a great experience to play to such a house.

Enthusiasm is a weak word for what runs riot. At the conclusion of each number, they applaud hysterically, each one raising the hands high above the head so that the camera may see. And there are no slackers, either. The entire audience, to a man, behaves like those little claques who are present at each opening night in the real theatre determined that their favorite shall receive an ovation even though the play be stopped. They all clap very fast, very loudly, and very high up. It is almost as if someone were giving them a signal.

It takes very little to throw a movie "audience" into a bedlam of enthusiasm. They are probably the easiest to excite of any audience in the world, not excepting the kiddies at "Beauty and the Beast." In several of our current feature pictures, the hero or heroine has been depicted as making a début before a blasé Broadway audience, and the acts which they have put on, and which have swept the crowd off its feet, have been acts which, to say the least, seemed hardly worthy of such a demonstration. In fact, some of them seemed hardly worth putting on at all.

In a feature picture a short time ago a well-known stage hoofer, now gone movie, literally knocked 'em cold with a dance routine which he himself has surpassed many a time at Sunday-night benefits. At its conclusion, the roof was shaken and the walls rocked by a thunder of applause such as could hardly have greeted Nijinsky on his first appearance in America.

A beautiful young daughter of a talented family is even now, in color, throwing what is supposed to be a typical Broadway revue first night into an hysterical fit simply by lending her charming presence (entirely as an observer) to an "Alice in Wonderland" ballet which, when it was done some years ago in the Music Box, was one of the milder features of the show. People not only applaud wildly but many jump out of their seats and cry "Bravo!" (It is perhaps too much to expect that they should cry "Brava!") and one feels that, as the happy young lady leaves the theatre, the milling crowds will unhitch the horses from her carriage and drag it through the emotion-seared streets of hardboiled New York. Nobody knows what ever becomes of the rest of the show, the curtain always falls on the riot, and the supposition is that the audience disperses in a frenzy and rushes out to toll bells and things.

Now all this is very charming, and it is good to know that somewhere in the world there are people who are so well behaved and easy to excite. But does it not explain why Broadway is losing its stars to Hollywood? What hoofer, on seeing an old-fashioned "off-to-Buffalo" step completely panic an audience, would not long for such a spot and determine to go after it? What singer, on hearing one verse and a chorus of a regulation counter-number bring the rafters crashing down on the head of the lucky performer, would not throw a few things into a bag and make for the Coast, where talent is evidently appreciated to the point of epilepsy? Even though they realize, as they are making the picture, that the audience is being paid seven-fifty a day for sitting there and that the applause is the result of a signal from an assistant director, nevertheless the audience is there and cheering and the applause is there and apparently incessant. After all, an actor is only an actor. So either those of us who constitute real audiences in New York must loosen up in our emotions and stop sitting on our hands, or we shall lose what few performers we have left.

And I'll bet that three out of the possible four readers who have stuck to this article to the end *still* think that I have been writing about audiences *at* the movies.

# "WRITERS—RIGHT OR WRONG!"

FOR quite some time now I have been worried about (among other things) my lethargy in the face of the important fiction of the day. I begin a novel by some new master of English prose, then turn ahead to find out how many pages there are going to be, and, when I start reading again, imagine my surprise to find that I have already skipped half the book! By then it is time to get up and go across the room for something, and the book gets lost.

I had been attributing this haphazard method of reading to some one of the six prominent flaws in my kidneys (which I have arranged in alphabetical order for the benefit of students on the subject) until the other night when I pulled Hugh Walpole's "Fortitude" out of the book-case and started re-reading it. I have just finished, and now I know that I am all right again. All that I needed was a good book.

By "a good book" I mean one of those books (you remember them) which have not only a beginning, but a middle and an ending. The characters are all designated by names, and each time one of them speaks, you know who is speaking. And the style, although flowery according to present four-letter-word standards, does have a certain swing to it which carries *you* along with it instead of your having to go back and find out what happened to *it*. It may be very poor form to like Walpole today (and don't think I'm not blushing), but when you've finished "Fortitude" you know that you've been reading a *book*. My theory is that this is because Walpole knows how to write a book.

There is no doubt that in many modern novels you get "a feeling" for things. You get a feeling for old Southern pappies soaking the blood off their knuckles, and you get a feeling for anchovy-paste in Mayfair. Once in a while you can recognize a character the second time you come across him. And, occasionally, a writer will let himself go mid-Victorian enough to write a sentence that will parse. But, when you put the plot, the characters and the style together in one bundle, you get a unit-effect something like those long tables of Swedish *hors d'oeuvres*. *It* really doesn't make up into a very nourishing meal.

People who begin sentences with "I may be old-fashioned but—" are usually not only old-fashioned but wrong. I never thought the time would come when I should catch myself leading off with that crack. But I feel it coming on right now. I may be old-fashioned, but I still feel that a writer has a certain obligation to his readers. If he is going to write a book (and Heaven knows there is no law making him do it) he might go at least half way toward making it understandable. That seems little enough to ask.

And I am just ill-tempered enough to maintain that a writer who doesn't make his book understandable to a moderately intelligent reader is not writing that way because he is consciously adopting a diffuse style, but because he simply doesn't know how to write; that's all. It is not my fault that I can't read his book. It is his.

# YOUR CHANGE

IT MAY be that my fingers were frozen when I was a very small child and have never quite thawed out, or it may be that I just become panicky at having a man look at me through a little window, but, whatever the cause, I am physically unable to pick up change which has been shoved out at me by a man at a ticket-booth.

I can scoop up change like lightning from a store-counter, and in the morning it is but the work of a split second for me to gather up the pocket-money I have left on the bureau the night before (possibly because there is so little of it), but let me stand in front of a ticket-window in a theatre lobby or a railroad station, with a line of people behind me, and a boy with a magnet could pick up a mound of iron-filings one by one quicker than it takes me to garner 20 cents in change.

People in front of me seem to have no trouble. Even women with gloves on do a better job of it than I do. I see my predecessors sweep up their change with one swoop, and I say to myself: "Come now, Benchley! Be a man! You can do it, too!" And then I buy my ticket, pass in my bill, and, when the rattle of the change sounds on the marble slab, everything goes black in front of my eyes, my fingers grow numb and I pick

*I pick and claw at each coin like a canary*

and claw at each individual coin like a canary. Sometimes I will get a dime almost up into the air high enough to get a grip on it, and then, crazed with success, loose my hold and off it rolls into the money-drawer or onto the floor. I would sometimes suspect that the man at the window had put some

sort of stickum on my partcular coins were it not for the fact that they roll so easily once I have lost my grip.

By this time the man behind me had pushed up to the window and ordered his ticket, shoving his money past me in an unpleasant manner. I frantically draw my pile of change over to my side of the window and there, in ignominious panic, scrape it off into one hand, or rather partly into one hand, partly down into the front of my overcoat, and partly onto the floor. Often I dash off without waiting to pick it all up, rather than subject myself to the scorn of the people behind me. I suppose that I leave thousands and thousands of dollars a year on ticket-counters and surrounding floors. I must leave them *somewhere*. I haven't got them now.

I do not know how to combat this weakness. I have thought of just handing my money, taking the ticket, and then dashing off with a cheery: "The rest is for you!" to the man. I have tried saying to myself, as I stood in line: "Why should you be afraid of a man behind bars like that? He is probably just as afraid of you." (This is not true and I know it.) I have tried pushing my whole hand under the bars and holding it open for him to drop the change into, but then I find that, as I close my fist on it, I am unable to get my hand out again.

I think the only way out for me is just not to try to buy tickets except at a ticket agency.

# INTER-OFFICE MEMO

I T WILL always be a mystery to me why I was asked "into conference" in the first place. I am more the artistic type, and am seldom consulted on the more practical aspects of life. I have given up wearing soft collars and can smoke a cigar, if it is a fairly short one, but I don't seem able to give off any impression of business stability. I am just one of the world's beautiful dreamers.

So when McNulty called me up and asked me if I could come over to his office for a conference with somebody named Crofish or Cronish of Detroit, I was thrown into a fever of excitement. At last I was going to sit in on a big business conference! I think there was some idea that I as a hay-fever sufferer, might have a suggestion or two on handkerchiefs that might be valuable. For the conference was on the marketing of a steel handkerchief which the Detroit people were about to put out.

So all in a flutter I rushed over to McNulty's office, determined to take mental notes on the way in which real business men disposed of real business in the hope that one day I might extricate myself from the morass of inefficiency in which I was living and perhaps amount to something in the business world. At least, I would have caught a glimpse of how things ought to be done.

Mr. Crofish or Cronish (whose name later turned out to be Crolish) was already there, with his briefcase open in front of him and a lot of papers piled up on the desk. He and McNulty were both so bustly and efficient-looking that it hardly seemed worth while for me to sit down. This conference couldn't last more than a minute and a half!

"Sorry to bother you, Bob, old man," said McNulty, briskly, "but we thought that you might be able to help us out a little in this scheme for getting the Beau Brummel Steel Handkerchief before the public . . . Sit down, won't you? . . . Perhaps Mr. Crolish can state his problem better than I can, and then we will get your angle on it."

Mr. Crolish looked at his papers and cleared his throat. "Well, here is the situation we are faced with," he began.

"Just a minute, Mr. Crolish," interrupted McNulty, "I think it might be well, before you begin, to find out from Reemis just what magazines we are going to use, so that Mr. Benchley will have a little better idea of what type of copy we shall need." And he turned to the telephone. "Get me Mr. Reemis, will you please, Miss Fane?"

Mr. Reemis's line seemed to be busy, so McNulty propped the receiver up against his ear and reached in the drawer for some cigars, while waiting.

"Another couple of days like this and spring will be here," he announced tentatively.

"That's right," said Mr. Crolish, which didn't leave much for me to say unless I wanted to fight the statement.

Mr. Reemis was very busy, so McNulty, still holding the receiver, tried something else to pass the time.

"Mrs. McNulty and I saw one of the worst shows I've ever seen last night. *Rolling Raisins*. Did you ever see it?"

I said that I hadn't and Mr. Crolish said that he hadn't but that he had heard about it.

"No wonder people don't go to the theatre more," said McNulty, "when they put . . . oh, hello! . . . Reemis? . . . say, could you step into my office for just a minute, please?"

While we were waiting for Mr. Reemis, McNulty explained the plot of *Rolling Raisins*. And, as Mr. Reemis was evidently coming into the office by a route which led him down into the street and up the back stairway, Mr. Crolish told the plot of a show which had opened in Detroit last week. I had just started in on the plot of a show we had once put on in college when Mr. Reemis appeared.

"This is Mr. Benchley, Mr. Reemis . . . I guess you know Mr. Crolish. . . . What we wanted to find out was just what magazines we are going to use in this Beau Brummel campaign."

"Well, there have been some changes made since we went over it with you, Mr. McNulty," said Mr. Reemis. "I'm not quite sure of the list as it stands. I'll shoot back to my desk and get it."

So Mr. Reemis shot back, and Mr. Crolish walked over to the window.

"They certainly are tearing up this old town, aren't they?" he asked. "Every time I come here there is a new building up somewhere. I suppose they'll be tearing down the Woolworth Building next."

"I understand they've started already," said McNulty, "but they don't quite know where to begin."

This was a pretty fair line and it got all the laugh that it deserved. The thing was beginning to take on the air of one of those easy-going off-hours which we impractical artists indulge in when we are supposed to be working. It was interrupted by Mr. Reemis "shooting" back with the list.

"Here we are," he said, brightly. "Now, as I understand it, this is a strictly class appeal we are trying to make and we don't want to bother with the old-fashioned handkerchief users; so we thought that—"

Here the door opened and one of the partners came in.

"Sorry to butt in, Harry," he said, "but have you seen this statement of the Mackbolter people in the *Times?*"

"I just glanced at it," said McNulty, ". . . you know Mr. Benchley, Mr. Wamser? . . . I guess you know Crolish."

Mr. Wamser and I shook hands.

"Are you any relation to the Benchley who used to live in Worcester?" he asked.

I admitted that I had relatives in Worcester.

"I'll never forget the night I spent in Worcester once," he said, seating himself on the edge of McNulty's desk. "We were motoring to Boston and a thunderstorm came up; so we put in at Worcester—what's the name of that hotel?"

"The Bancroft?" I suggested.

"I don't think it was the Bancroft," he said. "What are some of the others? I'll know the name if I hear it."

I said that so far as I knew there weren't any others since the old Bay State House had been torn down.

"Well, maybe it was the Bancroft."

Mr. Crolish suggested that it might have been the Worthy.

"The Worthy is in Springfield," said McNulty.

*Two young men bearing a lay-out came in*

CWYAS
WILLIAMS

At this point two young gentlemen bearing a lay-out came in.

"Sorry to interrupt," said one of them, "but do you want the package played up in this Meer-o page or just show the girl playing tennis?"

The two young gentlemen were introduced and turned out to be Mr. Rollik and Mr. MacNordfy.

"Hoagman is handling that more than I am," said Mr. Wamser. And going to the telephone he asked to have Mr. Hoagman step into Mr. McNulty's office for a minute. While waiting for Mr. Hoagman, Mr. Rollik asked the gathering (which was, by now, assuming the proportions of a stag smoker) if they had seen what Will Rogers had in the paper that morning.

"I can always get a laugh out of that guy Rogers," said Mr. Crolish.

"What I like about him is that he gets a lot of common sense into his gags. They *mean* something." It was Mr. Mac-Nordfy who thought this.

"Abe Martin is the one I like," said McNulty. Mr. Wamser was of the opinion that no one had ever been able to touch Mr. Dooley. To prove his point he quoted a fairish bit of one of Mr. Dooley's dissertations in very bad Irish dialect. Mr. Hoagman, having entered during the recitation, waived the formality of introductions and began:

"If you like Irish jokes, I heard one yesterday that I thought was pretty clever. I may be wrong."

He *was* wrong, and so got down to business. "What was it you wanted to see me about?" he asked, as soon as he had stopped laughing.

*I made unnoticed for the elevator*

"The boys here want to know whether the Meer-o people want the package played up in this lay-out or to subordinate it to the girl playing tennis?"

"Oh, you've got to play the package up," said Mr. Hoagman, thereby making the first business decision of the morning. This gave him such a feeling of duty-done that he evidently decided to knock off work for the rest of the morning and devote his time to story-telling.

The room was so full by this time that I had completely lost sight of Mr. Crolish, who was, at best, a small man and was in his original seat on the other side of the room, still sitting in front of his open brief case. Mr. McNulty was talking on the telephone again and seemed good for fifteen minutes of it. The rest of the staff were milling about, offering each other cigarettes, telling anecdotes and in general carrying on the nation's business.

I looked at my watch and found that I was already late for a lunch-date; so picking up my hat, I elbowed my way quietly out of the room unnoticed and made the elevator.

Later in the week I heard that McNulty had told someone that I was a nice guy but that there was no sense in trying to do business with me. I guess I shall always be just a dreamer.

# THE DEAR DEAD TABLE
# D'HÔTE DAYS

### *A Menu from Old Chicago*

I REALIZE as well as anybody that to talk about dieting at this late date is like discussing whether or not the polka causes giddiness or arguing about the merits of the coaster brake on a bicycle. Dieting, as such, is no longer a subject for conversation.

But the whole question has been brought to my mind with a fresh crash by the finding of an old menu among my souvenirs (several of the souvenirs I cannot quite make out—even if I knew what they were, I can see no reason for having saved them), an old menu of a Christmas dinner dispensed to the guests of a famous Chicago hotel in the year 1885. I was not exactly in a position to be eating a dinner like this in 1885, but some of my kind relatives had saved it for my torture in 1930. If you don't mind, I would like to quote a few of the more poetic passages.

The dinner was, of course, table d'hôte. When you bought a dinner in those days, you bought a *dinner*. None of this

329

skimming over the card and saying, "I don't see anything I want. Just bring me an alligator-pear salad." If you couldn't see anything you wanted on one of the old-fashioned table d'hôte menus, you just couldn't see, that's all.

This particular menu went out of its way. Even for 1885 it must have represented quite a snack. As I look at it today, I can only stand, hat in hand, and bow my head in reverence for the imagination, as well as the capacity, of that earlier day. Listen:

After the customary blue-points and soup, with a comparatively meagre assortment of fish (just a stuffed black bass and boiled salmon), we find a choice of broiled leg of mountain sheep or wild turkey. This is just as a starter. The boys didn't get down to business until the roast. There are thirty-six choices among the roasts. Among the more distinguished names listed were:

Leg of moose, loin of elk, cinnamon bear, black-tail deer, loin of venison, saddle of antelope (the National Geographic Society evidently did the shopping for meat in behalf of this hotel), opossum, black bear, and then the duck.

The duck will have to have a paragraph all by itself. In fact, we may have to build a small house for it. When this chef came to the duck, he just threw his apron over his head and said: "I'm going crazy, boys—don't stop me!" He had canvasback duck, wood duck, butterball duck, brant, mallard duck, blue-winged teal, spoonbill duck, sage hen, green-winged teal, and pintail duck, to say nothing of partridge, quail, plover, and some other of the cheap birds.

I am not quite sure what a sage hen is, and I doubt very much if I should have ordered it on that Christmas Day, but somebody thought enough of it to go out and snare two or three just in case, and it seems to me that this is the spirit that has made America what it is today. (And what is that?)

So, after toying with all the members of the duck family except decoys and clay pigeons, the diner of 1885 cast his eye down the card to what were called "Broiled," a very simple, honest name for what followed. Teal duck (evidently one of the teal ducks from the roast column slipped down into the broiled, and liked it so well that it stayed), ricebirds, marsh birds, sand snipe, reedbirds, blackbirds, and red-winged starling. One wonders why there were no ruby-throated grosbeaks or Baltimore orioles, but probably the dinner was sort of an impromptu affair with guests taking potluck on whatever happened to be in the house.

By this time you would have supposed that they had used up all the birds within a radius of 3,000 miles of Chicago, leaving none to wake people up in the morning. But no. Among the entrées they must have a fillet of pheasant *financière*, which certainly must have come as a surprise to the dinner parties and tasted good after all that broiled pheasant and roast pheasant. Nothing tastes so good after a broiled pheasant as a good fillet of pheasant *financière*. And, in case you didn't want that, there were also cutlets of antelope with mushroom sauce, stewed squirrel with dumplings, and opossum with a nice purée of sweet potatoes. (I suppose you think it is fun to sit here and write these names out, and before lunch at that.)

There then seemed to have come over the chef a feeling that he wasn't doing quite the right thing by his guests. Oh, it had been all right up to this point, but he hadn't really shown what he could do. So he got up a team of what he called "ornamental dishes," and when he said "ornamental" I rather imagine he meant "ornamental." They probably had to be brought in by the town fire department and eaten standing on a ladder. Playing left end for the "ornamental dishes" we find a pyramid of wild turkey in aspic. Perhaps you would like to stop right there. If you did you would miss the aspic of lobster Queen Victoria, and you couldn't really be said to have dined unless you had had aspic of lobster Queen Victoria. I rather imagine that it made quite an impressive ornamental dish—that is, if it looked anything like Queen Victoria, who was a very fine-looking woman.

Then, in a little group all by itself (after the pâté of prairie chicken, liver *royale*, and boned duck *à la* Bellevue), comes a strange throwback to the old days at the top of the menu, including boned partridge, snipe, duck (how simple just the word "duck" looks after all we have been through), and wild turkey. There seem to have been a lot of the birds who couldn't find places among the roasts and broils and so just took anything they could get down at the bottom of the card.

It is doubtful if many patrons, by the time they got down to this section, did much with quail or duck again. It is doubtful if they ever wanted to see the names in print again.

Now the question arises—what did people look like after they had eaten a dinner like that? Were people in 1885 so much fatter than those of us today who go around nibbling at bits of pineapple and drinking sips of sauer-kraut juice? I personally don't remember, but it doesn't seem that people were so much worse off in those days. At any rate, they had a square meal once in a while.

I am not a particularly proud man and it doesn't make an awful lot of difference to anyone whether I am fat or not. But as I don't like to run out of breath when I stoop over to tie my shoes, I try to follow the various bits of advice which people give me in the matter of diet. As a result, I get very little to eat, and am cross and hungry most of the time. I feel like a crook every time I take a furtive forkful of potato, and once, after sneaking a piece of hot bread, I was on the verge of giving myself up to the police as a dangerous character.

Now, all this must be a wrong attitude to take toward life. Surely there are more noble aspects (aspect of lobster Queen Victoria, for instance) than that of a man who is afraid to take a piece of bread. I am going to get some photographs of people in 1885 and give quite a lot of study to finding out whether they were very much heavier than people today. If I find that they weren't, I am going to take that menu of the Chicago Christmas dinner and get some chef, or organization of chefs, to duplicate it.

The worst that can happen to me after eating it will be that I drop dead.

# MEA CULPA

**D**URING the recent furor involving Father-and-Son enlistment in the Army and Navy, my own peculiar position was brought home to me, along with the *Herald Tribune* and the milk. This position of which I am speaking was not only peculiar; it was embarrassing.

I have a son who is apparently in the Navy. I am obviously *not* in the Navy, and possibly some explanation is due you taxpayers. A drag on the body-politic I will not be—at least not without stating my case.

In the first place, my son is two inches taller than I am, which makes me look pretty silly, even in civilian clothes. Especially as, for the moment, I have put on weight. Now the best that I could hope to be in the Navy would be a yeoman, because I can't tie knots, even in the simplest of dress ties. (You will notice that I didn't say "knots *an hour*." I'm not that dumb.) How would I look, a yeoman, saluting my son who is an ensign, two inches taller and quite a lot prettier? Imagination bogs down at the very possibility.

This, frankly, is the main reason why I didn't join in the Father-and-Son cavalcade. Other reasons follow in order:

1. I am the oldest living white man, especially at seven in the morning.

2. I still think of port-side as "larboard," because I was brought up on a whaler out of New Bedford (by Mioland).

3. My charge account at Brooks Brothers has been allowed to lapse, at the request of Brooks Brothers. This cuts me out of a uniform, and I see no reason for being in the Navy without a uniform. Do you? Dear?

On the other hand, if there is one, I used to swing a mean oar in a wherry, and was often admired by local trout as I spun under the Boylston Street bridge. I can also box the compass into insensibility. Maybe I am being just a silly sentimentalist in not joining up. Maybe I am just the man the Navy needs. Did you ever think of that? My father was in the Navy when there was no such thing as the Panama Canal, which meant that he had to go all the way around the Horn to get the morning paper. What am I doing sitting here in my cozy gutter—quibbling? Give me that application blank! And an eraser!

# "ONE HUNDRED YEARS
AGO TODAY—"

*Two Centenaries Which We in America
Must Not Overlook*

D URING the war there was a horrible type of mind
which did nothing, from morning till night, but
compute the number of days which had elapsed
since the struggle began, and compile tables of
"important events in the World Conflict."

Such specialized intelligences were usually employed in
newspaper offices, and found expression in daily columns
headed "The 1275th Day of the Great War." Then would
follow a snappy chronology, always beginning with *"June 28,
1914—Murder at Sarajevo of the Archduke Francis Ferdinand."* They never could seem to bring themselves to drop old
Francis Ferdinand, probably because he was one of the points
of which they were absolutely sure.

And now since the war has ended, these anniversary hounds
have been forced to scrape around for more data. Hence the
epidemic this year of centenaries of famous persons.

Family life in America must have been at its height during 1818 and 1819, judging from the number of people who are breaking into print now as having been born one hundred years ago. It was the Year of the Great Fecundity, especially in the genius crop. Hardly a day goes by but that we read of the celebration by the Gurble Society of America of the one hundredth anniversary of the birth of Chester M. Gurble, "the People's Poet," or see a column of selected quotations from the works of Mary Elizabeth Cogeshall Sampter, born just one hundred years ago tomorrow, at Truro, Mass. One cringes to think of the comparatively meagre line-up which we, of the present generation of parents, may have to furnish the centenary-celebrators of 2019 as material for a good time.

But in all this talk about Whitman, Kingsley, Lowell, and the rest, I am afraid that we run a danger of overlooking several anniversaries which mean much to American letters, perhaps more than any of those thus far celebrated. I have two such dates in mind, and it will be through no fault of mine if they are passed by without their share of special stories, reminiscences and quotations from the works of the men whose centenaries they are.

### JOHN BARTLETT

The one hundredth anniversary of the birth of John Bartlett, author of "Bartlett's Quotations," is rapidly approaching. Who shall say that it is without significance in the literary history of our country? I said *"Who shall say that it is without significance in the literary history of our country?"* As he himself has written of another (on page 115 of his collected works, Little, Brown, 1899):

337

> His life was gentle, and the elements
> So mix'd in him, that Nature might stand up
> And say to all the world, "This was a man!"

There is probably no writer in the whole course of our national literature who has made his influence so felt on other writers of his time (and of times to follow him) as John Bartlett. It is not an exaggeration to say that his words are in everyone's mouth wherever there is any pretense to culture in the English language. The hold which his works have taken on the minds of men cannot be overestimated.

And it is only just that it should be so. Where, in any literature, can there be found a writer whose range could include the production of such lines as:

> To each his suff'rings; all are men,
> Condemn'd alike to groan,—
> The tender for another's pain,
> Th' unfeeling for his own.
> Yet ah! why should they know their fate,
> Since sorrow never comes too late,
> And happiness too swiftly flies?
> Thought would destroy their paradise.
> No more; where ignorance is bliss
> 'Tis folly to be wise.          (page 382)

and then, in what might be termed the same breath, the conception of such a stanza as we find on page 679:

> Wee Willie Winkie rins through the toun,
> Upstairs and downstairs, in his nicht-goun,
> Tirlin' at the window, cryin' at the lock,
> 'Are the weans in their bed? for it's nou ten o'clock.

It is told of Bartlett that he wore the same sort of underwear winter and summer. One day, while waiting in Harvard

338

Square for the horse-car which was to take him in to Boston, he was accosted by one of the haberdashery-salesmen who infest those collegiate precincts.

"We've got a nice line of balbriggans in today, Mr. Bartlett," said the man, hoping to make a sale.

"Thank you, I never use them," was the quick retort, somewhat softened by a twinkle of the eye, which, however, the salesman did not see as Bartlett was looking in the opposite direction. The man went his way, and Bartlett took the horse-car to Boston.

Having seen this side of the man, it is easier for students of his works to understand the spirit which prompted the penning of those immortal lines:

> Oh why should the spirit of mortal be proud?
> Like a fast-flitting meteor, a fast-flying cloud,
> A flash of the lightning, a break of the wave,
> He passes from life to his rest in the grave.
>
> (page 561)

or, in somewhat different mood, but still displaying the same fire and deep insight into human hopes and aspirations:

> 'Twas the night before Christmas, when all through the house
> Not a creature was stirring,—not even a mouse;
> The stockings were hung by the chimney with care,
> In hopes that St. Nicholas soon would be there. (page 527)

Bartlett's creative life may be divided into three periods, all sharply differentiated and yet all, in a manner of speaking, similar. I shall refer to these periods hereafter as the Period of Preparation (1820-1840); the Sturm und Drang Period (1840-1897), and the Period of Revision and Introspection (1897-1905). It was during the Sturm und Drang Period that he published the work which stands second only to his "Quotations" in intensity and depth of feeling, viz., *"A New and Complete Concordance or Verbal Index to Words, Phrases and Passages in the Dramatic Works of Shakespeare; with a Supplementary Concordance to the Poems."* To one who does not know this book, a complete acquaintance with Bartlett has not been vouchsafed. It is within its pages that we find those lines so significant now to us in our present national unrest:

> He jests at scars that never felt a wound.
> But soft! what light through yonder window breaks?
> It is the east, and Juliet is the sun.

But it were useless to go on enumerating the priceless gems of thought which Bartlett has given us. It were a presumption to imply that the mind of the public is needful of their iteration. And yet, as his centenary draws nigh, let us not find ourselves so spent with our Whitmans and our Kingsleys that we have no paper streamers and siren-blasts for our Bartletts.

The second figure in American letters whose name I would bring forward for festive consideration on this one hundredth anniversary of his birth, is one which, I fear, is not known by reputation to many of us. And yet he is a man whose work, given to us anonymously, ranks with that of Bartlett in its far-reaching influence on modern English prose and verse. I am not quite sure of his name myself, but I feel no hesitancy in bringing an approximation of it to the public attention, for upon his writings rather than on any accident of nomenclature, rests his fame.

I refer to Amos W. Kent, the author of *The Standard Thesaurus and Treasury of English Words and Phrases.* Born in Sutton, Massachusetts, on August 27, 1819, Mr. Kent devoted his entire life, after his graduation from Harvard, to the compilation of a thesaurus which stands on equal grounds with that of Peter Roget, popularly called "The Thesaurus King," and, in many respects, excels the work of that Englishman, especially in its indices.

At a time when the categorical stanzas of Walt Whitman have been revived in every paper and literary journal in the country under the flimsy excuse that it was his one hundredth birthday, it is somewhat irritating to those of us who are admirers of Kent to consider how dependent Whitman was on Kent for nine-tenths of his material, and how slavish he (Whitman) was in his imitation of his (Kent's) verse forms (Kent's and Whitman's). Let us take one example. If the following quotation from Kent (page 375), written fifteen years before Whitman's "I Sing the Body Electric," is not the very essence of the Good Gray Poet's stock-in-trade, then the present reviewer will eat a hat furnished by any lady or gentleman in the audience.

(I sing the—)

> Cervical vertebrae, thoracic, the lumbar
> The sacral, the presternum, the mesosternum, the
>     scapula.
> The clavicle, humerus, radius, ulna, femur, patella.
> The tibia and the fibula and the long internal lateral
>     ligament.

Or again, on page 370, Kent antedates Whitman by at least ten years:

Man, male, he; manhood, &c. (adolescence) 131;
Gentleman, sir, master; yeoman, wight, swain, fellow.

Blade, beau, elf, gaffer, good man; husband, &c. (married man)
Mr., mister; boy, &c. (youth) 129.
Male animal, drake, gander, dog, boar, stag.
Hart, buck, horse, gib,—tom-cat; he-Billy goat.

It is when one considers these points in the work of Kent and sees them for what they are, and then hears the public adulation of Whitman, an obvious disciple, that the lover of truth must feel that he is in the presence of a great literary injustice.

Since then, we are on the look-out for centenaries this year, let us not forget to pay homage to these two cornerstones of American letters, Bartlett and Kent. Altogether now, fellers, three long Bartletts with three short Kents on the end! One—two—three!—

# A WORD ABOUT HAY FEVER

O N THE eighteenth of August, at 6 A. M., I celebrate the twenty-fifth anniversary of the advent of my hay fever. I plan to make quite an occasion of it, with field sports and a buffet lunch in a tent during the day and a *soirée de gala* after dinner with fireworks (including set pieces representing the different varieties of noxious weeds) and dancing for those who can. Twenty-five years of hay fever is nothing to be—would you believe it, I almost wrote "sneezed at" without thinking! Gosh!

On the eighteenth of August, 1905, I awoke at 6 A. M. (the reason for this unnatural procedure was that I was at a boys' camp at the time and a bugle had been blowing in my ear since 5:45) and realized that something was wrong. I realized that something was wrong because I sneezed nineteen times in rapid succession. One or two sneezes on arising is not abnormal, but nineteen indicate some derangement of the apparatus. "I must have caught cold," I said, and promptly went back to bed.

But as I got again within range of the straw-filled tick which served us hardy boys as a mattress, I realized that it was no ordinary head cold which had descended on me. I had heard and seen enough of hay fever among my tribesmen at home to know that the old Gypsy's Curse which was laid on the Benchleys generations ago in a dank Welsh cave had caught up with me, the youngest of the clan, and that, from that date on, I was to be marked with the red eye and the tender nose of the anaphylaxis sufferer.

If anaphylaxis (or hypersensitiveness to protein) were all that the victim of hay fever suffers from, things wouldn't be so bad. He could buy a bale of soft cotton handkerchiefs and fight the thing out by himself. The real suffering comes through his relations with the rest of society and from man's recognized inhumanity to man. In other words, he is a figure of fun.

People can have sunburn, hangnails, or even ordinary head colds, and their more fortunate mates will say: "Aw, that's too bad! Why don't you just take the day off and go home?" But the minute anyone with hay fever comes along, even though he be blind and gasping for breath, the entire community stops work and screams with laughter.

"Hay fever!" they say, holding their sides. "Boy, you ought to pose for a bunch of pomegranates!" or "What's the matter? Did you leave your eyes at home on the bureau?" People who are not ordinarily given to wise-cracking blossom out as the wits of their day when confronted with someone in the throes of a hay-fever attack. You wouldn't think there could be so many light-hearted, facile jokesters in the world. I can imagine no national calamity which would not be alleviated, no community depression which would not be shot through with sunshine, by the mere presence of a poor guy poisoned with ragweed pollen.

Hay fever has been going now for quite a number of centuries. Every year, along about August, there are editorials in the papers (humorous, unless the editorial writer himself happens to be a sufferer), and reports of conventions and newly discovered cures. And yet the ignorance of the immune citizenry on the subject is nothing short of colossal. Tell a man that the reason why you look so funny is that you have hay fever and, as soon as he has stopped laughing and has delivered himself of the customary *bon mots*, he will say: "Hay fever, eh? That's something you get from eating goldenrod, isn't it?" Goldenrod somehow always sticks in their minds as the sole cause of the affliction, although goldenrod is really one of the minor excitants and practically a soothing agent compared to ragweed and the more common grasses. But the non-sneezing layman will have it goldenrod, and goldenrod it is in song and story.

Then there is a great deal of good-natured incredulity over the fact that the first attack comes along about the same day every year. "You don't mean to tell me that it comes annually on exactly the eighteenth of August!" they say, poking the sufferers in the ribs. "That's because you are *looking* for it then. Suppose the eighteenth of August falls on a Sunday!"

They express no surprise that golden bantam corn comes along at the same time each year, or that the rambler roses on their porch are in full bloom every Fourth of July; but say that ragweed starts shedding its pollen every August along about the eighteenth, and they look at you suspiciously. I have struck, and will strike again, anyone who pushes me too far in this manner.

I do not know which is worse, to meet someone who knows

*The entire community screams with laughter*

nothing about hay fever and asks questions, or someone who knows just enough about it to suggest a remedy. The thing being as prevalent as it is, a lot of people have relatives who are victims. "I have a cousin who used to have hay fever," they say, "and he did something, I don't exactly remember what it was, but it was something you rub on your forehead, Cleenax or something like that—anyway, he hasn't had hay fever since he started using it." You never by any chance meet the cousin who has been cured, and you never find out just what this "Cleenax or something" was, but the implication is that if you don't follow the suggestion up you just like to have hay fever.

There is also quite a general, though extremely hazy, knowledge about inoculations. "Isn't there something that they shoot into your arm that fixes it up? A guy in our office had that done and is O. K. now." Well, there are plenty of things that you could shoot into your arm which would fix hay fever, among them a good, strong solution of bichloride of mercury; but most of the pollen serums which are used for this purpose have to be shot in every fifteen minutes from February 15 until November 1, and even then there is a very good chance that the result will be simply a sore arm in addition to hay fever. I tried it one year and have gone back to the good, old-fashioned eye-and-nose infirmity.

So, beginning with my twenty-fifth anniversary, I am going to take the aggressive. Instead of letting people say to me, "What's the matter with you? You look so funny," I am going to lead off with "What's the matter with *you*? You look awful." Just as Thoreau replied to Emerson, "Why aren't you in jail?" when the great philosopher asked him why he *was* in jail, I intend to make the immune ones explain why, with so many

347

charming and intelligent people wiping their eyes and sneezing, *they* are standing there like ninnies and breathing easily.

I shall either adopt this course or do as I have been doing for the past five years—retire to a darkened room, shut the windows, and tear bits of paper from August 18 until September 15.

# À BAS THE MILITARY CENSOR

*The Ride of Paul Revere—*
*As It Would Be Featured in Washington Today*

ONE wonders (especially if one is writing a story about it) just what would have happened if there had been a Committee on Public Information or a Military Censor during the Revolutionary War (1775-1783). How would Paul Revere have got his big news story to the people if he had been forced to deal through the channels of publicity which a modern news writer must traverse in our military organization? Following is a vivid word picture, giving the whole thing in detail:

Let us assume that Paul Revere and his little friend would have been allowed to execute their signalling stunt from the North Church steeple. As a matter of fact, the chances are they would have been arrested by the Salem Street Chapter of the Home Guard before they had waved one lantern aloft. We will concede that young Revere, on the opposite shore, has received the signal indicating that the British are on the way. His excuse for being out at that time of night is to inform the public.

But, being under a voluntary censorship not to disclose any military information without first submitting it to the proper authority for an O.K., he would ride quickly to the office of the Committee on Public Information, Middlesex Division.

On being shown into the office of the Public Informer (who, for the purpose of this story, would have to be staying late at the office that night working up a story on "How Our Soldier Boys Get Their Snuff") he would say:

"I have here a story on the imminent advance of the British troops which I think ought to get to the public as soon as possible or it will lose all of its news value. Do you suppose that I could get a release on it tonight?"

The Public Informer would take it and look at the first paragraph.

"Have you got John Adams' O.K. on this?" he would ask.

Mr. Revere would admit that he had just received the story.

"Well, I'll tell you what to do," would say the Continental Creel. "Leave the story here and I will have one of my men go over it for grammatical errors and then take it up with either Mr. Adams or Mr. Hancock, under whose department it comes. And, as it is a matter directly concerning military affairs, General Putnam ought to go over it first, also. I will be glad to put it out for you as soon as a decision has been reached. It looks like a good story to me. Come in tomorrow afternoon."

Although bursting with a desire to make himself the subject of a poem by dashing through "every Middlesex village and farm" that very night, our hero would have to spend the time between then and the next afternoon shooting Kelly Pool in the Boston Tavern, and telling the boys just what he thought about the Committee of Public Information.

On the following day he would gallop (he simply had to gallop somewhere, even if it were only back and forth from the Censor's office) and the Public Informer would explain to him how the matter lay:

"One of my men has taken it up with General Putnam, and the General is very much disturbed that such information should have fallen into civilian hands in the first place. He wants to see you at 9:07 tomorrow morning to ask you where you got it. In the second place, both the General and Mr. Hancock agree with me that to give this story out to the public at this time would tend to create an atmosphere of unhealthy pessimism. You say here, in the first paragraph: 'The British are coming!' Now that is direct military information, and might be used by the Tory element to inform General Gage that we know of his plans and the whole affair might be called off.

"Furthermore, it seems unwise to spread this broadcast among the citizenry just now. They might get panicky. General Putnam says that it would upset his whole system of defense if this became common talk on the streets.

"But I will tell you what I will do. You might leave the story here, and I can have one of my men work it over into a bully Sunday feature story on 'The Red-Coats in New England,' describing the various points of interest along the route that the British troops march, with pictures showing the house on the corner of the street near which they landed in Charlestown, and perhaps the town-hall in Medford. We have plenty of red-hot pictures like that in our Division of Photographs and a great story ought to be worked up on this piece as a basis. We will put it out for you through our regular channels, and most of the trade papers and farm journals in the country will carry it."

And thus, my children, you would hear, of the midnight ride of Paul Revere. But that is not all. Far from it.

It is an accepted fact that General Washington crossed the Delaware River. I think that I violate no confidence when I say that. Furthermore, it is conceded that it was a rather slick bit of work and done with a minimum of publicity and stir. And yet, had there been adequate military censorship think how much better it might have been done!

The Government would first have advertised in Trenton for bids on the furnishing of row-boats. It would have specified that these boats should be twelve feet, four inches long, with a four-feet beam, large enough to carry a dozen soldiers, with one boat equipped with a platform in the bow large enough for a general to stand on in a picturesque attitude. It would have specified that the firm offering the winning bid should have the boats on the New Jersey shore at 9:00 Thursday night, equipped with long poles.

Following this, a space along the water-front would be roped off and patrolled by Continental troops, so that no one could suspect that anything was going to happen in that vicinity.

In the meantime, the Military Censor would have got in his precautionary work and a notice would have been sent out to the editors of the various journals of the day, saying:

"It is requested that no mention, editorial or otherwise, be made of the intended crossing of the Delaware River by General Washington and his troops. In co-operating with the Government in this matter, the press will be aiding materially in winning the war."

The following news items, however, would be considered perfectly permissible, as no names would be mentioned:

"A New Jersey Port, December 23.—A soldier belonging to the ——th Regiment, which is quartered here temporarily preparatory to embarkation for a Pennsylvania port, was arrested last night for attempting to pass some Continental money. He was freed on bail on his promise to leave New Jersey with his regiment tonight."

"A New Jersey Port, December 23.—Two British spy suspects were arrested in the barred zone along the water-front this morning, charged with peddling milk without a license. They were questioned by officers in charge concerning their knowledge of the intended movements of certain troops across a certain river, and, although they protested that they knew nothing of the matter, this fact in itself was considered suspicious, as there was no reason why they shouldn't know, and they were therefore interned."

And by the time everything was ready for the crossing, no one would be in the dark about it except the men who were to cross, and their relatives at home. The British, incidentally, would have been on the opposite shore waiting for them, wearing badges labelled "Reception Committee."

On the whole, it seems lucky that General Washington and the rest of the Boys in Buff handled their own publicity by releasing news to the enemy and to the public at the same time, and letting Nature take its course. It has made history much more intimate.

# WHY DOES NOBODY
# COLLECT ME?

SOME months ago, while going through an old box of books looking for a pressed nasturtium, I came across a thin volume which, even to my dreamer's instinct, seemed worth holding out, if only for purposes of prestige.

It was a first edition of Ernest Hemingway's *In Our time*, the edition brought out in Paris by the Three Mountains Press in 1924, while Hemingway was just "Old Ernie" who lived over the sawmill in the rue Notre Dame des Champs. I knew that it must be worth saving, because it said in the front that the edition consisted of one hundred and seventy copies, of which mine was Number Thirty-nine. That usually means something.

It so happened that, a few weeks later, "Old Ernie" himself was using my room in New York as a hide-out from literary columnists and reporters during one of his stopover visits between Africa and Key West. On such all-too-rare occasions he lends an air of virility to my dainty apartment which I miss sorely after he has gone and the furniture has been repaired.

More to interrupt his lion-hunting story than anything else,

I brought out my copy of *In Our Time* and suggested that, in memory of happy days around the Anise Deloso bowl at the Closerie des Lilas, it might be the handsome thing for him to inscribe a few pally sentiments on the fly-leaf. Not, as I took pains to explain to him, that I was a particular admirer of his work, so much as that I wanted to see if he really knew how to spell.

Encouraged by my obviously friendly tone, he took a pen in his chubby fist, dipped it in a bottle of bull's blood, and wrote the following:

> To Robert ("Garbage Bird") Benchley,
> hoping that he won't wait for prices
> to reach the peak ———
> From his friend,
> Ernest ("——— ———") Hemingway

The "Garbage Bird" reference in connection with me was a familiarity he had taken in the past to describe my appearance in the early morning light of Montparnasse on certain occasions. The epithet applied to himself, which was unprintable except in *Ulysses*, was written deliberately to make it impossible for me to cash in on the book.

Then, crazed with success at defacing *In Our Time*, he took my first edition of *A Farewell to Arms* and filled in each blank in the text where Scribner's had blushed and put a dash instead of the original word. I think that he supplied the original word in every case. In fact, I am sure of it.

On the fly-leaf of this he wrote:

> To R. (G.) B from E. (-). H.
> Corrected edition. Filled-in blanks.
> Very valuable. Sell quick.

Now, oddly enough, I had never considered selling either book. I had known, in a general way, that a first edition of the Gutenberg Bible would be worth money, and that, if one could lay hands on an autographed copy of *Canterbury Tales*, it would be a good idea to tuck it away, but that a first edition of one of Ernie's books could be the object of even Rabelaisian jesting as to its commercial value surprised and, in a vague sort of way, depressed me. Why are not *my* works matters for competitive bidding in the open market?

I am older than Hemingway, and have written more books than he has. And yet it is as much as my publishers and I can do to get people to pay even the list-price for my books, to say nothing of a supplementary sum for rare copies. One of my works, *Love Conquers All*, is even out of print, and yet nobody shows any interest in my extra copy. I have even found autographed copies of my books in secondhand book shops, along with *My Life and Times* by Buffalo Bill. Doesn't *any*-body care?

What is there about me and my work that repels collectors? I am handsome, in an unusual sort of way, and speak French fluently, even interspersing some of my writings with French phrases. True, some of my copy, as it goes to the printer, is not strictly orthodox in spelling and punctuation, but the proof-readers have always been very nice about it, and, by the time my books are out, there is nothing offensive to the eye about them. And yet I have been told by hospital authorities that more copies of my works are left behind by departing patients than those of any other author. It does seem as if people might at least take my books home with them.

If it is rarity which counts in the value of a book, I have

*I have even found autographed copies of my book in second-hand bookstores*

dozens of very rare Benchley items in my room which I know cannot be duplicated. For the benefit of collectors, I will list them, leaving the price more or less up to the would-be purchaser. All that I ask is that I don't actually lose money on the sale.

There is a copy of my first book, *Of All Things*, issued by Henry Holt in 1922. (Mr. Lincoln MacVeagh, who engineered the deal, is now Ambassador to Greece, which ought to count for something.) It is a first edition, an author's copy, in fact, and has a genuine tumbler-ring on the cover. I have no doubt that it is actually the first volume of mine ever to be issued, and, as *Of All Things* has gradually gone into twelve editions since, it ought to be very valuable. Page 29 is dog-eared.

*Love Conquers All* (Holt-1923) is, as I have said, now out of print, which makes my extra copy almost unique. I doubt very much if any one else has an *extra* copy of *Love Conquers All*. It is a third edition, which may detract a little from its market value, but this is compensated for by the fact that it belonged originally to Dorothy Parker, who left it at my house five or six years ago and has never felt the need for picking it up. So, you see, it is really a Dorothy Parker item, too.

*Pluck and Luck* (Holt-1924) was brought out later in a dollar edition for drugstore sale, and I have three of those in a fair state of preservation. One of them is a very interesting find for collectors, as I had started to inscribe it to Donald Ogden Stewart and then realized that I had spelled the name "Stuart," necessitating the abandonment of the whole venture. It is practically certain that there is not another dollar edition of *Pluck and Luck* with Donald Ogden Stewart's name spelled

"Stuart" on the fly-leaf. Would a dollar and a quarter be too much to ask, do you think?

Faulty inscriptions account for most of the extra copies of *The Early Worm* (Holt-1926) that I have, lying about. It was during that period, and that of my next book, *Twenty Thousand Leagues Under the Sea*, or *David Copperfield* (Holt-1928) that I went through a phase of trying to write humorous remarks on the fly-leaves of gift-copies. Those copies in which the remarks did not turn out to be so humorous as I had planned had to be put aside. I have eighteen or twenty of these discarded copies, each with an inscription which is either unfunny or misspelled.

During what I call "my transitional period," when I changed from Henry Holt to Harper's and began putting on weight, I was moody and fretful, and so did not feel like trying to make wisecracks in my inscriptions. The recipient of a book was lucky if I even took the trouble to write his name in it. He was lucky, indeed, if he could read *my* name, for it was then that I was bullied into autographing copies at bookshop teas (this was my transitional period, you must remember, and I was not myself), and my handwriting deteriorated into a mere series of wavy lines, like static.

For this reason, I have not so many curious copies of *The Treasurer's Report* and *No Poems* hanging about. I have, however, a dummy of *The Treasurer's Report* with each page blank, and many of my friends insist that it should be worth much more than the final product. I don't know just how dummy-copies rate as collectors' items, but I will be very glad to copy the entire text into it longhand for fifty dollars. Thirty-five dollars, then.

And now I come to what I consider the choicest item of them all—one which would shape up rather impressively in a glass case a hundred years from now. It is a complete set of corrected galleys for my next book (to be called, I am afraid, *From Bed to Worse*) which I had cut up for rearrangement before I realized that I was cutting up the wrong set of proofs —the one that the printer wants back. I haven't broken the news to the printer at Harper's, and I may never get up the courage to do so (printers get so cross), in which case the book will never come out at all. Would that be a valuable piece of property or not—a set of hand-corrected galleys for a Benchley item which never was published? And all cut up into little sections, too! A veritable treasure, I would call it, although possibly the words might come better from some-body else.

But, until the collecting public comes to its senses, I seem to be saddled, not only with a set of mutilated galleys, but about twenty-five rare copies of my earlier works, each unique in its way. Possibly Hemingway would like them in return for the two books of his own that he has gone to so much trouble to render unsalable for me.